SUSTAINABLE ENLIGHTENMENT

Einstein's Razor: Seven Simple Steps to Awakening

Douglas McCarty

SUSTAINABLE ENLIGHTENMENT

Einstein's Razor: Seven Simple Steps to Awakening

Douglas McCarty

ISBN: 0983749507
ISBN-13: 9780983749509

DEDICATION

For Sookjae, Jamie and Jeannette,
my illuminations.

CONTENTS

INTRODUCTION

*L*ate September, 2006 in Eugene, Oregon still feels like summer. The sunny, brilliant days are getting shorter, but the rain for which the state is famous is still several weeks away. Weeks ago the unwatered lawns turned to straw on rock-hard ground, and the clay soil in the hills south of town is cracked and dry,.

"Dad, why don't you write this down?"

Son is on the phone. He has just begun his last year at Swarthmore and we are discussing some of the things he learned during two years away from his college, the first to study Chinese in Beijing and the second to study Chinese and Japanese at Harvard. In Cambridge, he chanced upon a "happiness" course and, despite my misgivings (at first glance, it seemed to be what we used to call a "gut course"), took it. But I was wrong about the course. He not only benefited greatly but introduced me, through that course, to the field of Positive Psychology. We chat about eastern philosophy and ways to get the best out of life. I am just finishing my explanation of "Karma" to him (see Chapter Nine, "Splitting the Mind"), a usable method for the oddball idea of Karma.

"Write this down? Well, I'm pretty much done, you have it now. That's all there is to Karma."

"No, Dad, I mean this stuff you know about. About happiness, meditation, how to be aware of the world. You know. It's really good stuff. People would be interested."

"You think so? Who?"

"Well, me, for one, and people I know. I'd like to have it to read. Seriously."

After raising two children who, during their teen years, often looked at me as if I possessed only the sense God gave to the lawn chair, this is quite a compliment. The idea gestates for a period of a few years, and this book is the result. For my children, and their friends, and maybe for some others, a simplified path to enlightenment during this life, provable and testable, a personal guide to awakening and Destiny.

*   *   *

If there is a sin against life, it consists perhaps not so much in despairing of life as in hoping for another life and in eluding the implacable grandeur of this life. ~ Albert Camus

You are a living miracle, but are you *living* a miracle? Your life story is a key chapter in an incredible chronicle of heroism and derring-do, an epic adventure filled with chance meetings and love and lust and hairbreadth escapes, but are you sometimes paralyzed with fear, or bored to distraction with your own existence? You don't need to be perfect or fearless, or physically powerful or saintly, or popular or charismatic, to receive your birthright now of a miraculous life, but you will have to change the way you see the world and how you think about things. You will have to spend some time and effort, but no money, really. Perhaps the entire process will take a few weeks. It's not much of a price to pay for awakening and enlightenment. You have a purpose in this life, you have a calling in this world and you have a destiny on this earth. It won't seek you out, but you can awaken to it, and you can start now.

So, what must you do?

You must first *come to your senses*. Literally. If you can gaze at a field of wildflowers and perceive their different colors and shapes, and open a jar of cinnamon sticks and inhale the spice's fragrance, then you have the innate ability to connect, *completely*, to the universe. Once you understand and practice this sensory connection, you are well on your way to enlightenment. You can take the next steps to think, express yourself, take action, find a deep peacefulness inside you, work at a true vocation (and not just a job) and achieve true, personal greatness. This last, your personal significance and splendor, may eventually become known to the world at large or be revealed to only to a few, and it will not matter one whit either way, because in finding and fulfilling your greatness you will create the true meaning of your life, and you will fulfill your destiny.

This book is not only a simple guide to personal enlightenment written in response to Son's request and with my children in mind, but also my thank-you note to Life itself. Or perhaps it is more of a love letter. In a sense, enlightenment, gratitude and love are all the same thing, or parts of the same thing. When I think about enlightenment—and not what is widely promoted as such, either on the internet or through various institutions—I am really thinking of how enthusiastic I am about my experience on the planet and how much I am in love with life, and how grateful I am for having a place here, even for a short while. Somehow, like any true enthusiast, I think everyone should feel the same way. As is the case with all of us, I could so easily have never been conceived or born, and Destiny might have snuffed out my candle quite effortlessly at any number of points in my life. We are so lucky, you and I, to be here at all. Like you and everyone else, I am living in this green and blue palace called earth, participating in this grand banquet I call "my life," on borrowed time. Knowing this makes existence all the sweeter and richer, and it makes it even more important that we taste and experience all that life has to offer us during the short time we are allotted.

But it is not just tasting and experiencing life that counts, it is not just perception, as you will see. Of course, perception is the major share of enlightenment, and once you get that right, you are doing, practically speaking, the lion's share of the work of awakening. Isn't that odd? Opening up your five senses to this reality in each unfolding moment, and practicing at getting *that* right, is the heavy lifting, so to speak, of becoming enlightened. After the perception— the full perception—of our beautiful world and all its manifestations and creatures, including ourselves, we now get the absolute privilege to take that perception—our own particular perception—and apply it through our thoughts, expressions and actions, and become the persons we were meant to be since birth. It is all free, too; all this will cost you is the effort it takes to change the way you think about things.

What exactly is an enlightened person, how can you describe a fully aware human being? That is a tough question, in fact, in that form it is almost too tough to answer. It's probably better to ask: What does an enlightened person do, what *can* an enlightened person do? How does an enlightened person think, act and react? Ah, now *that* is almost too easy to answer. An enlightened person perceives and is aware of her world to the utmost degree; she sees the world in all its variety, depth and beauty. The world now reveals itself to her, completely, each and every moment. An enlightened person takes these rich perceptions and weaves them into thoughts, expressions and actions which are in total accord with who she is. An enlightened person trains her mind through simple exercises to be always in control, and to be always calm, no matter the circumstance or obstacle or danger. Through the course of her existence, an enlightened person challenges herself to go farther, higher, deeper in her life through various quests, and by so doing, completes her own journey.

What good is it to be enlightened? Is there any real value to it? Reread the last three sentences of the paragraph above, slowly, and consider how your life might be different and better if you were always in total accord with who you really are, if you were always calm in the face of any challenge and if you could, throughout your life, claim and complete your true destiny.

Okay. But how complicated is it to do this, what are the hurdles? Well, enlightenment certainly is not something which requires a great intellect or sky-high IQ. You don't need to be Einstein.

Average intelligence will certainly suffice. Since 90% or more of all people surveyed happily admit to having above average intelligence (the so-called "Lake Wobegon Effect"), then so much the better. Also, you do not have to be particularly virtuous or beatific, you need not have started a non-profit organization to feed the world or save the spotted owl. Enlightenment is awareness, it is not sainthood. And, surprisingly, achieving enlightenment is not very complicated at all. In fact, what *is* complicated is to continue living an unenlightened life. The unenlightened life is a little bit like lying; when we start out, we think that we can smooth things out, or avoid a spot of trouble, by just fibbing our way through this one sticky patch. As time goes by, we find out that, in order to keep our machine of lies going, not only do we have to continue to manufacture fresh fabrications, but we also have to keep in mind not only all of the previous perjuries and prevarications we have invented, but also all of their various trajectories, in order that our "alternative" universe can hang together. Eventually, we learn that we are living not only a lie, but a grinding, complicated web of lies.

This is why, in an unenlightened state, we frequently feel lost, confused, unconnected and twisting in the wind. The world seems full of deceit and chicanery. That, however, is not the world, but rather the mirror we are holding up to ourselves, reflecting our own crooked existence. In life, in the end, it is so much easier to tell the truth, always, since the truth never changes and, as life rolls forward, all we need is to continue to see what is true and to stay with that.

Enlightenment operates in the same way, since, at its most basic, enlightenment is the process of connecting to the truth of the cosmos, and then interacting with it. And with no lies. We can all wake up from the lies and forgeries of our current misperceived existence, cast off their meaningless encumbrances, and cease keeping track of their useless trajectories, and we should all do this. Right now.

Once we take the first steps toward enlightenment, we realize that it is so much easier to live in its bright light than it ever was to stumble along in the murky dusk and deceptions of unawareness. We can now release all the burdens and excess baggage we have kept track of and carried for so many years, and step forward into our own awakened, aware and enlightened life, which has been waiting for us since the day we were born. In fact, we might just take a few minutes to contemplate five important awakenings.

*   *   *

In the beginning God created the heaven and the earth. And the earth was without form, and void; and darkness was upon the face of the deep. And the Spirit of God moved upon the face of the waters. And God said, Let there be light: and there was light. And God saw the light, that it was good: and God divided the light from the darkness. And God called the light Day, and the darkness he called Night. And the evening and the morning were the first day. ~Genesis 1:1-5.

There is no more beautiful passage written in the English language than these five simple sentences about the first awakening of the world, sentences fashioned from incredibly plain words, and mostly single syllables. *Form, void, deep, face, light, good, day, night.* Only four words bear the weight of even three syllables: *beginning, created, divided* and *evening.* And why is this collection of plain words so astoundingly beautiful? Because enlightenment is simply the most important and most exquisite explosion of beauty mankind can comprehend. It is the most wonderful thing that ever happened to us, and it is the most wonderful thing that ever will happen to us.

The Creation is the first enlightenment that we may consider, the moment when the universe left the void and perpetual darkness behind, and was transformed into a world of lightness and the first day. *Morning has broken, like the first morning.* Of course, this first cosmic awakening happened so long ago that we have difficulty comprehending it, except through some sort of metaphor.

*   *   *

The journey is difficult, immense. We will travel as far as we can, but we cannot in one lifetime see all that we would like to see or to learn all that we hunger to know. ~ Loren Eisely

We might contemplate a second enlightenment on earth, as our vertebrate ancestors—still fish, mind you—in the sun-drenched and tide-washed margins of the seas begin to focus up and out of the water for the very first time. The time? It is four hundred million years ago in the middle of the Paleozoic Era, 270 million years before the first primitive flower would bloom. The earth itself has already celebrated more than four billion birthdays unremarked, and water has been, for hundreds of millions of years, the only medium for life. It is under us, around us and over us as we swim and hide and try to reproduce, without any clue that there, up above us, is an entirely new and unexplored world. The new stuff and substance is not just more new territory, with that same dense, watery medium (seawater in three dimensions). No, this is completely new territory and a brand new medium: *dry* land and *cool, fresh* air. Imagine we are in a small group of the very first tetrapods, the linking creatures from finned bony fish to limbed amphibians, swimming and paddle-walking along the shallows near our birth.

The force of life has pushed us forward so that we can not only swim, but hold onto various seaweeds with our crude limbs, and even move ourselves along the shallow bottoms of swamps and tide pools, perhaps to hunt but most likely to flee creatures from the deep (I'm thinking sharks here, but that's just me). In one brief moment, a big wave drives our little band forward and we anchor ourselves in a tidal pool that momentarily drains and we find ourselves completely surrounded by nothing but air! What is this? What has happened to our world? We look around and we look at each other. I see Tom and Bill, and there's Harry just barely hanging on, but here everything is so different, so clear. What is this light, breezy medium, and why can we see so far through it?   It's a little frightening to us, at least to the extent that our primitive neurological system can process "frightening," and yet, at the same time (and with the same limitations) it is a little invigorating. It is, literally, an unexpected breath of fresh air.

But we are not the first visitors to dry land, just the first of our kind. Preceding us by several million years on terra firma are not only the fast evolving plants (first non-vascular, then seedless vascular plants, and finally, not long before our arrival at the land's edge, seed bearing gymnosperm plants) but also some early land arthropods. The hexapods—six-legged insects—had come first, but then crabs and spiders, centipedes and millipedes had also crawled ashore and adapted to the land and its atmosphere, and claimed it as their own. Perhaps in the moment before a wave comes to return us to the sea we stare, face to face, at a horseshoe crab, each of us wondering the same thing: "Who are you?" We tetrapods, already an invasive species in that first landing in a new world, have left the wet and cloudy and dense world behind, at least for a moment, and things will never be the same again for our descendents. This is our second awakening.

*   *   *

When the animals went ashore to take up life on land, they carried part of the sea in their bodies, a heritage which they passed on to their children and which even today links each land animal with its origins in the ancient sea ~Rachel Carson, The Sea Around Us

Our third awakening, foreshadowed by the cosmic beginning in Genesis and our ancestors' first visit to the airy atmosphere above the tidal pool, is, by earthly chronology, a very recent entrance into the light. Unfortunately, we cannot truly remember this event at all, although, strangely enough, people we are closest to—our parents— will witness it firsthand, and be transformed by it. It is the moment of our own birth. At the moment of delivery, too, we depart an undivided void, a place with no partition into light and darkness, and enter into a world of bright lights and strange shapes and faces and hard, sharp noises. We human beings are each, in our own way, a unique world, created in and then cleaved from the void and born into a new and grander world of contrasting light and dark, of sky

9

and earth and water, sun and moon and stars, and the living flora and fauna of our earth.

Oddly enough, we humans mimic the earth, since we each carry an inner sea almost identical to the Precambrian seas of three billion years ago, a sea which holds sodium, potassium, and calcium in almost the same proportions as the oceans are, even today. Our tears are the same salinity as seawater. And we carry continents as well.

We incorporate not only internal *seas*, with our salty blood and lymph systems, which are literally swimming with "servants" (our blood plasma carrying in nutrients and carrying out waste, busy red blood cells ferrying oxygen, and tireless white blood cells patrolling the blood, ready to attack any invader, platelets ready to repair structural damage, and our lymphatic system comprised of lymph fluid and lymphocytes), but we also contain external woodlands and deserts and marshlands, *terrae cognitae*, each with its own topography and each brimming with creatures. Along for the ride on and in each of us reside perhaps a thousand trillion visiting microorganisms, known collectively as our microbiota, which include bacteria, fungi and archaea, some of which help us and others who are simply micro-hitchhikers, who reside on and even in the layers of our skin, our saliva and oral mucosa and conjunctiva, and in our gut. We are not only miraculous creatures, but miraculous walking worlds. Each of us rules as the resident lord of our own rich and complicated world, and at the same time resides as citizen of a cosmos even larger, even more complex and beautiful.

*   *   *

You must live in the present, launch yourself on every wave, find your eternity in each moment.~ Henry David Thoreau

Our fourth awakening, and we are *always* here to witness it, visits us each morning as we break free from Erebos, the god of darkness, and escape Hypnos, the lord of sleep. This is the awakening we normally think of when we say the word. How miraculous not only that we alter our consciousness on a daily basis each morning from dormancy to wakefulness (and then fade again into oblivion each evening), but that we use our very consciousness to observe that alteration which we call "awakening." We may miss the precise moment of our diurnal awakening, but we recognize it almost immediately after it occurs. *Ah, now I am awake.* The world takes shape and shows depth in light and shadow now, the strange creatures and characters and landscapes of Dreamland vanish, receding into the darkness. If we carefully observe this fourth awakening, we will see that this juncture is very close to true enlightenment—for a few seconds, at least, we live immediately in the instant and see, hear and taste the world clearly without labels or judgments—things simply *are*, at least temporarily. This is a brief and evanescent clarity. We absorb the world in pure perception in these few moments and then, inexorably, our reactive brain clicks in and foresees daily schedules and plans and activities which crowd out our senses. *I'm still tired, is it Tuesday today, where are my socks, what time is it, what's on my list, have to get to bed earlier, not hungry at all, still, I should eat something, paper's here, I'll start with that. Big day today, lots to do, am I falling behind?* This transition time, when we get going or begin our day is usually the time that we surrender our perceptions and senses and our awakened state. We relinquish our true consciousness and engage a form of anesthetized autopilot for our lives, and lose contact with the perceivable universe. We might have only a passing relationship, if any, with that perceivable universe the rest of the day. Pity. We were *so close* to enlightenment at that moment, and now we are speeding away.

And so, to regain and sustain enlightenment, we need a fifth (and final) awakening, that of becoming awake and aware in each moment as it unfolds. This awakening, the fifth enlightenment, is what this book is all about. We will never do this perfectly, but even an imperfect awareness of each moment as it flowers and fades is enough for true awakening.

*   *   *

*I think I could turn and live with animals, they are so
placid and self-contain'd,
I stand and look at them long and long.*

*They do not sweat and whine about their condition,
They do not lie awake in the dark and weep for their
sins,
They do not make me sick discussing their duty to
God,
Not one is dissatisfied, not one is demented with the
mania of owning things,
Not one kneels to another, nor to his kind that lived
thousands of years ago,
Not one is respectable or unhappy over the whole
earth.* ~Walt Whitman, "Song of Myself"

When you think of an enlightened being, what image comes to mind? Do you hear absolute silence and see a saint, kneeling in prayer in a monastery cell, bathed in a heavenly glow from above? Or do you conjure the image of a Buddhist monk with shaved head, sitting in a full lotus position, staring with fixed eyes at a plain white wall? Or is it more the scene of a Hindu holy man, dressed like Gandhi, sitting by a river and instructing a group of eager yoga disciples?

For me, I sometimes think of my late, great, Husky, Stormy. He was silver and white, with a noble prancing carriage, at times he seemed more a regal stallion than merely our family dog. Just as Whitman said of the animals, Stormy was always placid and self-contained (except when he saw a squirrel or a possum), and he did not sweat his condition or lie awake in the dark and weep for his sins. Unlike many pet dogs, he was not really that *into* people, not even his own family; he preferred other dogs to play with and everything else to chase and woof at. He often ran away. During his thirteen plus years of life, he terrified innumerable squirrels and a few cats, and even managed to catch and shake two squirrels, one possum, and one unfortunate scrub jay (dazed and confused after a very one-sided altercation with our kitchen window) to their doom. He was not always victorious, however. Stormy was left bleeding after a 3:00

a.m. scrap with a raccoon who somehow had not received the script that said the dog was to be the woofer and all other creatures were to run away in fear.

Stormy was always looking at things with his bright blue eyes, cocking his head, and he had those amazing Husky ears which could turn independently to better catch sounds, that Husky radar array. I calculate that during his tenure on the planet, I took him for ten thousand walks, wearing out at least seven pairs of shoes. The vast majority of the walks were on a 1.5 mile loop in a nearby cemetery, and each time he was totally aware and completely in the moment as he sniffed the same tufts of grass, bushes and trees as if he had never been there before. He looked in the distance any time there was movement, searching for another dog and master— and whenever he saw a person walking *without* a dog he would look at me as if something was amiss. "What is the matter with that person, where is his dog?" he seemed to be asking.

Stormy was a master perceiver, but most of all he was a smeller. He smelled everything—the air, trees, rocks, the side of the house, beetles and bugs, people's hands and crotches, dogs' noses and anuses, dirty laundry, sidewalks and post boxes—several times if possible. But he was not much of a gourmet. Like his ancestors he wolfed down his food. He liked the texture of new grass, and its taste, and sometimes he grazed on it like a cow. He loved snow and would bury his snout in it, hold for a second, and then vesuviate up and scatter the snow in all directions. He pulled me, skijoring, on skis in the winter, and ran miles and miles in the wilderness in the summers where I hiked; he raced along the Oregon coast, tasting the water which was oddly salty, and looking at me, puzzled, as if asking for an explanation. The world aroused him when he was awake for his entire life, and when he slept, he slept beautifully, and then one day when he was thirteen and a half years old, he lay down and never got up again.

Stormy had a simple life, full of perceptions which he processed in the moment and sometimes acted on, or promptly forgot as he moved on to the next thing. He knew what he liked (walks, runs, real food, rides in the car to mountain passes) and was pretty much uninterested in the rest. He hated being brushed, and loathed being bathed. When the weather was hot, he knew where the coolest spots on the concrete slab patio were, and that's where you would find him. In the winter, when his second coat came in, he could have a beautiful nap right on top of a few feet of snow with the temperature in the teens.

And how long, you may ask, did it take Stormy to achieve enlightenment, how many years of concentration did it take my canine friend to learn to live in the present moment in full awareness of his surroundings? Did he frequently confess his sins and chant by candlelight? Did he have to study religious texts or shave his fur, and rise at 4 a.m. to meditate? No, in Stormy's case, after a lengthy period of puppyhood during which he did a variety of stupid puppy things, he basically lived as an enlightened Husky for the last eleven years of his life.

Now, I'm not completely serious, of course. I realize that human beings are considerably more complex than Huskies, and that we have a lot more going on both in the outside world and in the inner world. But, like Huskies, we are sentient beings who perceive and analyze input from the external world, think and express ourselves and act. The main difference is that, somewhere back in time we humans acquired this incredible consciousness which is mostly a blessing, but partly a burden, and sometimes even a curse. We are conscious not only of our surroundings and still somewhat in thrall to our instincts and reactions, like Stormy, but we also carry with us long memories of what has gone before (which forms part of our identity and our culture, but which also can leave us with smoldering resentments and crippling emotional baggage), an ability to think deeply (and to overthink, also), as well as an acute sense of time which projects into the future, a future which we can plan for (but one which also often causes us incredible worry and angst). Our consciousness enriches our lives beyond description (and can help convey us to our destinies) and yet, if not controlled, might enslave us and degrade us, as well.

Taking a cue from Stormy, Sustainable Enlightenment is going to make this entire enterprise as simple as possible. The goal is to get you this message as raw and unvarnished as possible, and keep the concepts and the prose as close to fresh planed lumber as I can. After reading this book, you should be elated and enchanted with the prospect of meeting *you* again and, through you, forging a deep connection to the universe itself. You will be impressed, but it will be your existence and your universe which will impress and delight you. You will wake up every morning astounded by the murmuring sound of *your* breathing and amazed by the soft feeling of *your* skin in the warm cocoon of the pillows, sheets and blankets on your bed. You will be dazzled by the rising of the sun and the glint of its miraculous light through the curtains, you will marvel at the eddy and dance of the tiny dust figurines in the morning sunbeams, and delight in the vague fragrances and sounds of the morning. This true awakening and awareness will happen the instant you gain consciousness, and will continue through the course of your day until that moment late at night when you surrender again to sleep.

*   *   *

ONE

How Simple It Is

After his first year of diligent effort, the ambitious young monk at a Zen monastery asked the abbot what he could do to achieve *satori*, or enlightenment, as quickly as possible. The grizzled abbot looked at the neophyte and told him that the key to enlightenment was 1) to really desire it and 2) to work very hard at it. He then prescribed a rigorous study and meditation schedule for the young man and told him to work at it for a year. At the end of this second year the young man sat with the abbot and asked the same question and received the same answer and prescription. This process repeated itself for five more years, at which time the young monk confronted the old abbot who happened to be sitting by the river. "I've done everything you asked and everything I could. No one here has studied harder or meditated longer than I have. It's been seven years now. When will I achieve enlightenment?" The old man looked at him and said, "It is true that you have worked very hard, but have you really desired enlightenment?" The monk replied that, indeed, he desired it more than anything.

The abbot then seized the young monk by the neck of his robe and thrust his head deep into a pool in the river so the young monk could not breathe. The abbot was incredibly strong, much stronger than he appeared and the young monk, no matter how he struggled, could not escape his grip. After a full minute the abbot let go and the young monk collapsed on the shore, choking and coughing. It took him several minutes to quell his anger and regain his composure; meanwhile the abbot sat quietly and watched the river flow.

"Why did you try to drown me?" he asked.

The abbot ignored the question and asked, "When I held you underwater, how much did you want to breathe air again?"

"What a foolish question," the monk said. "You know I wanted to breathe more than anything."

"That," the abbot said, "is how much you must desire enlightenment." And he instructed the monk to resume his studies and his meditation practice with renewed desire.

It's such a wonderful story, but it has almost *no bearing* on sustainable enlightenment. It's not "tough love" from a mentor or a football coach or a drill sergeant ("Drop and give me twenty!") or the command to dig deep and try harder that gets you there. Don't get me wrong, you have to want to be enlightened to achieve it, you have to want to be enlightened to get there, but you don't need to spend years at a monastery and suffer the abuse of the wise old abbot to achieve awakening. You don't need to suffer, really (although later I will explain that you will probably need to *persevere* from time to time, which is a different matter.) Everything you need, all the tools, you have already; you were born with them and you have carried them with you for your entire life, unaware perhaps that they were even there.

*   *   *

Nothing is so firmly believed as what is least known.
~Michel de Montaigne

Montaigne could easily have been writing about the leap of faith many people are willing to make when they come into contact with sellers of worldly success, spiritual self-improvement and even enlightenment. For example, the internet has a plethora of sites longing to sell you not only enlightenment but also a cornucopia of consumer goods to accompany you to awareness and an awakened state. At one site, "The Shop" was offering not only books and cds, but also t-shirts, chakra-balancing balms, angel cards, serenity beads, meditation cushions ($95.00 each!), meditation stones, chakra stone pendants, bracelets, stress relievers, herbal facials, lavender closet sachets, herbal teas, foot soaks and message beads.

Another site, a website of the "mind-power" variety, offered "a better you, a better world," with a menu of seminars, teleseminars, workshops, grad meetings, and teleconferences to transport you to the *better you & world*, and something they called "specials." If a *better you & world* alone was not enough, you could go beyond that in their "life system" and acquire a list of capabilities including, ". . . Deep Relaxation, Sleep Control, Clock Technique, Awake Control, Dream Control, Hand Levitation, Headache Control, Glove Anesthesia, Glass of Water, Mental Screen, Memory Pegs, Three Fingers, Mirror of the Mind . . ."

And, as if that wasn't special enough, they also offered something called "intuition training" which was not only *time-tested*, but, *tried and true*, and which would actually develop extra-sensory perception in the purchaser. This ESP course offered " . . . Deep Relaxation/Long Relax, Mental Screen, TeleMind, Holoviewing Technique, Connection to Purpose, Remote Viewing, OmniViewing, Projection to Tree during Season Changes, Projection to Leaves, Projection to Pet, Human Anatomy, Seeds of Purpose . . ."

It is not my intention to make fun, and certainly not to judge, but I am also not making this stuff up. Glove anesthesia? Hmm. And why would anyone ever wish to "project to leaves." What can this or other similar programs cost? Well, this particular one cost about $600 for the first two-day class. It also offered a Hawaiian cruise seminar complete with interior cabins, ocean view cabins and balcony cabins, for ascending prices. Imagine graduates of the ESP training course with holoviewing skills actually opting for cabins with views—why would they ever do that, since they could already see everywhere they wished.

*   *   *

Sustainability

Sustainable is the hot catchphrase as I write this book, 2010~2011. As used by corporations and city councils, "sustainable" probably has no more meaning than its immediate predecessors, "green" and "eco-friendly." It may have passed its half-life already, and be ready to give way to a new byword soon. Currently in the wide world, though, I think it means "good," in a somewhat vague sense. *Sustainable* in this book actually means *sustainable*, and there really is no other good word for it. So, we're going to stick with it.

Many self-help gurus and coaches promise you, for a price, the quantum leap forward into the *new you*, the improved *you* of your desiring. Of course after the seminars and fire-walking and the personal coaching sessions you end up with the *old* you, only somewhat poorer. For us, however, this will be different. First, we're not trying to get an instant epiphany or an immediate ecstasy, or a new you. We want to work with the old *you*, the *you* that you have always been, or perhaps the *you* which you were before you lost your way, and rediscover the tools which you have always had and still have today. You are enough, more than enough. Never forget that. Second, we want *you* to take each and every step you need to in order to awaken yourself. Neither this book nor any website will be your guru. You will be your guru, and all you will have to do to start the process each day is to wake up, breathe in the fragrance of the morning, listen to the sounds of the day, feel the terry cloth towel as your dry your face, see the sky and the clouds and be on your way. This enlightenment certainly is sustainable but, as you will read, whether *your* enlightenment will actually be sustained or not is completely up to you.

* * *

No Esoterics

The ability to simplify means to eliminate the
unnecessary so that the necessary may speak.
~ Hans Hofmann

There will no esoteric thoughts or impossible goals to deal with as we achieve sustainable enlightenment. We won't mention *hermeneutics* here, except for in this current sentence. I had a professor of Chinese philosophy in graduate school who used that particular word at least once or twice in each lecture; it must have been his favorite word. Each time he did, it took me a minute to recall what the word meant and, by the time I had thought about the way the professor used it, I had already missed the next two ideas he proposed. (It means, by the way, *the science of searching for hidden meaning in texts*. Meh.)

Although much of Yoga, Taoism and Buddhism is attractive and useful, once you begin to parse the dogma and dissect the philosophical discourses, those philosophies can go beyond useful and into useless pretty quickly. For example, in Yoga, the ultimate goal is to actually achieve something called *moksha*, or liberation from the cycle of reincarnation, while Taoism posits that, if you align yourself correctly with the five elements (fire, earth, metal, water, wood) you can attain the exact opposite, to wit, physical immortality on the earth. No release, ever, I suppose.

In Buddhism, the esoteric concept of non-dualism generally means that there is no separation in the cosmos, there is no *you* and no *me*, that when we sit and see a tree or a stream that the separation between us and the object is an illusion. The idea of non-dualism, some ineffable state of being which is neither physical nor metaphysical, however, is simply an esoteric and philosophical concept of little use to anyone living in the real world. Of course, one of the main issues keeping us from enlightenment is that we are too cocooned from life and the universe, and too disconnected. We need to be connected. However, if you actually believe that there is no *there* out there, you can wander over a cliff and meet the *there* pretty quickly. And with a thump. If everything is an illusion then driving your car into a stone wall will do nothing to the fender at all, and the air bags should not deploy. Werner Herzog made a movie ("Grizzly Man") about a young man in Alaska, Timothy Treadwell, who believed that he was one with the grizzly bear. Treadwell routinely got much closer to the great predators than he should have and would coo and yell at the bears, believing, I suppose, that he had bridged the dualistic divide between Homo Sapiens and Ursus Arctos Horribilis. That worked until one day a grizzly ate him and his girl friend, and bridged that particular divide forever. We do not get reconnected with the universe by making up some patently false but incredibly complex fairy tale about duality. To the contrary, we have a rather elegant solution to the re-connectivity conundrum: we get reconnected with the universe, quite simply, by *reconnecting* with it. Sustainable Enlightenment will show how.

There are any number of abstruse theories we can think about to pass the time of day on a sunny afternoon, but for *sustainable enlightenment* they are of little use. Is the cosmos tiny little strings at its tiniest and curving space at its largest? What good is it to know that a particular star is shining from 100 million light years away, while its neighbor is shining from only 30 million light years' distance? Is "time" an illusion? Knowing that won't stop clocks from ticking or your favorite dog from growing old. If you are making a meditation bench, a *seiza,* out of a piece of 2" by 6" fir, what real difference can it make whether its quantum components are waves or particles? We prefer to ground sustainable enlightenment firmly in perceivable reality, not only because we have to live in reality and not in some ineffable state, but mainly because it is in reality that we will re-discover our own powers and light, our true enlightenment.

*   *   *

Witchcraft, Magic and Mysticism

Mysticism is the mistake of an accidental and individual symbol for an universal one. ~Ralph Waldo Emerson

The average man, who does not know what to do with his life, wants another one which will last forever. ~Anatole France

Mysticism is the pursuit of direct communion with the ultimate reality or God, or the pursuit of a spiritual reality which cannot be reached through one's intelligence or senses. One description of the "mystical process" takes the seeker through five stages: awakening, purgation, illumination, helplessness and, finally, union with the godhead. Another statement claims that meditation is such an advanced practice for Buddhists that it can only be entered into after several lifetimes. That could only make sense if we had even a vague idea of which lifetime we are currently experiencing; is this lucky number seven, or do we have to wait for two more to pass before we can start chanting "Om"?

With human beings, often the more preposterous the claim, the more likely people are to embrace and believe it. Would you like to "quantum jump" to a parallel universe where you are living out a parallel life? There's a program for that. Or would you prefer to travel into the center of the earth or beyond the galaxies, turn yourself into a bird and soar above canyons, engage in a "mind-meld" with someone thousands of miles away or hundreds of years in the past? Yes, there's an offering for that. Would you like to pray an obscure verse or incantation and have your real estate and bank accounts grow as if by magic? There's an app for that. While you are at it, why not achieve unity with the Infinite? Why not, indeed? Sign up for the October enlightenment cruise seminar which will also visit seven Mediterranean ports of call.

Commonly, mystics and magic seekers, unhappy with their current universe, opt to believe that our existence must, somehow, be not exactly real, but rather some sort of barrier or wall (I suppose it is rather like sheetrock) which separates us from the ultimate reality and, again, union with the godhead. Well, this reality is real and you can prove it quite easily. Light a candle and put your hand over it. It will not take you very long to conclude that this world is indeed real and, in at least one location, perceptively hot. In any event, this universe is certainly real enough for sustainable enlightenment.

The mystical journeys and magical realities of the Kabbala, the Sufis, and the shamans and others may, after all, be no more than a form of self-induced mental illness. Plants and drugs and methods used during shamanic and other "mind-expanding" ceremonies have included cannabis, peyote, ayahuasca, psilocybin mushrooms, datura, fasting, vigils and sleep deprivation, sweat lodges and vision quests, some of which are hallucinogenic, poisonous and even life-threatening. We will stay clear of all that. Nothing about enlightenment will be dangerous, poisonous or remotely life-threatening.

There is no indirect or gentle way to say this: we will encounter nothing magical or mystical about sustainable enlightenment. Sorry, no witches' brews here. If you have read this far, then you already know that anyone wishing to flee this reality, no matter its manifestation, is on the wrong track. Sustainable enlightenment means embracing, fully, and immediately, this reality, with a clear head and a sober mind.

*   *   *

Simple Pleasures, Simple Treasures

'Tis the gift to be simple, 'tis the gift to be free,
'Tis the gift to come down where we ought to be. ~
Joseph Brackett

The subtitle of this book, "Einstein's Razor," is Einstein's statement (actually a paraphrase) that "things should be as simple as possible, but no simpler." Einstein never called it a razor; the razor is a reference to an earlier razor, Occam's Razor, which posits that, when you are confronted with a problem or a puzzle, "the simplest explanation is likely to be the correct one." So, let's accept the razors of Albert Einstein, and William of Occam, let's agree that *enlightenment should be as simple as possible, but no simpler.* There is no need to delve into "clock control" or a "mirror of the mind". Enlightenment is achievable, and sustainable, because, at its core, it can be understood as either a relatively simple, two-step process (receiving and processing or, as I like to think of it, "mining and manufacturing") or an only slightly expanded, seven-step process explained in more detail in Chapters Five through Eleven, which is the entirety of this book. And anyone can do this.

That's it. That's all. It really is this simple. Is it easy? Well, *easy* is a different question, but it is considerably easier (not to mention, less expensive) than the internet scammers, the life-coaches, the self-help promoters, the meditation centers and other organizations out there would like you to believe. Can you do it yourself? Strangely enough, the answer is: you can *only* do it yourself. Enlightenment is the only absolutely, no ifs, ands, or buts about it, do-it-yourself project. Unlike other DIY projects, such as installing a new sink in your guest powder room or granite counters in your kitchen, awakening is one project where you cannot hire an expert to come into your house and, for a price, do the contract work for you.

> *There are many people who reach their conclusions about life like schoolboys; they cheat their master by copying the answer out of a book without having worked out the sum for themselves.* ~ Soren Kierkegaard

You—and you alone—have to do the work; there is just no way around that. What is more, once you learn how to do the work, you must continue to do the work every day for the rest of your life. But the work of enlightenment is not heavy or particularly onerous work, not at all. In a sense, awakening or enlightenment is a life sentence, but a very nice life sentence. You don't reach awakening or enlightenment, receive a diploma for your wall or a license to put in your wallet, and then go on to other projects. Awakening *becomes* your project, your life's work, which is good, since it is the single most important thing you can do with your life. Awakening, enlightenment, is, after all, your destiny. All else, as you will see, becomes secondary. Awareness is your daily practice. You do not get your *awareness license* validated one day and then go on a two thousand dollar "continuing enlightenment seminar" cruise every two or three years to get re-certified. You renew and revalidate your awakening every single day.

The good news is the "work" is very pleasant, in fact, it is delightful. I hope to convince you of this by the time you finish Chapter Five. The lion's share of the work, practicing perception, requires no extra time from your life and eventually no extra effort, while it yields incredible rewards in and of itself. Eating an apple, going for a walk, riding a bike or jogging on a path, or simply driving in your car to and from work, or raking wet leaves in the garden or washing pots and pans after dinner or folding the laundry, while fully perceiving the inputs of the universe, is simply a wonderful thing to do, in fact, at that particular moment it is *the* most wonderful thing to do. The rest of the "work," meditation practice, takes only a little bit of time out of your day (just ten to fifteen minutes which you can quite easily find) perhaps for four or five days a week. Other than this time, the *work* takes no time and costs nothing, which means sustainable enlightenment is practically free in every sense. Of course we know this already: enlightenment should be as simple, and as inexpensive and as time-efficient, as possible, but no more so.

Here is another thing you won't get from the enlightenment industry: you don't have to buy, or even read, this whole book, as short as it is. If you will read the Introduction and the first five chapters carefully, and then feel smart and confident enough, you might be able to skip the rest. Once you have grasped the central position of the senses in this process, the remainder can be rather intuitive. I've tried to make the whole book easy to read and enjoyable, and valuable, but I'm not forcing you to read it, or even buy it. Maybe you can get it from the library. (It does, however, make a wonderful gift for a loved one . . .). After you read this book (okay, I believe you will want to read the whole thing, because I have made it as simple as possible, but no simpler), since awakening is a do-it-yourself project, you will most likely want to adapt and modify certain of the concepts described here. You may wish to reorder some of the steps, or create your own practices to hone your perceptions, or combine certain other steps or even leave one or two out. That's fine. It is your light, it is your awakening, it is your enlightenment, after all.

As to the structure of this volume, I hope you will read through the second chapter where I convince you (I think) how miraculous you are, and how deserving you are of an entirely awakened and enlightened existence, along with some other introductory information that did not seem to fit elsewhere. Most people forget how wonderful they are; the second chapter is here to remind them. You have to start with an understanding of and an acceptance of your own fabulous, and unlikely, existence. The third chapter is a very short "executive summary" of how enlightenment works. You might want to skip ahead now, read that chapter, and then come back. It describes in a sort of shorthand what enlightenment is, what enlightenment actually means, and what we can expect from it, but I include it mostly to give you two images to keep in mind as you read further. The fourth chapter is a parable. The fifth chapter, "The Doors of Perception," goes into some detail on how to focus perceptive powers (vision, hearing, smell, taste and touch) on the universe around us. Perception is the connection; perception is all the magic we will ever need. Perception is the first, primal act of awakening, and it is our sole interface with Reality. If you accept your life as a true miracle and then do only this—fully perceive— and nothing more, you will have conquered perhaps seventy percent of the enlightenment challenge. Enlightenment is, for the most part, awareness. And awareness is, almost completely, perception. We know this because when we say with regret, "I wasn't aware (of how you felt, or the situation, etc.)," what we are saying is, simply, "I failed to perceive."

If you decide to continue reading after Chapter Five, Chapters Six through Eleven walk through how to use the raw material of your perceptions to achieve what we can call "applied awareness," or more correctly, "awareness applied." *Awareness applied* means, using the harvest of your perceptions, you will practice thinking, expressing yourself, taking action, and then focus on meditating, working and, finally, taking up larger and longer, more sustained challenges to reach desirable goals, processes I call "quests." It is not only knights or adventurers who go on quests; fully enlightened people make quests an integral part of their lives.

* * *

But First, Are You Experienced, Have You Ever Been . .?

We might paraphrase Jimi Hendrix's words us to inquire whether or not we have ever been enlightened, or awakened? So, have you ever been awakened, have you ever felt enlightenment? Yes, in a word. Of course. Most of the meaningful turning points in our lives have been awakenings, even if they did not last very long.

For example, in addition to our daily awakening from evening's slumber, we awakened the first time as a baby we saw and recognized our mother's face, or when we took our first steps, or the first time we said a recognizable word and got the reaction desired (bottle, cookie, to be picked up and held, etc.). We awakened at the age of seven when we ran like the wind on the playground or tasted the sweet nectar of a honeysuckle blossom at the back fence, or the first time we noticed winter giving way to spring and then to summer, or felt the mysterious brush of lips during our first puppy love kiss or wept inconsolably at our first broken heart. We might have been shaken awake with an athletic achievement we had or an adventure of the mind, or when Clyde, the family beagle, was struck and killed by a car, or our first journey alone far away from home, or the perfect vacation with a barbecue on the beach and a sunset that still defies description, or a concert with our friends, or a perfect dinner party.

There are actually so many moments in our lives when we glimpsed through the door clearly, and viewed, if only for a moment, the richness and fullness of life, that it would be difficult to list them all for even one person. The bad news is these moments remained discrete, rare and evanescent, because we had no way to sustain them, to connect to them for very long, or to link them together with other "awakenings." The good news is, if we can be *there* once fleetingly, and if we have the wherewithal and the tools to experience this awakened zone, this enlightened state for separate moments, then we have the power to live there. Always.

*   *   *

Happiness

Will I be pretty? Will I be rich?
Here's what she said to me:
Que sera sera, whatever will be will be.
~ Ray Evans, "Que Sera, Sera" lyrics

Many people confuse enlightenment with happiness and comfort, conjuring a slightly sleepy looking lama (not *llama*, but come to think of it, the expression—that heavy lidded, enigmatic smile—may be similar), thinking that the cure to unhappiness must be happiness. The cure for discomfort, then, must be comfort. But happiness is very fleeting, and happiness is an effect, something which has a cause. And comfort leads, inevitably, to ennui.

We sometimes fill our hearts with envy and then mistake the object of envy's desire as the one key possession which will grant us happiness. *If I were an important surgeon like Dr. Jones, then I'd be respected and I'd be happy. If I only had a new car instead of this junker, then I'd be happy. If I only were more beautiful, or if I had a steady boyfriend, or if I even had a date for New Year's Eve, then I'd be happy. I see big houses all the time, if I only lived in one of those mansions instead of my little apartment which forbids pets, I'd be happy and I'd be comfortable. I need a yard and a dog to be happy.*

I like happiness as much as the next person, but happiness isn't something you achieve and then sit back and wallow in forever. Happiness is like the warmth given off by a fire or a fine cast iron stove in a cabin. You work hard, build a nice fire, cook dinner, eat and then bask in the warmth. *Voilà*, happiness. It is an effect, not a process or a thing. It comes and goes. It is only happiness, after all.

Surprisingly, rather than bringing comfort and happiness, awareness and enlightenment are at least as likely to be associated with discomfort and, for lack of a better word, unhappiness. Why is this? If you are out at six a.m. for your standard run, first there is the cool or even cold air against your face and the somewhat labored motion of your torso and legs as they begin to warm up while you push against gravity and through the pressurized atmosphere. Your run includes a somewhat long and steep hill, and now when you are in the middle of that hill your mind begins to wonder where the end could possibly be, and has this hill somehow become steeper than before, and maybe today is the day you can stop halfway up and just walk to the top? For the morning run's first twenty minutes (and you still have at least forty minutes more to go before you return home), you are *never* comfortable and you are *never* happy. Those feelings are never in the cards for your six a.m. run.

You are uncomfortable and you are struggling—you are, in a word, unhappy. But discomfort and unhappiness won't stop you from being completely *aware* at this moment, you should clearly see the grit and the fir needles on the path, you should perceive the sun's kaleidoscopic rays dappling through the trees, feel the breeze, feel the sweat beading on your forehead and back and sense as it begins to drizzle down your skin. You should feel your lungs start, as they always do at this particular point on the hill, to quicken and to gasp for air, and just begin to feel the slow build-up of lactic acid in your quadriceps and calves. No, there is nothing *comfortable* or *happy* about this moment or the four minutes of increasing struggle which have led up to it or the final six-minute push to the crest of the hill, but there is no reason why each of these moments, hundreds of them on the struggle up the hill, should not be moments of pristine and clear awareness and enlightenment.

*　　*　　*

Testing, One, Two, Three

Do not believe in anything simply because you have heard it. Do not believe in anything simply because it is spoken and rumored by many. Do not believe in anything simply because it is found written in your religious books. Do not believe in anything merely on the authority of your teachers and elders. Do not believe in traditions because they have been handed down for many generations. But after observation and analysis, when you find that anything agrees with reason and is conducive to the good and benefit of one and all, then accept it and live up to it. ~ Buddha

Everything in Sustainable Enlightenment is provable. You don't need to take anything on faith. You can and should examine each step and prove it to your own satisfaction. If I tell you (and I will) that the world and you are both almost unbelievably miraculous, then think about it and see if you can prove it to yourself. Or, try to disprove it. What chain of chance had to occur for the cosmos to form, for the stars to explode and for one or more of those massive explosions in our quadrant of the universe to settle and cool into our solar system, for life to surge forward and flourish over all the earth, for all of your great-great-great-great grandparents to meet (yes, all 64 of those individuals who comprised the 32 couples who, six generations later, have miraculously led to you)? One hundred or two hundred years plus ago, how did your paternal progenitor (whose surname you acquired at birth) travel across an ocean and then part of a continent, and how did his bride-to-be get to the same spot at the same time, how many would-be suitors did they each meet and reject (or be rejected by), and why did their match work, at least long enough to create and nurture the next generation of ancestors in your remarkable descent?

If I tell you (and I will) that your first and most vital connections to the world are your senses, test that and see if that is true. We know that even a little bit of total sensory deprivation can lead to hallucinations, depression and severe anxiety. Some of these effects can happen in as little as fifteen minutes. Apparently cutting a person off from his sensory connection to the world can be a more effective form of torture than, well, what we normally think of as torture.

When you are alone one day, check the time and find an interior closet in your house that you can darken completely. Leave your watch and telephone on the dresser. Set up a folding chair inside, and close yourself within it. Sit there in the dark as long as you can and, when you have had enough, emerge and check the time now. A seeming eternity in a dark closet was no more than a few minutes, right? Perhaps modern medical and scientific theories about dreaming are all wrong. In trying to figure out why we dream and what purpose the dream state serves, scientists may be presupposing a function ahead of their theories. We know that the act of sensing things is vital to our safety in the world and to our continued existence (smelling the breath of a mountain lion or the musk of a ripe bear, recognizing the half-hidden shape of a boa constrictor in the tall grass, or sensing the movement of a predator at the river's shoreline, could make the split-second difference between living to breed or becoming a crocodile's brunch). Since we know from sensory deprivation studies that people quickly begin to go mad when deprived of their sensory connections, might it also make sense that, even when we are resting and replenishing our bodies in an unconscious state, were we to turn our senses *completely off* during sleep for a period of even a few hours, we might lose the moorings of our minds? Our dreams with vivid characters and activities may simply serve to keep our selves and senses alert and connected, albeit to an "alternative" and "unreal" universe, and prevent the onslaught of "madness" while we sleep, and have no other purpose (interpretative, de-fragging, etc.) at all. Perhaps we dream, not to accomplish anything, but simply to keep from going crazy each night. We awake, sane, and simply trade one set of sensory connections for another.

As you read this short book, test each of these seven steps against what you *know* to be true. Can you control your thoughts and intentions and, if you can, how does that affect your life? If you feel hurt and ignored by someone you love, can you not imagine that person caught up in some problem you are not aware of, and forgive him or her, without knowing more? Then the hurt feeling disappears, correct? Have you ever found the peace which you sought within a religious setting or retreat? Can you control your expressions and actions? Does simple meditation allow you to see more clearly who you really are? Can you see your choice of vocation in a new, clearer light? Can you understand the steps to undertake, and the ultimate value of, a series of quests in your life? This is the testing you must do and, like all of this enlightenment process, no one else can do it for you. It is a do-it-yourself activity.

*   *   *

The Secret

When imagining an "enlightened" person or a sage, most of us have the image of a guru chanting in a cave or a priest earnestly praying in his monastery cell while fingering rosary beads. We imagine that these icons of enlightenment are not actually doing *anything* at the time except sitting there thinking and perhaps chanting or repeating silent prayers over and over. It is very passive. And we know that we don't have time in our own lives to spend hours every day lost in our chakras and our chanting. But enlightenment is physical. In fact, I'd say it is 90 percent *physical*, it is 90 percent *doing* things or, more correctly, it is the doing of things and the *how* of doing things. Actively perceiving, expressing yourself and taking physical actions throughout the course of a lifetime—that's enlightenment. Therefore, if enlightenment is 90 percent physical actions of one sort or another, then the mental part of enlightenment can only be 10 percent of the process. That's math for you.

Again, the physical part is how you sense things, how you express yourself, the actions you take, how you choose to work and how you accept and carry out challenges throughout your life.

When we look at the (already much smaller) non-physical or mental part, which is just ten percent of the whole, you will see that even *that* is actually 99 percent *how* you think, that is, *how* you process all the external sensations you receive (including all filters you have set up) and *how* you review (which is a sort of *re-perceiving*) all of the thoughts, expressions and actions you have undertaken and are undertaking, in order to test them against your inventory of sensations and thoughts and intentions, in an endless iterative loop. It is also *how* you conceive and plan your quests as each presents itself to you. The last remaining part, the one percent of the mental part and only one tenth of one percent of *enlightenment as a whole*, is meditation practice, the sitting and mulling and focusing that most people imagine is the main path to enlightenment. That's right, if we were to draw a comparative chart of enlightenment, the biggest 90 percent piece (let's make this a tall pyramid, almost an obelisk) would be "Physical," and then the squat 9.9 percent pyramid next to it would be "Thinking," and the 0.1% flattened pyramid, so thin you can barely see it, would be "Meditation". (It looks rather pitiful, like a thin slice of white bread, flat-fried in a skillet.) So you will want to meditate ten minutes or so a day, maybe five days a week. This is very good news since the vast majority of us simply don't have an extra 400 or more hours a year to use for quiet sitting.

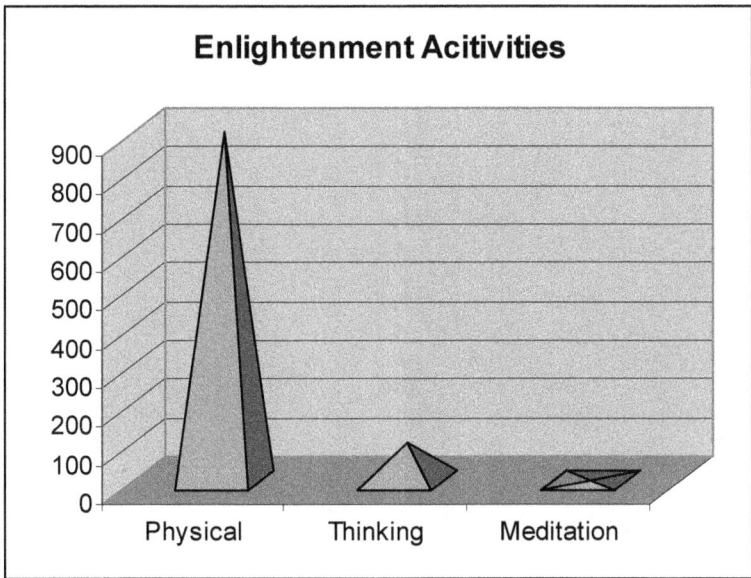

Enlightenment Acitivities

So, the popular myth of the guru or enlightened one pictures him doing something which is, *at most*, one tenth of one percent of getting enlightened. We don't meditate our way to enlightenment; we take specific actions to get there.

That's it, that's the end of this chapter. We must try to keep it as simple as possible. But no simpler. Now, let's introduce you to your miraculous self.

*   *   *

TWO

Miraculous You

You are *fabulous*. Not, "you look fabulous," but you *are* fabulous, wonderful—*miraculous*, even. You are simply a miraculous wonder. No, I am not trying to "pick you up" or "set you up." This is no advertising scam, your very existence is a miracle. You are *miraculous*.

Whether you are young or old, fit or unfit, as happy as a clam on the seabed floor or as depressed as a wet, spun sock in the washing machine, the fact that you are standing or sitting here, reading this, means that you are absolutely, undeniably miraculous. And, as a true miracle, you deserve a truly miraculous life. Is that how you describe your life today? Is it how you would describe your life every day? The one truly miraculous life which you deserve—the only way to live miraculously—is to live wonderfully awakened, fully enlightened, and blissfully calm, all of the time.

Before I get into exactly how you will get to where you want to be—that truly aware and enlightened state—let's talk some more about you.

When I tell you that you are a miracle, standing there, am I just buttering your toast or shining your shoes? No. Am I just trying to sell you this book? Maybe. I *am* trying to sell you this book, or at least trying to sell you on reading this book, but I am not "just" trying to sell you this book. Read a little more and decide for yourself. Actually, the fact that you are a miracle is empirically true, which means I can prove it to you, or rather you can prove it to yourself. Right now. Pinch your arm—gently, after all, you are touching a living miracle—you have perhaps 100 trillion cells made up mostly of a few of the simplest and most abundant elements on earth. Four of them—oxygen, carbon, hydrogen and calcium, account for about 95 percent of what you are. Put another way, you are 75 percent water, 18 percent carbon and a relatively small amount of calcium. Surprisingly, the calcium in your bones, your heavy duty infrastructure, the frame which holds you erect as you climb that mountain trail, is only about 1.5% of you. As marvelous as you are, not one thing in you is rare, however; you contain no cerium, no samarium and no gadolinium, no rare earth elements at all.

Imagine that you have a 40-gallon fish tank. Now fill it with 16 gallons of water, add 30 pounds of coal (maybe two shovels full) to represent your carbon components, and two and a half pounds of dried bones (okay, no need to find human bones, desiccated beef ribs will do) to represent your calcium. Those 162 pounds of material represent about 95% of a 175-pound person, chemistry-wise. The other 12 pounds or so of you is just a bunch of other chemicals, and very common ones at that. Nitrogen, phosphorus, potassium, sulfur, some table salt and a little iron. It is not a very impressive or exotic recipe. Regrettably, in material terms, there is just nothing very special—or miraculous—about you. It is not the shopping list of your chemical structure which is miraculous, however, but rather how it is all arranged, and, that is, *very carefully*. You may not know this, but certain of the chemicals and compounds you contain and absolutely need in order to live, if they were suddenly released into your blood stream, would kill you almost instantly. Fortunately, miraculously in fact, the potassium, the phosphate and the myoglobin are locked away and, barring some unfortunate accident (such the pinning of one of your limbs under a boulder or heavy machinery for an extended period of time, something which is called *crush syndrome*), they will stay locked away, doing their thing, enabling you to function as a miraculous human being, and not kill you.

Somehow this relatively short and simple grocery list of some very common elements is *all* that you are, materially speaking, but this *stuff* is organized by tiny genetic instructions into an amazing creature—you—who can not only read this page but can also walk, run, ride a bike, swim, hum a tune that was just on the radio, swing on a trapeze, swoosh on a toboggan, paddle a canoe, skin up and ski down a snow-covered volcano, tell funny stories, tell sad stories, cook a meal, remember to turn off the lights, laugh, cry, hug, snuggle, do something incredibly brave or something incredibly foolish, and choose among seven types of lettuce at the market. Look at the stuff you've assembled in that aquarium once more, look at 95% of what you are, and think of all the things you can do with one hand tied behind your back. Is it amazing? Yes. It's miraculous.

Do you want or need to be more miraculous? Simple as pie. How on earth did you get here? Think about the chain of chance that brought you *qua you* here. Your father, Thomas, sitting in Kentucky in October of 1950, was about to be drafted into the Korean Conflict, so he decided to enlist instead. Thomas was only alive at that point, however, because a hunting incident which occurred in Pike County near Fishtrap Lake in October of 1940, when he was ten years old, sent a bullet one inch over his head—a head which he had lowered exactly 1.4 seconds before to check on his boot stuck in the autumn muck—instead of propelling the bullet through his brain. At twenty, in the military, Thomas opted for some special training you have never been quite clear on and, by the time he was a qualified whatever, instead of serving in Korea, he was sent to a base in Germany. There, in late 1951, Thomas met the woman who was to become your mother, Agnieszka. And she was only there, working as a translator-secretary on the base, because *her* father, Stanislaw, had the great luck and wisdom to take his wife and four-year old daughter out of Torun, Poland in 1937 and find work in England. Had they stayed in Poland it is very likely that none of the family would have survived. Your mother, quadrilingual in English, Polish, German and Czech, was nearly nineteen when she met your father and they fell in love, married and returned to the U.S. to live, eventually, in St. Petersburg, Florida.

You are the fourth of six children. You were born in 1959, before birth control became widely available. Had birth control been available, your parents could have experienced all those passionate nights in steamy Florida without any consequences other than the après-sex cigarette. They smoked Pall Malls, by the way. Luckily—miraculously from your point of view—the consequence instead was *you*. You are the merger of Agnieszka's egg of the month (in this case it was September, 1958) and a single, intrepid sperm cell from Thomas. Scientists tell us that in each male "try" (in medical terms, "ejaculate") there might be as many as 40 million swimmers. We cannot know how many times your parents "embraced" in September of 1958, so we don't really know the exact ratio of "swimmers" to the single gold medalist, but let's assume that it was five times. Your unique (and miraculous) genetic makeup, a large portion of who you are and what you do, is because the meeting of a 200 million to one shot, pardon the pun, and the ovum of the month. Of course, another, different swimmer could have breached the castle rampart, and perhaps in a later month, say, December. But the result, while it might have been someone as like you as either your older sister, Jill, or your little brother, Robbie, would not have *been* you, of that we can be sure. You—that is, your exact genetic combination along with your unique experiences in the world you grew up in, your environment, your history and the sequence in which it all has happened up to now—never existed before, and will never exist again.

You are feeling a bit more miraculous by now, I assume. What? Well, yes, I know, this is not *technically* your story and your history, and it's not mine, either, but each of us has an even *more* complicated story which involves an incredible chain of chance on both the cellular and human historical levels. Still not convinced? Okay, how about this?

Sometime in the late 1760s, a Scots-Irish baby is born in Northern Ireland. His parents christen him Michael. We don't know the details, but the region has been aflame since the English first brought their lowland Scots immigrants across the Irish Sea to take the Catholic lands in Ulster. Michael grows up speaking the Scots dialect and, to escape the hard life, violence and famine, joins the tens of thousands of his countrymen who migrate to the North American continent in the eighteenth century. In his particular case, sometime in the 1780s, Michael lands in the port of Philadelphia and, unwelcome there, finds his way west to Fayette County in

Pennsylvania, and meets and marries a Pennsylvania Dutch woman named Susannah Foreman. Birth records show that they have five children, and the last, whom they name Michael for his father, is born in 1803. In 1816 the elder Michael dies. The records are a little unclear but young Michael marries Sarah Shanabarger sometime around 1820 at the age of seventeen, a union which produces seven children during the ensuing nineteen years. Sarah disappears from the record in the 1840s, perhaps a victim of childbirth fever or dysentery. Michael's second wife, Virlinda Hancock, gives birth to two more children, Lewis and Malinda, in 1846 and 1848, respectively, but then she also disappears from the records. Did they divorce? Did she die? We don't know. A census taken in 1850 shows Michael in his household, married now to a third wife, one Minerva Gault, ten years his junior, who is raising the four younger children. Minerva has no babies which survive in the records. In 1863, at 60 years of age, Michael dies of dysentery, and his youngest boy, Lewis, is seventeen years old. At some time in the next five or six years, Lewis works his way west to Wheeling, West Virginia, gets passage down the Ohio River through Parkersburg and Huntingdon and lands on the western shore of the Ohio in Greenup, Kentucky, where he will eventually become the superintendent of schools. He meets and marries Eliza Collins in November of 1872. They have seven children, and their last is born on February 27, 1887. They christen him *Chester Arthur* in honor of our twenty-first President, who has died just three months before. He is "Jummie" or "Jum" as a boy, but as an adult he will always be known as "C.A.".
C.A. is the seventh child of the eighth child of the fifth child of Michael from the eighteenth century and the old country.

C.A. leaves Greenup and moves east to Charleston, West Virginia where he meets and marries a young woman named Odessa Mae Chandler, in 1917. He is thirty, she is twenty-five. Their first child is born in May of 1918, a boy, and they name him William Louis. Thirty-six years later he will become my father. Although William Louis McCarty is born during the great influenza pandemic of 1918-19, that particular plague bypasses his household. He will grow up and fly more than forty bombing missions for the Army Air Corps in Africa, Italy and Germany during the last two years of World War II. Many of his fellows never return, but he does, about nine years before I am born, the fourth of five children. Counting all the way back, I am the fourth child of the first child of the seventh child of the eighth child of the fifth child of Michael McCarty of Northern Ireland from the 1760s. I carry the progenitor Michael's full surname, McCarty, on my birth certificate and passport, and I have his DNA in my cells, but because of the generations which have passed, the progenitor's DNA contribution to me comprises only 3.125% of my code. The other 96.875% of me comes in equal fractional shares from the rest of the tree, that is, 3.125% from each of the other 63 people who make up my great-great-great-grandparents' contributing generation. Each of them has an incredible chronicle, too. Unfortunately, I do not know much if anything about those lives.

More miracles. Although I personally have lived a comparatively safe life, I have actually escaped, narrowly enough for me, death at least five times. In 1956 when I was two years old, my older brother (Don was three at the time), believing he had discovered hidden candy, shares some rat poison with me (sharing is caring) and we are rushed to the hospital to have our stomachs pumped. That particular nightmare is probably my earliest memory. In 1971 (see Chapter Eleven) I come perilously close to peeling off the Grand Teton for a several hundred foot drop into Idaho, which certainly would have ended my seventeen years' residence on the earth. In August 1978, on our honeymoon, my wife and I are nearly swept out into the East China Sea and to our death. We were just body-surfing off the southern coast of Cheju Island during a vicious, post-typhoon riptide. It takes us 10 minutes of hard struggle just to fight our way the forty or so yards in to shore. In August 1983, my wife, infant son and I are holding reservations on the very last KAL 007 flight from New York to Seoul, the one which, you may recall, will be shot down by the Soviet Union in the early morning hours of September 1[st.] We will be spared only because we are so poor that I renegotiate to extend an extra two weeks in New York at my summer job, and we cancel our seats on the doomed flight. Finally, en route to a cross country ski trip in Nikko, Japan in January, 1992, as I stop to chain up our Mazda and am crouched on the road's narrow shoulder trying to suss out the detailed Japanese instructions, a Toyota Landcruiser slides across an icy intersection and plows into a car perhaps six feet from where I am sprawled. If that vehicle is not there, the skidding SUV will turn me into a newspaper item on page 12 somewhere and a memorial service. Look back at the miraculous chain of chance in just these three paragraphs. Two hundred and fifty years of unlikely happenings and chance encounters, implausible journeys and improbable loves, passions and lustings and anguished labor pains, hairbreadth escapes and white knuckle squeezes, all of which have brought me here to have this conversation with you. And your trip here has been at least as improbable, implausible and miraculous, if not more so.

Very quickly, because I want to get to *your* enlightenment soon, let's at least discuss our palace, this improbable earth. Think about the miracle of your 175 pounds of superbly organized (but absolutely mundane) chemicals living on this small but spectacular blue planet, perfectly situated about 90 million miles from its home star in a corner of the cosmos (and a not very important, or central, corner, we are told), with its own perfectly sized moon which creates the tidal movements in rivers and estuaries, which brought and deposited concentrations of key chemicals into the coastal sounds, bays, seas and oceans, key chemicals which formed the original earthly soup of life more than three billion years ago. Our earth is protected from constant attack from space flotsam by one terrific, oxygenated atmosphere which burns up most of said flotsam well before impact; it acts like a science fiction "force shield". Yet if the oxygen content of our atmosphere were only a few percentage points higher, we are informed, most of our terrestrial forests and other flora would simply burn up during incredible forest and plains fires every year or so, and the land would resemble burnt toast. It turns out that 21 percent oxygen in an atmosphere is close to perfect. We have plenty of oxygen to breathe and grow, but not so much as to barbecue everything on earth once every few years. We also have a miraculous axial tilt (thank you very much, again, Mr. Moon!) which gives our temperate areas stable seasons, and a magnificent molten iron core and magnetic field which protects life on earth from the murderous charged particles contained in deadly solar winds.

In short, you are an improbable creature and a living miracle, born of a chain of impossible chance along an immense journey of earthly life, alive on a miracle planet, and able to perceive and marvel at a myriad of incredible things. You should be content and alert, and you should feel enthusiastic about each day; you should literally kick up your heels and jump for joy. Your life should be robust and authentic, full of achievement and self-realization. Your life should be a daily manifestation of your destiny unfolding. You should act generously to your friends, family, colleagues and the world around you, and feel gratitude every waking moment of every waking day, and even be grateful every night while you sleep and replenish your miracle self.

Does this describe you already? If so, then close Sustainable Enlightenment now and put it back on the shelf, and congratulate yourself. You are already completely aware, awakened and enlightened.

If, on the other hand, you have down days and middling days, if you sometimes or often feel like the world is passing you by, if every day brings at the very least some new annoyances and irritations which ensnare you, and if you sometimes have vague and haunting fears, then you might want to read on for a few pages. If you regret some of the things you have done and resent some of the events which have happened to you in the past, and you grieve for lost family and friends, feel physically heavy and burdened and slowed by life, if you sometimes wake from night-dreams and day-dreams in anxiety and fear, and if you wonder at the purpose of it all—your birth and life so far—and where it is all heading, then Sustainable Enlightenment can help. If you daydream about wealth and power and fame, and resent that others have them and you do not—then maybe there is a solution inside this book. If we can agree that your entire life is, in fact, a *miracle*, then at the very least you are entitled to experience a miraculous life, an awakened life, an enlightened life which is truly rich each and every day you are here. Not only should you be and feel all these wonderful things, but most miraculously of all, you have always had—and have now—within you, everything you require to achieve it all, and within a very short time. Let's explore how, together.

All enlightenment is *awareness applied*. Stated just slightly more fully, enlightenment is our active, daily practice to do several things: to use all our senses to perceive our universe as fully as possible, to think and intend enthusiastically, graciously and generously, to express ourselves correctly, and to act correctly, to train our minds to be totally aware, to pursue a correct livelihood and to exert ourselves over extended periods to attain more complex goals, something we call "quests". Do we need to be especially virtuous, or saintly (you know the type) or ethereal or other-worldly? Is the road to enlightenment harsh and grueling; is it a rocky path of suffering? No. We can be flawed, we can err, we can be proud, lazy, impatient, hungry, lusty, angry, jealous and envious, and still get there. We won't be putting on hair shirts or punishing ourselves physically; we can stay in our agreeable homes and earn our living in well-lit and comfortable workplaces. We're talking about enlightenment and awakening, not abstinence, puritanism or sainthood. Speeches, seminars, webinars and cruises will not take us there. We can get there, of course, but we have to get there on our own.

Can we seriously mean that anyone can achieve enlightenment? Yes, practically speaking, yes. Yes.

*   *   *

The Buddha

When Siddhartha Gautama left his kingdom in 563 B.C. to search for what later became known as Buddhist nirvana (the end of suffering) and enlightenment, it took him six years of travel, intensive study, asceticism and, finally, meditation to achieve his full awakening. It is interesting to note that Christ became a Christian at birth, we are told that even as a child he was unusually good and spoke on equal terms with the elders, but it took Siddhartha thirty-five years to become the first Buddha (and therefore, the first Buddhist). Although some temples today have curricula for the laity to study Buddhism for weekend retreats and courses of up to six months or a year at their sites, nowadays it probably takes at least five continuous years of hard study to be ordained a basic Zen monk, and often longer. Most serious Buddhists I have met say it takes a lifetime of diligent study of the dharma to have any hope of reaching nirvana, let alone awakening and enlightenment. I've never met any "organizational" Buddhist ever who said he/she was a Buddha (literally, an "awakened one"), or even getting close. Many seem to think it might take more than one lifetime, and they seem comfortable with that.

We are left to conclude that, with over six billion people on the planet, almost nobody here is actually awakened or enlightened. Nor could they be, since enlightenment is just *so hard* to reach. If this is true, then awakening itself has to be considered an "epic fail," in modern parlance.

However, what if there is an enlightenment which any of us can achieve, without joining a monastery or a temple, without committing years to study ancient and profound religious texts and indecipherable koans, and within only a few weeks or a month, and one which we can carry through—sustain—all the days of our lives? What would it take to achieve this kind of enlightenment? Have the clergy and the monks and the writers and the scholars—not to mention the promoters and the scammers—made it too difficult, too esoteric, too inaccessible and too expensive for the average person?

*   *   *

The Path to Heaven

It used to be very complicated to get to the Christian heaven. If you were a Christian in the old days, fire and brimstone awaited you when you slipped up in life, a celibate priest took weekly confessions of your human frailty and transgressions, you needed near perfect attendance at Mass, you needed to say any number of Hail Marys and Our Fathers while fingering rosary beads, and you needed the last rites administered to you when you were *in extremis*. Unless you were a scholar in those days, you couldn't even understand the words of the scriptures or the path to heaven—that was left to the Papal hierarchy and cognoscenti. Most of your understanding of the scriptures came from cathedrals and their paintings, statuary and stained glass depictions of the Creation, the Holy Family, various saints and the Last Judgment. It could only help, of course, to purchase a "safe passage" to Paradise when a travelling salesman, such as Johann Tetzel, knocked on your door to sell you an "indulgence." The best I can make of an "indulgence" is that it was sort of a purchasable "golden passport" into paradise, like a three- or five-day pass you might buy at Disneyworld.

A millennium and a half into this type of Christianity, Germany's Martin Luther in 1517 takes one good look at Johann Tetzel standing at his door in Wurms and figures out that we can pretty much bypass the Pope and the priests, the confessions, a lot of the rites, the ritual phrases and the bead thing, and we should be able to read the scripture in our own language, and we can tell the indulgence-seller to go pound sand. To Marty, there is no reason why a religious advisor (soon to be known as a Lutheran "minister" or "pastor") needs to be celibate. Why shouldn't a pastor take a wife and have children? After all, God created man and woman and made them attractive to each other. Martin Luther leads by example, so to speak, by marrying his own sweetheart, Katharina—a former nun— and moves into what had previously been a monastery, and they begin having children of their own. Talk about "in your face." Take that, Rome. Katharina is quite a catch, because when she isn't giving birth to the young Lutherans (six!) she keeps busy with the farm and even takes in boarders to help make financial ends meet. Perhaps "behind every good man is a great woman" is actually an early Lutheran doctrine. Most importantly, the Church's convoluted and twisty path to heaven, like some 16th century turnpike in France, is replaced for the Protestants with a smoother, less curvy interstate, which Luther calls "Justification by Faith through the Grace of God". He might as well have called it "Route One," though.

About a century and a half later in England, George Fox, the son of a country weaver, begins to think that even Protestantism with its church organization and ministers and stone cathedrals is a touch unwieldy. He has the brainstorm that 1) church rituals can be discarded, 2) anyone guided by the Holy Spirit can act as a minister, even women and children, without any theological training, 3) since

God is everywhere, the idea of a "church" as a specialized, single-use building is absurd, and religious ministry can occur anywhere on the surface of the planet, and 4) since God is within us, we can follow the spirit within and not have to worry too much about the details of the Bible or what the priests or ministers tell us it is supposed to mean. This group becomes known as the Quakers, and their path to Heaven might be termed the autobahn.

So it only takes the church (well, a small part of it) about 1,650 years to wend its way back to something which was there, all along: Luke 17:21, "The Kingdom of God is within you." Now might be a good time for a Quaker-style movement for individual awareness practice, aimed at simplifying and speeding up our own awakening and enlightenment.

*   *   *

What's in Enlightenment for Us?

Life has loveliness to sell,
All beautiful and splendid things,
Blue waves whitened on a cliff,
Soaring fire that sways and sings,
And children's faces looking up
Holding wonder like a cup. ~Sarah Teasdale

What might awakening or enlightenment mean for us, in practical terms? *Practical* is an odd word to use here, since so much of what we will gain will be beyond "practical" in any sense of that word. Of course, words themselves present difficult issues—*the Tao that can be spoken is not the true Tao*—and words are unwieldy utensils for describing accurately what the actual goal of sustainable enlightenment is, but in the universe of books, words are all we have.

As noted above, when we are aware and enlightened, we will have highly developed perceptive powers so that we are fully engaged in life's loveliness, and we will see, hear, smell, taste and feel more and more. Every moment of every day we will perceive directly more and more not only of the richness of the material world, but also the relationship of related objects and entities, and the relationship of seemingly unrelated objects and entities, and our own miraculous place in the material and metaphysical world. Because our world will become so much richer, we will feel "wealthier" in the true sense, and feel grateful for the tremendous gift that is literally our birthright—life itself.

Everything, in effect, will begin to be illuminated. Negativity, skepticism and unpleasantness will begin to vanish from our minds and our experience in life, and our thoughts and intentions will become more and more robust, authentic, generous, gracious and enthusiastic. Because we now directly comprehend the richness of everything which surrounds us and is available to our senses, we will feel a deep gratitude for every element of our world (which we will now perceive more profoundly than ever before) and this feeling will make our lives more bountiful than any king's or billionaire's. More and more we will speak and express ourselves in accordance with the thoughts and intentions just listed, true and correct thoughts and intentions *which will be our own.* Our actions, like our thoughts, will similarly become enthusiastic, generous and gracious, and our bodies, minds, and spirits will grow strong and rich. We will be able to concentrate our minds, focus and find inner peace through meditation practice; we will soon find that meditation practice need not be limited to a quiet room but can be done anywhere at anytime. We will find it easier to work and easier to find that kind of work which is suited to us, and we will take pleasure in our livelihood, comprehending and understanding how our work is part of the entire web of our lives and, indeed, the universe. Finally, we will be able to concentrate our intentions and our actions into extended efforts to achieve greater goals—quests—which will be in line with who we really are and who we are becoming.

In a certain way, we will have the training of a master clockmaker who can open any clock and understand the entire clockwork. Things in the world might still dismay us, such as when the master sees that a part of the clockwork is stuck, or bent, or broken and needs to be repaired, but nothing will surprise us. We will understand to the tiniest detail (look, smell, feel, taste, texture, history and aesthetic), the nature of every *thing* in an instant, intuitively and not intellectually. This nature, or truth, of each thing is called the "suchness" of a thing, and it includes all of its own attributes and all of its relationships to every other thing.

For example, we hike along a mountain stream in the early spring and we will perceive it as an agglomeration of water molecules which are themselves agglomerations of tinier particles, atoms, which are themselves agglomerations of even tinier subatomic particles and waves. Back above the molecular level, we will perceive this water, which fell as snow last winter, melted into the soil and now percolates up through the aquifers and gains force and speed as it careens down this particular mountain's gully, icy cold and numbing to the touch, with a slight tang of decayed leaf and soil and an aftertaste of certain minerals. The water gurgles and pops and rushes forth, and at night the dark skin of the stream is illuminated by sparkling starlight, and moonlight, and in the morning the surface goes muted and dull in the fog, and in the later morning the fog burns off and the watery façade shines again with blinding brilliance; downstream now in serene pools, the clear water refracts the light making some stones appear bigger as tiny fish dart around. This kind of understanding, which is really just a tiny representation of what we will actually understand about the stream, and which will be immediate and instantaneous, and which only begins *in a kind of shorthand* to delineate our awakened knowledge of one tiny stream (out of millions) on one mountain (out of ten thousand), is just one isolated instant and instance of our perception from an awakened state. Multiply this enhanced perception by all the streams, mountains, trees, bushes, meadows, blades of grass, squirrels and wrens and nuthatches, possums and raccoons and deer, rocks and forests and lakes and oceans, villages, towns and cities and automobiles and trains and airplanes which we might see. Seeing through the veneer of all things to their individualized suchness will make our lives immediately fuller, richer and deeper. How could it be otherwise?

*   *   *

What's Not In Enlightenment for Us?

An oak tree is an oak tree. That is all it has to do. If an oak tree is less than an oak tree, then we are all in trouble. ~ Thich Nhat Hanh

A little boy goes camping at the lake with his parents. After the youngster falls asleep, a young couple arrives at the next campsite, sets up their tent quietly and goes to sleep. The next morning the boy wakes before his parents and walks to the campsite next door. He sees their tent and their car, a brand new, candy-red Corvette. He has never seen a car like this, although he has seen a television show where a red flying saucer landed on earth. He believes he is looking at a flying saucer now, and is more than a little excited, and somewhat afraid. Where did it come from, can it go a million miles an hour, does it have ray guns mounted on its deck, what do the aliens look like, and what do they eat? Can it sail on the lake or dive under it like a submarine? He feels a hand on his shoulder and, fortunately, it is his father. "Dad," he whispers, "is that a flying saucer?" "No, son," his father says, a little wistfully, thinking of his car, an aging minivan, "but it sure is a nice car."

Later that same morning, while walking with his mother on the path around the lake, the boy sees a yellow banana slug and asks if it is a poisonous snake. His mother tells him, no, that it's only a forest slug; it goes very slowly and it can't hurt anyone. He wants to step on it, but his mother stops him, explaining, "She's not hurting anyone, and she may have little ones at home waiting for her. They would be sad if you stepped on their mom, wouldn't they?"

Let's contemplate the sports car and the slug for a moment. First, we "value" the slick car at sixty or seventy thousand dollars and "value" the slug at nothing. Second, although a candy-colored sports car may look like it can fly through space, on closer inspection, we see that it has four treaded tires, a couple of doors and a steering wheel. If we pop the hood we'd see a familiar (if very nice!) engine, carburetor, etc. If we were to turn it over like a turtle, we'd see a drive shaft, a gas tank and an exhaust pipe—all very familiar. A car is just a car, after all, and it can't blast off or fly or sail on or beneath the water. We should not be fooled by surfaces or our own desires; things are what they are and are limited to what they are. And that includes us.

Now the slug, which is so much slower and, to most people, so much uglier than the Corvette and almost everything else in the world, is so far superior to the automobile that it scarcely needs describing. After all, the slug is alive and has its own awareness. A slug can do, and does, something the Corvette can never do: sense the world (through two sets of feelers, one for seeing and one for smelling), decide where it wants to go, and take action to get there. Unlike the Corvette, which is the true parasite (although we can call it a high maintenance "tool") and needs manmade roads to get anywhere (not to mention man-provided gasoline, oil, replacement tires, brakes, regular service), the slug paves his own way with his own mucus, feeds and fuels himself and can even hibernate underground during the winter in certain temperate climates.

When we think about enlightenment, or awakening, we need to remember that, like the Corvette, we are only what we are. The sleekest, finest car in the world is still a gasoline engine with a power transfer unit driving four rubber encased wheels along macadam or concrete pathways. No matter its aerodynamic lines and composite materials, it is never going to be a spaceship. Just an automobile. The same is true for us.

All any exalted Rolls Royce, or the humblest sedan, ever will be is a car. As humans, even though we can dress ourselves up in silk dresses and worsted wool suits and lather ourselves with lotions, and apply makeup and fragrances, in the end we are simply human beings. Consider a simple toaster, its two slots with heating elements, metal case, cord and plug. There's only one thing to do with this device: plug it in and toast something "slottable." We can't "imagineer" it into a radio or pneumatic drill, or wish it into a television.

Although I believe I have made a convincing case that we are all, indeed, miraculous, our vision is still limited to the visible spectrum and our ears cannot discern ultrasonic or infrasonic sounds. Our terrestrial enlightenment, at its best, will only be human enlightenment, and that will necessarily exclude any claim that, by reaching some sort of uber-state, we will stop the cycle of reincarnation, see into the future, travel into the past, jump into a different dimension, or attain eternal life. Enlightenment and meditation promoters who are trying to sell you any of those powers along with their t-shirts, beads, webinars and cruises are taking advantage of our tendency to dream away our limitations and dream our way into magic. We are sentient beings who have certain powers of perception, the ability to think and analyze, the means to express ourselves, the capability to act using our bodies and our tools, and the ability to discipline ourselves to do certain things (meditate, pray, and endure certain amounts of "suffering") over extended periods without immediate reward. What we have is limited, but it is more than enough to achieve enlightenment, and to sustain enlightenment throughout our lives.

When we are enlightened, our lives won't suddenly be perfect, just immediately better; and annoyances may still annoy us and irritating people may indeed still irritate us, or a part of us, but it will not matter so much, or perhaps begin not to matter at all. We won't be any richer in dollar terms, unless something in our enlightenment "unblocks" obstacles which have kept us relatively poorer. This is not a get rich quick scheme; it is a *get aware quick scheme* only.

*   *   *

A Little Background, a Little Structure

East meets West. As a teenager in the suburbs of Philadelphia, I liked the Tao and the Buddha; I think most young men in the West have a thing for the Far East at some point. It might begin with kung fu or karate. I watched Bruce Lee movies and *Kung Fu* on TV; I was entranced by the juxtaposition of calm and danger. Although I played football, wrestled and ran track in high school, and later rowed on the university crew team, I also meditated and wrote poetry. I started learning Tae Kwon Do in the summer of 1972, and bought a white plaster Buddha at a novelty shop and painted it red. I kept it in my room during my first two years at college in Charlottesville but, when I departed in May of 1974 for a year in Spain, I gave it to a girl I had dated a few times.

My interest in Taoism and Buddhism grew exponentially when I joined the Peace Corps in 1976 to become a middle school teacher in Korea. During weekends and longer school vacations I hiked and climbed and camped out in the Tae Baek Mountain range, always stopping and sometimes staying at Buddhist temples and hermitages. I conceive this little book to be a straightforward explanation for anyone who might like a mercifully short and economical guide on how to perceive and then illuminate their personal world so as to attain the fullest and richest life possible right now. That is really what awareness, awakening or enlightenment is. If we can perceive things as they truly are, and apply that awareness diligently via thoughts and actions, and meet everything the world presents with calm and serenity, then we can become true visionaries and true life masters.

I was brought up attending Presbyterian services and now attend Catholic Mass almost every Sunday with my wife, but I have achieved at this point a position in the Christian world of lapsed. I'm no better in the Buddhist world, I am afraid, since I found group meditation sessions not to my liking, and I do my learning and my practice on my own, so there are no strange sounding titles in my name, such as *roshi* or *rinpoche*. I am not interested in hierarchies, whether organized by state, institution or church. I am not a monk, a guide or a guru, just an average meditator writing a book.

For structure I have borrowed some bits from Yoga and Taoism, and reconfigured the eightfold path from Buddhism. I see it a bit differently than others do; after all I am seeing it through my prism, not theirs. In my view, it is important to get to meditation (which is comprised of mindfulness and concentration) sooner than last, so it's now the fifth step. I'm using this structure to streamline what is really important, and put it in a format which is easily accessible. My hope is to show how relatively simple this clarity can be.

In the East, eight is an interesting number. In India, there are eight "limbs" in the yoga sutras (yama, niyama, asana, pranayama, pratyahara, dharana, dhyana, and Samadhi), which act as a short list of commandments (non-violence, truthfulness, non-covetousness, abstention and non-possessiveness, cleanliness, austerity, study, etc.), as well as instructions for postures, breathing and meditation. In the Sinitic world, eight has a particularly lucky significance, as the Chinese ideograph shows two simple slashes, pointing up toward heaven (八). Its sound, "ba," indicates richness and wealth. Just to illustrate how seriously they take this *octophilism*, the Beijing Olympics opened on August 8, 2008 (8/8/08) at 8:08:08 p.m. in order to achieve maximum good fortune for the host country. Apparently, it worked, since by the completion of the games China scored more gold medals and achieved a higher total point count than any other nation.

Seven is our lucky number in the West, and when it came time to settle on a structure, the last two steps (right mindfulness and right concentration) from the eightfold path seemed to fold, as it were, into one another.

This is a book for anyone of any religious persuasion, and for those with none at all. The process and practice of enlightenment in our daily lives can supplement religion and belief, but at the same time present no conflict. The afterworlds of heaven and paradise are beyond the interest and scope of this book. I am interested in awakening fully in this world, and invite you to do the same. These seven steps are not discrete, separate items, however, but rather a series of simple practices where the first, perception, lays the foundation for, informs, and leads directly into the second, how we should think and intend. Of the seven steps, we already know that the first practice of full perception is by far the most important. It is the gateway to clarity and enlightenment, it is our connection. If we manage to perceive the world in all its richness, and do only that, then we will be at least partly aware and partly enlightened. If we fail to do that, then we will never achieve any clarity at all. You can not expect your refrigerator or television to work if it is not connected to a power source. Human beings are no different.

It seems quite natural, then, that once we perceive clearly, we will be able to think correctly. The third step will be to speak and communicate in the correct way. And once we perceive, think, and speak correctly, then it should be easy, or at least easier, to follow this virtuous momentum by taking actions in line with our thoughts, intentions and speech. Now we are on a juggernaut, and our next task will be to train our minds through correct meditative practice. If you wish, you can expand meditative practice and take it quite a distance, but for me, I believe the simplest practice is more than sufficient.

After that, we will be ready to evaluate what we are doing for a living, which is really simply applying all of the prior steps to the question of how we interact with our community and the world, and how we provide for ourselves and our families on a daily basis. The world is what it is, and unless we are to become mendicant monks or the guys at a stop light with a cardboard sign saying "Please Help," then we have to make our way in it. But what is the good of making a living if by doing so we lose our way? Finally, we learn to concentrate all our powers on more sustained challenges and expeditions in the undertaking of specific *quests*.

It takes relatively little time to learn these steps and begin the awakening we want. The path will be clear. Once we begin the awakening process, we will wish to remain awake and aware for a lifetime. Eventually, with a little practice, we will, in fact, repeat these steps every day without even intending it or realizing it. Again, it is not the case that we have to labor with these steps for all the decades of our lives in the hope that somehow, at the very end, we will be awakened on our deathbeds. It does take perhaps a lifetime to put them into practice, but it is an *awakened* lifetime which becomes almost fantastically rich, beautiful and satisfying from the very beginning. As we go through the decades in our lives, already aware to a large extent and growing more and more aware every day, each practice will put each of life's stages into more clarity and will bring more sense, satisfaction, fulfillment and peace to us. Windows and doors will open and the world will make more and more sense. Once we master these seven steps, then each day we begin again in the current moment by first perceiving fully, ordering our perceptions, and then intending our universe correctly. And so it goes.

*   *   *

The Tale of One Bullet, Two Thousand Years, and Fifty Four Generations

In the early morning of July 14, 1978 in Hiroshima, Japan, I take a bullet. Just 500 miles away but almost 2,000 years before, in 18 B.C., when Judaea is still a client kingdom of Caesar Augustus' Rome, still twelve years before it will be absorbed as a Roman province, and some fifty years before the crucifixion on Golgotha, the second wife of King Jumong of Koguryo (present-day northern Korea) is fleeing the royal court to the south with her two sons, Onjo and Biryu, to Korea's Han River basin area, to what is present-day Seoul. There the brothers separate, and Biryu and his followers continue further west into the marshlands to found his kingdom (near present-day Incheon), but Onjo remains in the dryer and more fertile area with ten loyal followers. He names his kingdom for them, calling it *Shipjae* (The Ten Vassals), and his kingdom thrives. According to the ancient records, among the king's vassals is a man named Jon Sop, who will become the very first progenitor of the Jon clan (the "Jongson Jon") of Korea.

In the salt marshes to the west, King Biryu has chosen poor terrain for his realm, recognizes his mistake and now covets *Shipjae*. He invades his brother's kingdom, hoping to reign over all, but Onjo defeats him. Biryu commits suicide in shame, and King Onjo accepts the vanquished into his kingdom, which he now renames "One Hundred Vassals" or *Paekche*, one of the three great kingdoms of early Korea.

Not much more is known about Jon Sop's life in early Paekchae, but his tomb can be found today in Seoul's East Gate District. The descendents of this first Jon progenitor prosper in farming and small trade for seven generations. The eighth generation progenitor, Jon Son, is born in 704 A.D. (Just doing the math, it seems a generation or two might be missing here, but that's antiquity for you.) At some point during his life Jon Son will receive a grant of lands in the county of Jongson, in Kangwon Province, and move his clan there.

From this time on, the meticulous genealogical records will always refer to this clan as the Jongson Jon.

From the death of Jon Son in 755, during the next 1100 years and forty-two generations, from the eighth to the 50th progenitor, Jons will be born and live, strive and thrive and marry and farm and engage in small business enterprises, and suffer and die in Kangwon Province. History itself will march on, the Paekche Dynasty (18 B.C. to 668 A.D.) will give way to the United Shilla Dynasty (668 to 935), which will give way to the Koryo Dynasty (918 to 1392) which will give way to the Chosun Dynasty (1392 to 1897). In the late Chosun Dynasty, in 1838, a firstborn boy named Jon Sayo is born to the 49th progenitor. This 50th progenitor will grow up and marry a woman from the Kang clan, and their first boy, named Yongsu, will be born in 1862. Yongsu, the 51st progenitor, will also marry a Kang, and their first boy, Taegun, will be born in 1890. Amazingly, Jon Taegun will also marry a Kang, and their first child, Uyong, a son, will be born on January 11, 1913. Uyong, the 53rd progenitor, will live through the Japanese occupation of Korea, the Second World War and liberation of the peninsula, the Korean War, the rebuilding and growth of the Korea, all the way to the advent of computers and software (one of his four surviving sons will found two small software companies) and the cusp of the twenty-first century before his death in May, 1999 at the age of 87 in Kangwon's provincial capital of Chuncheon.

Eighty-one years before Jon Uyong's death, however, on March 3, 1918, on the western bank of the Yalu River in the Manchurian city of Andong (present day Dandong, China), a baby is born. Yun Choljung and his wife, Koreans, have migrated to Manchuria from Korea several years before by ferry from the port of Incheon in search of economic opportunity. It is a dark era for Korea, which will be oppressed by Japan as the colony of Chosen for forty years until liberation in August, 1945. The baby is a pretty little girl, however, a bright spot of hope in dark times, and they decide to name her *Anja* for the city of her birth. By the spring of 1950, Yun Anja is now thirty-two years old, married to thirty-seven year old Jon Uyong (yes, the 53rd progenitor) and is already the mother of five children, four boys and a daughter. The children are now the

54th generation of Jons to be born in Korea during more than two thousand years. Life is good for the young family, and the future is brighter than it has ever been. They live in Chuncheon in the now independent Republic of Korea, and have been living peacefully there in the newly liberated nation for almost five years. However, on June 25, 1950, North Korean forces cross the thirty-eighth parallel and unleash war's hell on the peninsula. Uyong and Anja are forced to flee the city, pushing all their belongings in a wheelbarrow, the older three boys (ages seven, five and three) walking while the parents carry a two-year old daughter and the baby boy, strapped to their backs in the Korean traditional style. The refugees walk for five days until they come to the town of Janghowon in neighboring Kyonggi province, which is away from the brutal swath of the war and where they have relatives. Within a year, the little girl and the baby boy will die from scarlet fever, and thirty-three year old Anja will go nearly crazy with grief. But life is strong. With the Korean War now in a stalemate, the family stays in Janghowon, and they struggle to pick up the pieces of their life. On October 16, 1952, Anja gives birth to a new baby, a pretty little girl, whom she names Sookjae, and three years later she will give birth again to a new baby boy, her last child.

The bullet which I take that July morning in Hiroshima in 1978 is actually the bullet train, the *Shinkansen*. I have many things to think about that morning as the train speeds west toward the port of Shimonoseki where I will wait a few hours for a ferry ride back to Korea. Like the train, my life is speeding up, and I am going to be married, and soon. On the *Shinkansen*, you must stare far out in the distance to see anything, if you try to see the houses and trees going by at eye level, close by, you will get a nasty headache. The bullet train is a little like life: you get on and before you know it you are zipping by trees and rivers and towns so quickly you can't see a thing, it's all you can do to stare into the future to try to catch a glimpse of where you might be going, and perhaps think about where you've been. Where you actually *are*, at any one time, is a mystery. I settle into my seat and drink a small, plastic bottle of warm green tea. For almost three weeks, even travelling mostly by hitchhiking, sleeping in occasional train stations, youth hostels and at the homes of drivers who just plain take pity on me, Japan has been extremely expensive and I am almost out of money. The tea is a luxury, but it doesn't do anything for my empty stomach, and I regret the expense. Serendipity brought me into contact on the first day of my Japan trip on June 20 with a travelling salesman named Kengo. We had bonded, strangely enough, because I knew all the words to the theme song, "Rawhide," which happened to be Kengo's favorite song. We had sung "Rawhide" from outside Shimonoseki north along the Sea of Japan almost to Matsue It turned out that Kengo had been a college kendo (Japanese wooden sword) player, captain of his team, and he had actually competed in a match with the great author, Yukio Mishima, who was a fine writer but, in fact, a poor kendoist. At the end of my travel, I found myself returning through Hiroshima, and I had stayed two nights in Hiroshima with Kengo and his wife, Fujino.

In any event, on the morning of July 14 I bid adieu to my hosts, and am only eight days away from my wedding day, July 22. I will walk down the aisle in a Catholic church in western Seoul on one of the hottest days I will ever experience, an atmospheric fact aggravated because I will be dressed in a navy blue suit and obligatory white gloves. No air-conditioning, perhaps there will be one floor fan. My fiancée and I will be married by a Catholic priest who will never once say my name correctly, or even the same way twice, during the ceremony ("And, do you, Daniel Winston, take . . ." "And, now, David Wilson, you may . . ."). Standing outside the church will be the 53rd progenitor, Jon Uyong and his wife, Yun Anja, waiting to give away their only daughter, Sookjae. The 54th progenitor, Sookjae's eldest brother, Shinjae, will be there as well as her three other brothers.

The exact locations are lost in history, but this church cannot be too far from where Paekche was first founded by King Onjo and the first progenitor, Jon Sop, one thousand nine hundred and ninety-six years earlier.

I like this story, it is my wife's story and part of my history, and forms half of the legacy for our children, Son and Daughter. Koreans are unusual in their detailed record-keeping of ancestors, marriages, births and burial spots, as it is part of the Confucian devotion to and gratefulness for the lives and struggles of one's ancestors. However, even without any records, both you and I, in fact, also reach back 60 or 70 generations to a progenitor from the time of Christ. You and I could not be here, having this conversation, if it were otherwise. In addition, you and I also go back another 500 or so generations to a Cro-Magnon progenitor, perhaps one wearing sandals woven from wild grasses, one who spends part of his life painting in caves. Finally, DNA studies tell us that about 2,700 generations ago (assuming 22 years per generation, or 60,000 years ago), just after the Toba eruption, the human population on earth for some reason was reduced to between 1,000 and 10,000 "breeding pairs" in Africa, and it is there we can probably look to find the original progenitor of our clans. We all have magnificent histories, you and I, even if most of the documentation has been misplaced.

*　　*　　*

Time is All We Have

A man with outward courage dares to die. A man with inward courage dares to live. ~Lao-Tzu

One evening some years ago, I met a dying man. It was at a tennis facility, and a new player and I were playing singles. He seemed to be having trouble with one of his hips, yet he was unwilling to stop. It was the first time I had met him. He spoke with a slight accent, the kind which has been worn away by decades living outside his country, so much so that it was impossible to tell which part of the old country he was from.

"You know," I said, "if your hip is hurting, maybe we'd better stop."

"No, let's keep going."

Okay, I wasn't going to push it. He was a genial man who looked to be in his early sixties. After I hit another passing shot winner he winced in pain.

59

At last he shrugged and said, "Maybe you're right."

As we approached the net and shook hands, he said, "I received treatment today, a shot in the butt, and I think that's what's holding me up."

I looked at him as if to say, "Really?" just giving him the opportunity to explain further if he wanted, or not. It was an opening for him. I am not one to pry. He said, "I used to get them, the shots, in the stomach, and that wasn't too pleasant. Not sure if I like them any better in the butt."

He paused and glanced at me, as if gauging how interested I was, or was not, in his condition. He was very matter of fact about this treatment, as if he were describing getting his car washed. I waited. I was interested, but only to the extent that he wished to talk.

"You see," he said, "I have cancer. It's in the bones now, L-3 and L-4."

I didn't know what L-3 and L-4 were exactly, but I guessed they were vertebrae. Two of the lumbar vertebrae, I supposed. That would make sense.

"Actually, you see, I'm dying, and these shots are helping me slow it down. There's no cure, not for this. It's actually why I moved to Oregon, you have this euthanasia law here, that's quite helpful."

We spoke a little more as we stood there, and then more in the cool evening air of the parking lot. He had been diagnosed with cancer in 2003, and it had spread to his bones, the vertebrae. It had been eight years, now, and he had told no one, only his ex-wife and his daughter. If he told his mother, he said, he thought it would kill her, so she would not know, at least for now. Through it all he was quite steady, as I noted, very matter-of-fact. He seemed to be at peace with his condition as he explained that every morning when he woke up it was a reason to smile, *he was here for another day.* At some point, when the pain became too much to bear, he would opt for the peace of death over the pain of life. It seemed very rational. He was writing a book, he said, or rather a manuscript, which was to be given to his friends after his death. Its purpose was to "explain some things."

I did not ask him which things he was going to explain; after all, I barely knew him. And yet I felt a connection, and also some gratitude. I was being allowed into the inner world of a stranger, to know a secret truth which he was keeping from his friends and family, except for two people. I seemed to be the third. We never know what difficulties and tragedies we may face in the future. I was interested in his approach to his own, how he found the courage and the will to attend to daily life, in the face of such an immutable sentence. Would I one day face something similar?

Now, people have told me things, of course. Decades ago, as a young man hitchhiking through the United States, Europe and Korea and Japan, drivers would often open up and, over the course of a long journey, tell their stories to a hitchhiker. I learned many things from people which I am sure they would not have told others, tales of betrayal and sadness, failure and loss. But this was no driver offering an anonymous confession to a person he would never see again.

"Everyone is dying, you know," he said, "it's something that begins to happen the moment you are born. Life is about living, but it's also about dying. Most people just don't know it yet. So, when I go, it will be my choice, but only after my circumstances have changed so much for the worse that it won't be much of a choice, in the sense of choosing options. I will deal with it—I am dealing with it now. Only I know, when I choose, it will be my time."

Life was about dying, that was true. Our cells were dying every day, and every single thing I am right now, today, will be dead and swept away within three years, each cell replaced by a new one. I did not have anything to offer, and there was an awkward pause. I thought his approach showed a remarkable awareness and enlightenment. I thought of my father, who died at age 62 of a heart attack, a massive one. I was away at graduate school at the time, and in my mind I have this picture of him on the ocean, snarled up in some kind of ropes, harpoon lines like you imagine Captain Ahab in Moby Dick, rolling over one last time, and then being pulled down into the swells. I don't know why I think of it that way, since he collapsed on the kitchen floor that morning in 1981 and was rushed to the hospital. It's just the image I have of him as his heart stopped, and then everything else did, too.

Life and death. Death and life. And between those points on a life's line, we have the time and the opportunity to choose. Do we wait passively and sleep through life, or do we elect to awaken and find meaning now, this instant? Will meaning find us, and only in the shallowness and disappointments of our lives, or during some deathbed revelation? Or will we actively seek out life's richness and bounty by simply awakening to it?

All we have during this life is the time we are given to spend alive and awake and conscious, all we can truly control is how we will perceive, think and act. That is it, that is the sum total of every human life which has ever existed or will exist—perceptions, thoughts and actions. How will we perceive the world, how will we think and how will we act? Will we master ourselves and our life experience, or will we ourselves be mastered by other forces? Existence is the great gift, the miracle of each person's life, and it is up to us individually either to shrink from the gift and experience life as not only a tragedy, but as a shallow tragedy, or to rise up to accept existence, to realize our great gift as a triumph against impossible odds, and to witness and to enjoy the miracle of it all.

If you are reading these words then life is upon you, in full force. What are you really seeing now as you lift your gaze from these words? What do you hear, smell, feel and taste? Are you in a bookstore, or in a cozy chair, or rumbling along on a commuter train? This is your life, now, and it is happening to you each and every moment, until it ends. The pendulum is swinging and the clock is ticking. Are you really alive, are you satisfied with everything in your life, or would you like to master it, really master it, for however long you have?

*   *   *

THREE

The Executive Summary

Happy families are all alike; every unhappy family is
unhappy in its own way. ~Leo Tolstoy

If Tolstoy had written about enlightenment, he might have said, "Unenlightened people are all alike; but each enlightened person is enlightened in his own way." Even if two people, fully aware and enlightened, walk the same forest trail a few minutes apart, each will perceive the universe differently, become aware in a different way, and apply that awareness in a distinct, individual manner. In awareness you connect everything you have witnessed, and all your experiences, with the real world through perceptions, and become enlightened in your own way.

Here are two simple ways to think about the entire enlightenment process, two images we might wish to keep in mind. The first is *mining and manufacturing,* and the second I call *dual engagement.* There is nothing particularly earth-shattering about either of these metaphors, but they may be helpful to keep in mind as guides as we go along.

*   *   *

Mining and Manufacturing

Everyone knows what yellow Post-it® Notes are, and perhaps most people know that they are a huge moneymaker for the 3M Corporation, but relatively few people remember that 3M stands for

"Minnesota Mining and Manufacturing". The little semi-sticky notes were originally a solution for which there had been no obvious problem, in fact, for six years Spencer Silver, who had invented the "repositionable adhesive" as it was called, could find no use for it. It was only when one of his colleagues, Art Fry, was daydreaming about how to efficiently bookmark his hymnal, that the Post-It Note was born. And why yellow? Apparently, the lab next door to the Post-it® Note team had a slew of yellow paper on hand.

That is an interesting story, and it reflects the chain of chance which can take us from place to place, good places, that is, if we are open to ideas, but I am noting it really to bring up the commonplace usage of older, industrial wordage, *mining and manufacturing*, a phrase almost from the buggy whip era. In our information and social networking age, *mining and manufacturing* seems a little out of date. But, like mining and manufacturing, the path of enlightenment is also a two-part process, the first of "mining" useful minerals, that is, using all of our powers of perception to fully absorb everything which the universe presents to us, each and every day. Then, through discipline, action and practice, we "manufacture" the products which will be vital to us. These products will be thoughts, inspirations, expressions and writings, actions, calmed minds and disciplined bodies, correct career paths and bigger efforts, or quests.

This minute, very few of us are really using our "mining equipment" to extract the precious minerals we need; our drills and shovels are idle, our manufacturing facilities are empty of raw materials and our processing machinery sits, gathering dust. But once we learn to "mine" (perceive) all that which the universe offers, we will find ourselves with an incredible bounty at our fingertips, and the stockyards and storage facilities we were all born with will rapidly become filled to overflowing. Unlike mineral exploration in the physical world, our own precious ores are in plain sight, each and every day, where we live and work, play and sleep, and those minerals have been there all along. We need not search the world over, use complicated mapping systems, drill test holes or do complicated calculations as to the feasibility of and likely payback from the proposed extraction of ores. We know that extracting these valuable ores from our perceivable universe will not only be feasible but, with practice, simple. We know that these "seams" from the universe are thick and rich with pure minerals and priceless gemstones. We won't need to go to the financial markets and make PowerPoint presentations to sell shares in our enterprise. We won't have to give up control to venture capital firms or be buffaloed by investment bankers. We will own all of the productive resources we will ever need, immediately, and have them at our call at all times.

And now, with our raw materials piling up, waiting for us, once we learn how to turn on the switches in our internal equivalents of the sorters, graders, crushers, the blast furnaces and converters, and the stamping and milling machines, we will find that, like the industrialists of the last two centuries, we can create marvelous products from what is stockpiled in the yard, but products which are so vital to our existence that we will marvel that we could have ever existed without them.

*   *   *

Dual Engagement

A second image to keep in mind is also industrial in nature, but more modern, one of a device with a two-part engagement, if you will. Perhaps we can visualize a large, sleek machine encased in stainless steel with a single, large cog extending beyond its casing. This cog is the only interface we have with the universe, and it is a metaphor for our perceptions. For most people, the cog sits there and is either unengaged or only intermittently engaged. Visualize it as slowly rusting away. In order to fully perceive the universe we must engage *our cog* with the *great cog* of the universe. We must reach outward, we must deal with the real, physical universe as it is, and we do this by simply "engaging," that is, by putting into gear, all of our perceptive powers: visual, auditory, olfactory, gustatory, tactile, and other, secondary perceptions or senses, which we will discuss later. By perceiving, we get our gear to mesh with the "universal cog." This is step one, to connect to, or to engage with, the universe.

I have already mentioned once and will return to again St Luke's familiar aphorism, "The Kingdom of God is within you." However, that is only half true or, in a fashion, less than half true. The kingdom (enlightenment) is within you, but it is also without you, that is, it is also outside of you, and by sheer volume both of "stuff" and effort, it lies *mostly* outside of you. You must first connect via your senses to the outer world, the "real" world, and only then can you begin to work, *within you*, with that sensory data to find enlightenment. Paulo Coelho's incredibly popular story, The Alchemist, is a parable of this truth. Originally one of the tales told by Scheherazade in 1001 Nights, "The Ruined Man who Became Rich Again through a Dream," Coelho's modern version tells the story of an Andalusian shepherd boy who, inspired by a dream, travels to Egypt in search of his destiny and fortune, and suffers many misfortunes only to find that his destiny and fortune were back at his pastoral home, all along, actually buried in the ground there.

Step two of *dual engagement* is to face inward, to look inside our vast machine, and simply engage the self. Having linked ourselves to the universe without, and having found a never-ending, rich source of the raw sensations, images, energy and truth from the universe, we now link those perceptions to the operations within, and take part in daily practices to create our thoughts and inspirations, our outward expressions, our acts, our mindfulness, our careers and our big, defining quests. Our machine is now connected and running beautifully, seamlessly, bringing in rich perceptions from outside and feeding them into a disciplined and peaceful clockwork inside.

Before we begin the real work, the first step, however, let me tell you a short parable.

*   *   *

FOUR

The Parable of the Banquet

Every second is of infinite value. ~ Goethe

Slight not what's near through aiming at what's far.
~ Euripides

Peter and Paul were poor orphaned brothers, nineteen years old, struggling to make a living, actually struggling just to eat something, in western Pennsylvania during the 1930s. They had shared a tiny room in a boarding house near Uniontown, but were now so poor and desperate that they joined others squatting in an abandoned coke oven. They hired out as day workers on farms or wherever anyone would pay them, or simply knocked on doors asking for work or food. They would accept anything, they would take a few coins, or meals and some food to take home, or an old coat or, in fact, just about anything offered.

One hot August day, a magnificent car pulled up to the coke oven and a man in a suit got out. He saw Peter and Paul sitting in the dust, leaning against the brick wall, raised two fingers and then lowered them at the brothers. He then, without a sound, indicated they should get into the back seat of the vast automobile.

"You two are hungry, is that correct?" the man asked when they were seated.

"Yes, sir."

"My name is Wilson, and this," he said, indicating the driver, "is Mr. Davis. You two have been invited to dinner at a mansion. You need do nothing other than accompany us to the dinner. Is that acceptable?"

The brothers looked at each other and then nodded. They rode in the back, almost afraid to say a word as the car began the long trip into Pittsburgh and toward the east end of town. Paul, who was the more forward of the two, at one point, asked, "Sir, what kind of car is this we're riding in?"

"This? This is a 1930 Pierce-Arrow. Do you like it?"

"Yes, sir. I'd love to have one of these someday."

"Well, you may have to hurry. The company that makes them is failing."

For the remainder of the ride Wilson and Davis spoke breezily of the weather, the towns which they passed, and many things which the brothers could not hear. Paul marveled at the car and the scenery as it passed, wishing he could own this car, or at least be the driver. Peter simply absorbed everything about the car, the softness of the seats, and the breeze in the lateness of the day. "This is surely fine," Peter thought.

The Pierce-Arrow drove through many small towns and then along a river and finally into the city. More miles and finally, the car stopped in front of what seemed to be a castle. Wilson instructed the brothers to enter this building where they could bathe and put on fresh clothes which had been laid out for them. When they were clean and ready, Wilson reappeared, inspected them and escorted them to another, larger "castle." It was not yet dark and Wilson held a large printed card.

"Can either of you read?"

"Not very well, sir, but a little," Peter said.

"Well, then you may look through this menu card at your leisure. It's five-thirty now and we will begin the banquet at six o'clock, on the dot."

The twins looked at the card (although the boys only knew perhaps half of the words):

BANQUET

Cocktails and Hors D'oeuvres: (6:00 pm)

Pomegranate with Gin
Garnished with a Kumquat
Triangle Terrine of Beet and Orange

Supper (6:30)

Lemon & Rosemary Fingertip Towels

WHITE WINE SERVICE: *various*
Amuse Bouche:

Paté of Duck Stuffed in Dried Plums

Course I
Ravioli Pillows with a Sage Sauce, Garnished with Italian Parsley

Course II
Salad Puffs filled with Waldorf Salad

Course III
Pheasant breasts, with Chanterelles and Morels
Served in Miniature Casserole Dishes

Course IV
Carrot/Tangerine Soup with Diced Beet Garnish

BEER SERVICE: *various*

Course V
Rack of Lamb Roasted with Pesto

On a Bed of Crimson Lentils with Herbes de Provence

Course VI
Sea Foam: Conch, Lime Mousse Garnished with Trout
Roe and Beet and Caviar

RED WINE SERVICE: Burgundy

Course VII
Short Ribs Braised in Stout with Vegetables

Course VIII
Skate in Burre Noisette with Champagne Gelée

Small Cherry Peppers stuffed with Breaded, Herbed and
Baked Chêvre

Course IX
Roasted Pork Tenderloin Encrusted with Hazelnut Paste
and Unsweetened Cocoa
Beets in Filo with Ricotta

Course X Intermezzo- Pear Sorbet

WINE SERVICE:

Course XI Cheese

CHAMPAGNE SERVICE:

Desserts XII

Lemon Cookies dusted with Black Sugar
White Chocolate Cheesecakes with Strawberry Sauce

The boys could easily make out certain words, "breads," "water," "lemon cookies," "cheese," "beets," and "pork," but many others were unfamiliar. Why did they use so many foreign words? Were they really going to eat a "mouse"? The item, "Skate in Burre Noisette with Champagne Gelée," was a complete and total mystery.

The brothers—who appeared to be the only guests—were seated at 6:00 pm and served the cocktail pre-course by a butler. At six-thirty, the butler brought the first course. Paul, who always was the hungrier of the brothers, no sooner received a drink and something to eat than he had swallowed it. Peter, on the other hand, looked carefully at each item, from every angle, savored each smell and tasted either a tiny sip or a small bite, and seemed to be testing everything.

The butler noticed this as he replenished Paul's servings, which Paul almost immediately downed. The butler asked Peter if everything was all right.

"Yes, sir."

"You seem to be examining each dish; I hope they are to your taste."

"Oh yes, sir. I've never had anything like this, and don't know as I ever will again. I'd just like to take my time with it, that's all."

"Very good, sir."

The meal continued much the same, but somewhere between the beef and the seafood course, Paul finally became sated and began to wonder what would happen when the meal was over. Would they have to change back into those dirty overalls? Would they be driven off the property and left alone in the city to fend for themselves? Would they be punished by the police? Could they stay here at this castle, at least for the night, or maybe get a position on the grounds staff? Was this even real? He had eaten so quickly that he had not actually tasted anything so far, and now the edge was completely off his hunger and the flavors seemed to run into one another. He hadn't bothered with the card and didn't know now whether this was the 6th or the 8th course, and didn't much care. He was growing more and more skeptical. What he cared about now was this growing anxiety that soon the meal would end, and perhaps they would be accused of something, and then the brothers would be in trouble.

Meanwhile, Peter kept savoring and eating slowly, looking carefully at each item as it was placed before him, referring back and forth to the menu card which he had placed next to his place setting. Occasionally, he would ask the butler how a certain item was to be pronounced, what kind of word it was and where it came from, and what it actually meant, nodding slowly when he got the answer, and then returning to the task of savoring each new dish. Peter was relieved when the butler pronounced one of the words as "mousse" instead of "mouse" and said it was a kind of pudding. Peter, unlike Paul, was not thinking about when the evening would end or what would happen then, he was too involved with everything as it was unfolding to worry about that. He did not wish to miss any of *this*, while senselessly worrying about *that*. Besides, no matter what happened in the future, he would always have this, if only he could remain focused on it.

When the pork was about to be served, Wilson took a seat across from the twins and smiled.

"How are you enjoying your meal?" he asked Paul.

"It's fine, it's been, yeah, great. But what happens next?"

"I'm sure I don't know. That will be up to someone else, perhaps someone from the family," he said, nodding toward the upstairs of the grand home. "And you, Peter, you seem to be enjoying your meal."

Peter looked up from the pork. He had been tasting it and then reading the card, trying to see if he had ever tasted hazelnut and unsweetened cocoa before. He had certainly eaten pork, but why had they made a crust of nuts and chocolate for it, and why didn't they sweeten the chocolate? He liked it, it was very delicious, but it was also very different from all the other dishes.

"I'm sorry, Mr. Wilson, I didn't hear your question. I mean no disrespect, I guess I was kinda lost trying to figure this pork thing out."

"No, that's no problem at all. I'm very happy you are so absorbed."

"Absorbed? I'm amazed. I didn't think anything like this even existed. Do you folks eat like this all the time?"

Wilson laughed. "No, my good fellow, even the rich don't eat like this all the time. It's a special meal, but I may say that you seem just the type of person this kind of banquet is made for. Someone who takes it bite by bite, if you know what I mean."

"Personally, I hope it never ends," Peter said. I know it will, it has to, but I just hope it doesn't. Anyway, if it's all right with you, I'll just sit here and see it through."

"But of course, that's the meaning of it all, after all. Just sit here and see it through, Peter, bite by bite. And, are you not concerned, like your brother, about what happens at the end of the meal?"

Peter put his fork down and paused. He picked up his napkin and wiped the corners of his mouth. He blushed, slightly, at the question, as if it might expose him for a rube or a hick.

"You may find me a fool, Mr. Wilson, since we've been sitting here for nigh on two hours, but I haven't had a chance to really think about that. I suppose I should, but it seems that someone's either just put something under my nose, or I've take my first bite, or I'm looking at that card trying to figure out what they were trying to do with the flavors and such, or I'm taking a second tiny little bite to see what I missed on the first go-round, or I'm getting a sip of something with a brand new color and taste, or I've finished the dish and I'm still thinking about it when that butler fellow brings me something I've never seen before, and takes away what I just had. It's almost a race for my eyes, nose and tongue to try to keep pace with what's happening next."

The butler approached and took Paul's half-eaten plate of pork and motioned to take Peter's. Peter raised his palm, requesting with the gesture that he be allowed to keep the plate and his drink a bit longer. The butler nodded with a slight bow and left with Paul's dishes.

"Am I supposed to be thinking about later tonight," Peter asked, "and whether or not Mr. Davis is going to be driving us back to that coke oven?"

"What do you think, Peter?"

"Well, sir, if it's all the same to you, I'll just sit here and finish this pork and then see if that butler fellow is going to bring me something else. The card says it's going to happen, and I'm just going to believe that for now."

"Very good, Peter. I believe you are making the wise choice."

* * *

FIVE

The Doors of Perception

If the doors of perception were cleansed everything would appear to man as it is, infinite. ~William Blake

Epictetus noted that, since we have two ears and one mouth, we should listen twice as much as we speak. But we have, not only two ears, but also two nostrils, two eyes, and tactile receptors running the length and breadth of our skin. Our one mouth, we might point out, is not simply home to our powers of locution, but is also the seat of our taste receptors, and also the home of even more tactile receptors. Clearly, from a purely physiological point of view, we are designed much more to sense and perceive the world than we are to say anything about it.

Perception is an iterative process, the more you sense the world and interact (via your thoughts, expressions and acts), the more aware and awakened you become, and the better you will now *sense* the world. And, if you do it right, you become not just aware of the thing (flower, bee, fragrance, silk texture, sour taste) sensed but, through it, directly connected to the universe which is manifesting it this moment, in a continuing dialogue between the cosmos and its highest living consciousness (well, that we know of)—you. When we think about how we might truly validate our lives and achieve our destiny, we are mostly talking about perceiving all that we can, and bearing witness to the universe itself. This is not "witnessing" in the religious sense, and it is more than just "witnessing" in the judicial sense. Pablo Neruda wrote his autobiography, *Confieso Que He Vivido*, "I Confess That I Have Lived," and that is the title each of us should be happy to write on our own memoirs, even if those memoirs are published only secretly within our souls. A person with a truly validated and successful life can, at almost any point in his life say, "I swear that I have lived, and as proof of this statement, these are the myriad things which I saw, this is what I smelled and here are the flavors I tasted, this is what I heard and what it sounded like, and this is what I touched and this is how it felt. The world has dazzled me each and every day, and made me utterly grateful for the privilege. These are all the perceptions I have been entrusted with during the my time this far, and I can still sense them almost as new and fresh as the day I first perceived them I stand before you as a witness. Now, based on those perceptions, let me tell you what my thoughts were, and how I expressed who I was and what I believed at that time, and let me tell you the actions I took, the purpose I discovered and the destiny I created, and how all of this is my life."

*   *   *

The Suchness of Every Thing

Tom wakes up every day for five years to an alarm buzzer and then a radio station informing him of the day's commuter traffic patterns, the weather and a summary of what passes for the morning news. He eats almost the same breakfast every day: toast, jam, a glass of orange juice, and on his drive to work he stops at a drive-thru coffee stand for a double latte. Each day Tom greets everyone with some variation of the same salutations and phrases, and each day it rolls more glibly off his tongue, and sounds a little tinnier and emptier. "Hey, how ya doing?" "Heya." Sometimes there's a little news banter, or some political banter (but only with those of a similar persuasion), or a little sports banter. Banter, banter, banter. A minute or two after each *conversation*, if you can call it that, all is forgotten. Lunch comes and goes in a blur, as do a few meetings, more banter and finally a drive home reversing the exact route he took this morning, stopping at a grocery store or the Chinese takeout place to get some food. Sometimes Tom is caught up on his life, his bills, his personal to-do list, and at other times he is behind and vaguely stressed about it all.

Today is the anniversary of five years like this—it passes without notice—and it is difficult to pinpoint what Tom has done with all this time. He seems to be treading water, or running in place. There has been no richness in his life, no beauty except for a few hours each year on his annual vacation: one particular sunset seen from a beach in western Mexico three years ago, a beautiful early evening shrimp fry at the Outer Banks last year, but nothing else he can recall. He feels vaguely heavy, tired, worn out.

Tom has lost five years of his life. There is a beautiful grove of trees on his commute; he has never seen them. Ten years ago—five years before Tom moved here—the town council built a lovely park with several nature trails, and along some of the trails great care has been given to label trees, bushes and flower beds; Tom has never been there. There is a bicycling group comprised of people Tom's age who meet every Saturday morning to go for interesting rides exploring the town and its nearby environs, sometimes stopping for brunch or lunch at comfortable, funky places off the beaten track. Tom has never been on one of these rides, either.

Tom has gone through most of his life, but particularly these last five years, with his perceptive powers turned off. He hasn't read any new authors or listened to any new music, he hasn't tried any new food, he hasn't expanded his area of expertise or responsibility at work, and he hasn't taken any courses or joined any clubs or associations which might expand his horizons. His body has gotten softer, and flab has accumulated around his middle. When he gets bored, which is several times an evening, he turns the television on and clicks through the channels, then turns it off. Tom hasn't been out of breath once in these five years; the closest he came was walking a hundred yards of fairway when the guy he was golfing with had taken the cart to the other side to look for a lost ball. Tom opens his eyes in the morning and thinks he sees, he sips his latte and thinks he tastes, he takes a test-whiff of some cream in his refrigerator and thinks he senses odors and smells, he rubs his chin after he shaves in the morning and thinks he feels, he takes notes on a telephone call about a sales prospect and thinks he listens. But his perceptors have been turned off for years, perhaps for decades.

Do you know someone like Tom? Were you once Tom, or are you still Tom? Tom has lost five years of his life, and is about to lose five more years, unless he changes what he is doing. To save your life, you must first savor your life.

*   *   *

On November 4, 2010, a Thursday, I ran for three hours through the various segments of the city trails here in Eugene. At one point, about one hour into my run I was on the steep incline which ends at the summit of Spencer Butte, a thousand feet or so above our town, and I felt a gentle caress on my shoulder. Throughout the run I had taken care to look through the dappled sunlight at the grade, dampness and texture of the trail, as well as the leaves which had all turned and were beginning to fall. With every breath I tasted the sweet dampness of rain from the night before, the fragrance of rain-soaked fallen leaves and fir needles and trail duff, a smell which reveals its life sustaining process of decay. It is only out of this thin, rotting biological layer that we, all life, draw sustenance and can survive. I could feel my legs pumping hard and my lungs working in rhythm and, as I said, I suddenly felt a gentle caress on my shoulder. Now, during the entire run I had not seen or heard anyone except a few squirrels and scrub jays, and I knew that no one was around me. At the trailhead there had been a sign, "Cougar Sighting" telling users that a cougar had been spotted above the trail in March, so I was already on medium alert.

The touch startled me and I turned in time to see my caresser: it was a very large maple leaf which had taken that exact moment to detach from its branch and fall onto my shoulder, rest there for just a moment and then drop to the ground. Relieved, I looked at it for a second, not wanting to stop my run, and yet, it was so interesting to be touched in this way. The leaf was bright yellow but not yet dry—

still soft and a bit rubbery, it measured perhaps 10 inches across at its widest, and it lay now among its fallen brothers and sisters. I smiled to myself and began to run again.

The leaf's caress was a tiny moment of beauty which enriched my life for an instant, and enriches my life still. On my runs, or hikes, or long bicycle rides, or drives in the car, I practice being open and aware to the possibility of individual beauty happening against the backdrop of overall beauty. And we can find that beauty almost anywhere, if we allow ourselves to be present at each moment, and to perceive everything. It is then that the entire world will begin to put on its magical display of detailed beauty and truth for us, something which can best be called the "suchness" of things. (As a side note, the Japanese have a term, *"mono no aware"* [物の哀れ], which is often translated as the "pathos or the sadness [of the ephemeral nature] of things," but that concept of "suchness" is too loaded. Everything has its suchness, even the oceans and mountain ranges, which scarcely can be said to be ephemeral, at least on the human scale.) Buddhists use the terms "tathata" and "dharmata" to describe suchness, and sometimes it is translated as the "thusness" of life, but for our purposes, "suchness" will suffice. Suchness does not, of course, always have to be associated with nature or aesthetic beauty. Work has its own suchness, as does a simple prepared meal, the shape and shine of dishes and the feel and sound of fabrics. Breathing has its suchness, as does humidity, the feel of pulling wool socks up over your ankles, and the whistle of a tea kettle. Later on my run that day I first smelled and then saw the carcass of a bloated raccoon, road-kill, in the short weeds by the side of the road. He might have crawled there with his last breath, or been thrown there by a car's force. The crows and turkey vultures and other scavengers would soon find it—if I could perceive it, then they would arrive, too. This smelly carcass had its own suchness, and I was thankful to have perceived it.

The ancient Greeks had a term, *epiphany*, for a sudden enlightenment, the solving of a puzzling situation, or the sudden realization of the grander meaning of something. Christians use *epiphany* in the sense of a religious epiphany, the most important one being the revelation of the divinity of the infant Christ to the

magi.   And any sudden and serious spiritual illumination is an
epiphany. James Joyce used a secularized version of epiphany in his
short stories to show his characters coming to a new understanding
of things, often to their great sadness (see "The Dead").   And
sometimes the Buddhist term "satori," enlightenment, is thought of
as epiphany.

But full perception and comprehension of the suchness of our
everyday universe is not nearly so grand an idea. It is an everyday
thing, almost an every moment thing. If we practice all seven of the
vital steps we may at last achieve an overall epiphany or a satori.
But full perception of the suchness of all things, gathered through
our senses, correctly, is not so much an epiphany as it is the moment
to moment data collection of everything in our universe—a mining
operation—that is, a constant connection to the everyday magic of
the world.

*   *   *

The Poetry of Suchness

나의 벗이 몇인가 하니 水石과 松竹이라
동산에 달이 오르니 그것이 더욱 반갑구나
그만두자 이 다섯 외에 더하여 무엇 하리

*You ask how many friends I have? Water and stone, bamboo
and pine.*
*The moon rising brightly over the eastern mountain is a
happy companion.*
Enough! Besides these five, what else could I ask?

from "Five Friends" a *sijo* by Yun, Seondo, Korean poet
(1587-1671)

Poets, particularly Asian poets, are masters at catching the suchness
of a moment and, through their short and imagistic poems, give us a
window into our suchness as well.

Around 760 A.D., during the Tang Dynasty (or viewed another way, about 600 years before the Italian Renaissance, and 800 years before Shakespeare), Du Fu (Tu Fu, 712-770) wrote a poem describing a solitary goose who has become separated from his flock:

孤雁

孤雁不飲啄
飛鳴聲念群
誰怜一片影
相失万重云
望盡似猶見
哀多如更聞
野鴨無意緒
鳴噪亦紛紛

The Solitary Goose

The solitary goose neither drinks nor eats,
He flies about and calls, missing the flock.
No one remembers now this lone shadow,
They have lost each other in the layers of clouds.
He looks into the distance, and he seems to see,
He is so distressed--he thinks he can hear the flock.
Unconsciously, the wild ducks start to call,
Cries of birds are everywhere confused.

Notice how compact the original Chinese is, it takes only forty syllables (characters) to write what takes English well over 80 syllables to express. As you read this poem, think about how few details Du Fu includes, and how many he makes you provide. It is dusk, I think, but the poem nowhere says that. It seems to take place on the edge of a lake, lush with reeds; again, that information is not in the poem. We can almost see the lone goose, looking first in one direction, then another, listening to false alarms, getting more and more disappointed and frustrated. He spreads his wings as if to fly, then stops, thinking better of it, growing more and more desperate.

And in unconscious sympathy a different species, the wild ducks, begins to call out. This is a poem of witnessing, I like to think: the poet has created a minimalist scene but, by requiring the reader to provide things from his own life, reveals a sad moment in all its drama. Without its flock, the solitary goose will be dead within a day or so; this is the cruelty of Nature.

And here is a tiny Japanese poem, from perhaps the most famous haiku poet, Basho (1644-1694). He uses just three elements, a single crow, a bare branch, and the scene of an autumn evening, and then asks us to fill in all the details from our own personal library—the shape, the lighting, the background, the sound of the wind, any autumn smells:

枯枝に
烏のとまりけり
秋の暮れ

A solitary
Crow on a bare branch-
Autumn evening

Do we paint our background as mostly sky, that is, are we looking *up* at the bird and branch, or do we have half sky and half land? Are we above the bird and the branch, on a ridge, peering down into a valley? Do we have tall mountains in the distance, or rolling hills, or a flat landscape? Do we put in a lake, or perhaps the setting is near the sea? What hour of evening is it? Is it just dusk with a darkening sky, or is it a night lit by a moon, or is it a moonless night? Where do we witness this from? A tiny house? A roughly built tea house? Can we smell anything? A charcoal brazier, brewed tea, hot sake? In my version, there is a cold night wind beginning to blow down through the valley, rustling the leaves. What is in your version? What Basho is getting at with this sketch is to use his very simple framework, a tripod, really, and draw forth from us everything else, the entire *suchness*, of the scene. Poet sketches the scene, reader provides the suchness. Each of us reads the same poem, but your particular autumn evening with a crow on a branch will be different from mine and everyone else's; this is not just the truth of the poem but the truth of the world, the suchness of the life experience itself.

Westerners often find Asian poetry and, particularly, haiku, with their stark images, to be devoid of emotional content, because we fail to understand the interactive nature of the forms. We are not used to interactive poetry or art; we usually get the whole thing filled in for us. Compare a thick, heavy oil painting (say, a Rembrandt landscape with windmills, or a Van Gogh night scene) with its light, almost feathery Asian counterpart: a few brush strokes of black ink on a piece of rice paper depicting a single bamboo or a branch of plum blossoms. We can immediately understand the excitement and pathos of the "Charge of the Light Brigade," because Tennyson has laid out the commotion, devastation and tragedy of the scene, and he even tells us how we are supposed to feel with exclamation points ("Honor the charge they made! / Honor the Light Brigade, /Noble six hundred!"). Compared to Basho's interactive exercise and Du Fu's only slightly more descriptive poem, Tennyson's verse is like watching an action film. But life, if we wish to perceive it fully, requires our participation, and asks for interaction.

An American poet concerned with the suchness of things, William Carlos Williams, wrote a famous short poem called "The Red Wheelbarrow":

> so much depends
> upon
>
> a red wheel
> barrow
>
> glazed with rain
> water
>
> beside the white
> chickens.

It is the best American poem of the suchness of life that I know. I like it quite a bit, but would actually prefer it without the first two lines. Read it without the first two—editorial—lines, and see what you think.

We don't usually think of Ernest Hemingway and Du Fu or Japanese haiku writers in the same breath, but the great novelist constantly sought to portray the truth and, although he never referred to it in so many words, the *suchness* of life. He was a tremendous witness of life in the first half of the twentieth century. In the very first paragraph that he wrote for <u>A Farewell to Arms</u>, he conveys *suchness* perfectly in four sentences composed of the simplest of words (summer, mountains, pebbles, boulders, etc.):

> In the late summer of that year we lived in a house in a village that looked across the river and the plain to the mountains. In the bed of the river there were pebbles and boulders, dry and white in the sun, and the water was clear and swiftly moving and blue in the channels. Troops went by the house and down the road and the dust they raised powdered the leaves of the trees. The trunks of the trees too were dusty and the leaves fell early that year and we saw the troops marching along the road and the dust rising and leaves, stirred by the breeze, falling and the soldiers marching and afterward the road bare and white except for the leaves.

Or this gem, from <u>A Moveable Feast</u>:

> As I ate the oysters with their strong taste of the sea and their faint metallic taste that the cold white wine washed away, leaving only the sea taste and the succulent texture, and as I drank their cold liquid from each shell and washed it down with the crisp taste of the wine, I lost the empty feeling and began to be happy and to make plans.

No one can read Hemingway's passages without interacting with them, bringing one's own remembered rivers, mountains, troops, dirt roads, fresh oysters and the catalogued taste of cold white wine, and unconsciously finishing the scene with even more personal details such as the hour of the day, the furnishings in the house, sounds, a tablecloth and wine glass at a French brasserie, re-creating for oneself in that instant a unique experience.

*   *   *

Perceptions Trump All

*Convictions are more dangerous enemies of truth than lies .~*Friedrich Nietzsche

When we perceive correctly, we do not need to categorize or label anything. In fact, labeling any perception will be the eventual destroyer of that perception. Labeling can ruin it almost immediately. Initially it may be difficult to understand this, but it is critical to do so. But we so love to label things, to "organize" the world. Maybe we get this attitude during our "terrible-twos" when we walk around in a soggy diaper ordering mother and the family dog to do our bidding. *Mommy is mean to me, Fido is a bad doggy.* Labeling gives our egos a sense of power and order over the world, and we love to have power and order, since that feeling helps us to conquer our innate fear of the chaos of the universe, and make a kind of temporary sense of it. But what we call the chaos of the universe is its own exquisite power and order and, instead of trying to command the universe to listen to us, we should be turning our perceptors on and connecting to it. Like King Canute, we will quickly find that ordering the ocean's waves to stop is a fool's errand, or a toddler's tirade, indeed.

Perhaps we never grow up, though, because even as adults we continue to glue puny labels on everything, to impose our order on the universe. Good, bad, pretty, ugly, impressive, depressing, valuable, worthless, delightful, disgusting, chic, stupid, awesome, crazy—these names abet the delusion that we are masters of the world, and that we somehow need not be subject to it. Even seeing a flower bloom and labeling it "perfect" or "beautiful" can be a mistake. Bear with me for a moment, as this concept may go against everything you think about perception.

Let's start with the three primary colors, red, green and blue. Anyone with a pulse will understand that red is not better, or prettier, or more dignified, than green. Green is not superior to blue, and not one whit more honest than red. These colors simply *are*. When you perceive them, you simply perceive red, green or blue. If you study optics, you will know that when green light and blue light come together they produce sky-blue, or cyan. When red and green light come together, they produce yellow, and when red and blue light come together they produce magenta. Cyan, yellow and magenta are neither superior to nor subservient to the primary colors of red, green and blue. Again, they simply are. All the myriad hues you can achieve through repeated blending and shading of these six colors are, similarly, without comparative merit or demerit. When you add all three primary colors together as light, they become white. When you subtract all three colors from each other, they become black. White, or black, for that matter need not be labeled beyond their identifying names, either.

Do you have a favorite color? Why? Is it because magenta highlights your dark hair? Fine. And you avoid yellow because it washes out your complexion? Okay. But that favoritism has nothing to do with perceptions, correct perceptions. And it is fairly easy to see, at least with the perceptions of these myriad colors, plus white and black, that labeling them is nonsense. The thing is, labeling *any* perception is similarly nonsense, as it will interfere with and eventually blot out the perception. One day, you walk along a forest trail in the early spring thinking, ah, this is good, green is good, and then you miss the dappled yellow light shining through the trees, or the slick gray surfaces of the rocks, or the cyan sky. Or you smell the faint scent of pine needles warmed by the sun, but miss the moist smell of the moss, as it perfumes the lower branches of the scrub oaks. The arctic is not more beautiful than the desert, the ocean is not better than the mountains, and the New Hampshire farm with the nifty looking stone wall is not superior to the Virginia horse farm with its rambling wooden fences. Or vice versa. For awareness and enlightenment, we have to *connect*, to let all the sensory perceptions in without barriers or filters or labels, and be ready to loll around in them without dividing, categorizing, valuing or judging.

The world is constantly creating a dazzling display of perceivable phenomena that no one person can ever hope to actually perceive even a small part of. Let's suppose that you decide to rise early one morning, hike up to the top of a hill or a butte in order to watch the sunrise. It sounds like a simple enough excursion, and you hope to absorb all the sensory output of the sunrise this particular morning. So you set your alarm, awake in the dark, and make your way in the fresh cold morning air toward the observation point. Every step of the way you are glossing over all kinds of perceptions—the morning smells of your bedroom and house, the sounds of getting dressed and opening and closing the door, the stars still sparkling in the sky and the moon setting in the west, the slight taste of toothpaste in your mouth and the frigid air now drying your hands and beginning to chap them, the cold air in your nostrils and your lungs now working as you push your body up the trail.

You perceive none of this because you are focused on your footing and the time your watch says. Fifteen minutes into the hike, you realize now on the trail that you will arrive at the viewpoint with almost five minutes to spare and you see the sky in the east is visibly growing lighter. Finally, atop the promontory, you wait a few minutes and then observe the sun's light blazing up out of the horizon, rising up against some ragged clouds, turning them first dark purple, then red, then orange and now emerging with a yellow and white light at the center of the fireball. The sky is no longer black but now a rich blue. Taking a deep and somewhat satisfied breath, you start on the trail back down toward town, happy and even a bit smug in your excursion. But you haven't head a single bird singing or the wind in the trees; you never even saw the moon, which is now only a pale ghost disappearing in the west, and you didn't smell the cut grass or the faint wood smoke from neighbors' houses.

You haven't done anything wrong, of course. No one can actually fully perceive the rich cornucopia the world creates instant by instant. It is simply enough, at this point, to know and remember this fact.

All enlightenment begins with rich perception, and all valid perception is *true* and *infallible*. Perceptions are never wrong, they never need correcting or editing, and they never cause any harm. Sunlight illuminating the forest and glancing off a leaf and its neighbor stone is never wrong, never incomplete, never in need of anything. An ocean wave which starts miles off shore and builds and then breaks over some rocks is always complete and perfect. You cannot say the same for thoughts, words or actions.

When we perceive something, again, we know one truth: things just simply *are*. We never need to put any specific value on it, and we don't have to take ownership of it, either. If we smell a yellow rose and its fragrance floats up and fills our nostrils with that sweet indescribable scent, we don't have to take possession of that smell, to name it "lovely," or "noble," or to try to describe it in terms of odd remembered spices or fragrant woods, or compare it to the roses of our grandmother's garden or to a sachet from our favorite aunt's house or to anything else. It doesn't have to be owned or twisted or named or compared. We have to release those intentions and simply perceive, for that moment, the sweet fragrance of the yellow rose. We should wrap ourselves, not in ourselves, but in the vast canvas of the universe:

> *A man wrapped up in himself makes a very small*
> *bundle.* ~ Benjamin Franklin

Later, when we discuss thoughts and actions, we will revisit the seemingly odd truth that thoughts and actions will always be inferior to perceptions. Why is this so? First, perceptions are superior because they take us outside of ourselves and connect us to the universe. We can't stay engrossed in ourselves and our minutiae when we are connected to the cosmos. Thoughts are internal to us, and actions are personal to us, and only consequently interactive with the universe. Second, perceptions are always true, but thoughts, which are derivative of perceptions, will only sometimes be true and, even then, often only partially true. And actions, which are derivative of both perceptions and then thoughts, are therefore doubly distant, and twice as likely to veer off the path.

For thoughts to be correct, they must be based on perceptions and constantly retested against them. Thoughts, even if they start out right, can go wrong. A perception, properly perceived, never needs to be enhanced, retested or amended. The touch of silk carpet is always the touch of silk, the mountain ridge in late afternoon is always the mountain ridge. Also, thoughts arise from the mind (admittedly a miraculous mind), but a mind whose fecundity pales in comparison with the richness of the perceivable universe. Even the most profound thought there ever has been (perhaps, *I think, therefore I am*, or $E = mc^2$) is not even one thousandth as true and important as each of the almost 1.5 trillion sunrises which the earth has witnessed, or the hundreds of trillions of waves which have risen and fallen in the oceans and on the shores of the continents throughout the eons.

A perception need never be checked as to its veracity. A perception simply is. The truest thought we ever have, however, is more like the trajectory of an airliner flying westward across the Pacific; it must be constantly checked and readjusted, or else we will never get to Tokyo. Even if the trajectory (thought) is absolutely, 100 percent "true" and on course when we lift off from LAX, if we don't monitor and make changes within the first 300 miles and every few hundred miles thereafter until it's time to land, we will not only be off course, but will stray farther and farther off course with every minute of flight.

Metaphorically, we can think of any perception as a GPS reading, a perfectly triangulated and true statement of where we are at one moment. And, we can think of any individual thought as a map and compass bearing we take when climbing in the mountains, perhaps while attempting to find our way back to the access trail we used to hike in two days ago. We take a reading on the compass, recheck to make sure we are using the correct magnetic declination and note the features of the nearby and not so nearby mountains on our topographical map. This is our concept, our idea, our thought, our working conclusion. *I think we're here.* We follow the knife edge of a ridge line and then, at what seems like the correct point, we turn south and take a likely looking trail down into the thick woods. At some point, though, the trail peters out, and we need to reopen the map, and retake our bearings. That is, we need to recheck and recalibrate our "thought," based on what we now perceive. The mountain that should be to the south of us, is it there? Yes, good. And if we came off the ridge we thought we were on, then we should be no lower than 6,000 feet. We must be here, at 6,000 feet—that is our "belief" and our "thought." But our GPS says we are now at 5500 feet and a quarter mile south of where we "know" we "are" on the map. The GPS is a true perception. Can we afford to continue with our "thought" and ignore our perception?

This is the problem with thoughts, ideas, beliefs and concepts. Even if we base them on true perceptions at the time, if we do not constantly check and recheck them against new, true perceptions, a error in bearing of only one or two degrees can rather quickly take us miles and miles off course, towards cliffs or into gullies, into ravines which may lead us to unseen dangers. Blindly following thoughts is also part of the truth behind the popular definition of insanity: doing the same thing over and over and expecting a different result. When we latch onto a thought and, despite evidence from our perceptions (if we believe we are even listening to them!) that our thought is not bearing the fruit we expected, we often stay with our thought which is, step-by-step, leading us off the path. That is always a crazy thing to do.

In terms of actions, I am not sure what man's greatest deed ever was. Perhaps it was the discovery of some great truth, such as Newton's discovery of the three laws of motion—inertia, acceleration and re-action—or Columbus' discovery of a new world in 1492. Great as these actions supposedly were, they are nothing compared to your ability to discover and uncover the perceivable universe itself with each breath and in each unfolding moment, a million times or more in your own lifetime. Each perception, tiny as it may be, is the spring from which the river of awakening flows.

It is likely that some people, or many people, won't be immediately convinced that *mere perceptions* are not only pivotal to our enlightenment but, fundamentally, the key to the achievement of our destinies. In almost every instance, however, as we have seen, perceptions are vastly superior to our thoughts and actions. We humans instinctively want to bypass the obligatory first step of connecting to the world via our senses, the real work of perception. We would rather jump headlong into the crafting of thoughts and the taking of bold actions, even if we lack the crucial inputs, the perceptions, necessary to think and act correctly. *Ready, Shoot, Aim.* I did something like this as a child, when on a birthday I received a plastic model airplane kit with a tube of glue. None of this *measure twice, cut once, follow the directions* detail work for me. No. I pulled out the largest of the extruded pieces and put the instructions to one side, intent on joining the fuselage together— after all, it was the biggest piece—and I didn't look for a toothpick with which to apply the tiniest amount of the glue necessary, I simply squeezed the tube and put a glob on the most obvious joints and pressed. Nor did I wait for the glue to dry. Instead, I put the fuselage to the side and found the wing pieces, and started working on them. The impatience of youth. Well, you know, my little disfigured and glue-smeared airplane ended up looking nothing like the color photo on the box. I was eight-years old and in a hurry to proceed.

We love our thoughts, and want to jump to them, in part because our thoughts take almost no effort to create, and in part because we can stretch them out and tie them in bows or fisherman's knots. Ironically, though, when you get right down to it, our thoughts can be so *thoughtless*. We are their masters, they are our slaves. And, possessing this slave thought of ours, we are ready to take action, cross a Rubicon or hack through a Gordian knot.

Unmoored thoughts are the Silly Putty of our minds, an easily accessed and endlessly amusing form of entertainment. Having fashioned these chariots in our wainwright's shop, we propose to ride them around the world. We fancy that we can control these vehicles, so our thoughts give us a godlike power to carry us afar. Our nimble and unrestrained thoughts can focus in on the incredibly minute world of our pantry or soar beyond this galaxy to worlds unknown. *Look, I have created a new thought, and I am its lord.* Like some drawing by Escher, however, our thoughts can look logical for a long time and then, poof, disappear into illogic. But the jasmine scent of a flower cannot become false, nor can the sound of a gust of wind through a pine forest ever betray us. We can train ourselves to perceive fully, but we will never attain the power to order our perceptions around, or believe we are their masters.

The most degrading news for some of mankind (but not for me) is that not only is perception the first and most vital step for *homo sapiens* to achieve enlightenment, but after all, almost all forms of life actually actively perceive in some way or another. That is right, it is not just the primates and mammals, and also the birds, reptiles, amphibians, fishes skates and sharks who perceive, but even the plants in the earth and floating in the sea perceive as well. Our ego's greatest desire, it seems, is to constantly set our species separate and apart from—above—all other forms of life. How uncomfortable it was, and sometimes still is, when human life is compared to other terrestrial animal life, such as the primates or perhaps the larger sea mammals. *My good fellow, are you actually proposing that we are no better than the apes? That we are simply monkeys with clothing? Balderdash! And you say dolphins might have an intelligence on par with our own? Preposterous!* But it is even worse to learn now that the lowly plants not only perceive, but even *prepare to perceive.*

Scientists have discovered that photosynthesizing plants will, each night before the dawn's light, begin to stockpile certain proteins to use once the sun arrives, in the same way as we might pack the car the night before a big trip, in order to depart without delay. Once the sun rises, the proteins will bind and, after a series of activities, engage in a number of actions, including priming the plant to strain toward the light. For sun-worshipping plants, maximizing their "quality time" with the light, their personal source, is paramount. Several years ago we planted quite a few sunflowers in our flower bed. By the time the young flowers were blooming, they all looked east, their comical faces straining in anticipation of the sun rising, and then would follow the sun to the south and slightly to the west during the course of the day. This continued for several days until their stalks stiffened and they stared for the remainder of their lives south by south east.

And if the initial and most important step toward achieving our own enlightenment—perception—is something that even sunflowers or snow buttercups do on a regular basis, isn't that a bit depressing? Well, no, unless we stay hoisted atop our own arrogance. It is quite exhilarating, and more proof that we are not separate from the billion years or so journey of life that goes back even before the first photosynthesizing plants, but rather an integral part of it. We literally and figuratively stand on the shoulders of hundreds of millions of generations of perceiving life. We should be proud of where we come from, and delighted to continue the tradition.

*　　*　　*

Synesthesia

Vladimir Nabokov, author of <u>Lolita</u> and <u>Speak, Memory</u>, was a synesthete. When he read or saw certain numbers or letters, they actually produced individual colors in his mind's eye. It was not that the numbers and letters were vaguely associated with the colors; they in fact *produced* the colors in his mind. For him, the sibilant sounds of "c" and "s" were both light blue, but actually two different shades. Scientists today believe that the proximity of the areas of the brain responsible for recognizing letters and numbers on the one hand, and colors on the other, may be responsible for synesthesia. It appears that when a person's brain articulates a number or letter and it fires off a synapse, and in a synesthete that particular firing may somehow trigger or cross-activate a synapse in the color recognition area. Apparently, synesthesia is not limited to letters and numbers; some synesthetes find that their auditory and gustatory senses may be triggered by letters or numbers. When one of these synesthetes hears certain types of sounds and variations of music, she might hear them in color, and when one reads or articulates certain words, he might actually taste them.

It is unclear how many of us might be full synesthetes, but estimates are as high as three to four percent of the population. How wonderful it might be to have this extra dimension of perception.

But even if we are not technically synesthetes, isn't it likely that our brains and our lives have created in each of us a unique and very large set of cross-activations of senses and memory? When you think of the ocean, what does it smell like to you, what are its sounds, how does it appear, can you feel the sand, and are your parents or siblings there with you? How individualized and marvelous our perceptive powers are. We are, each of us, unique witnesses to the world. What an honor to have been chosen for this task, and we should all feel grateful to be here. We probably don't know exactly how the universe and our senses and our brains interact, but it is clear that each of us bears witness not only to a marvelous universe, but to an individualized and separate one as well.

*　　*　　*

Delusions of Grandeur and Insignificance

Do you know or have you ever met anyone, a co-worker, a boss, a teacher, a minister, or a relative, who has an inflated sense of how smart or good looking or valuable he or she is? Does that sound like someone you've had close contact with, at the job, at church or at a family gathering? And do you know or have you ever met anyone with a poor self-image, one who has a deflated sense of how smart or hard-working or good looking he or she is? Of course you have. The world is filled with people who hold exaggerated opinions of themselves: the boss who can't manage his own staff of seven but takes their ideas and work as his own in front of his own boss, and believes himself to be manager of the year; the out-of-shape older woman wearing clothing meant for someone twenty years younger and thirty pounds lighter; and the unmanageable young employee who thinks he can solve all the problems of the company in a single day, but finds it difficult to show up on time and complete his own relatively simple tasks. The world is also filled with people who do *not* believe they are smart enough, attractive enough or capable enough to do a job, to establish a solid relationship with a desirable soul-mate, or to strike out on their own and blaze their own path in a new city or new state.

But what about us? Are we either deluded about how good we are, or deluded about how inept we are? Usually we see others very clearly but as for ourselves, not so much. Although we need to see ourselves clearly, that does not mean that we need to be overly critical. Later on, in the fifth step, we will focus on how to split our minds so that we can use the "observer-mind" (which I later call the "commander") to watch over us and see us as we really are. There's no reason to be hypercritical, however, just because we can observe ourselves from a third party point of view. In fact, what we want to do is to observe ourselves as we would observe someone we care for deeply. This is sometimes hard to do, but it should not be, since we should care for ourselves more deeply than we care for anyone else. After all, we won't be able to care for, or love, anyone else until we have figured out how to care for ourselves in the deepest way.

In a certain sense, delusion is the human condition. From the time we are born we often delude ourselves about almost everything. The baby in his first months sees no separation between himself and the rest of the world; his mother and father exist only as extensions of his senses and his desires. When he cries because he is hungry or uncomfortable, it is to move these *extensions* so that they may satisfy him—change a diaper, bring food, perhaps rock him gently until he can sleep. The two-year old often bosses her world around, *mommy do this, mommy do that.* Later, in teenage, we often think we can take possession of another person by giving her a ring and claiming, "She is my girlfriend," the same way a few years before we said, "This is my bicycle." Parents and teachers sometimes work to further the illusions and delusions we have, when they opt to enable rather than instruct young people. A big part of growing up through late youth and into adulthood is learning that certain things were always delusions. Everyone does not have the potential to be an A-student, or National Merit Scholar. We are not invulnerable, and must be careful with speed (cars, skis, skateboards, bicycles), and we not only can never possess another person ("She is my girl friend"), but we often cannot really *know* another person.

People in the enlightenment "business" often play on human nature's incredible laziness, our great desire to get something for nothing, or next to nothing. It is a well-known and standard selling ploy: state a need or desire (money, success) and then inform the "target" that is is 1) not his fault that he does not have it yet and 2) he may have it all as soon as he pays to attend the seminar or buys the software and learns what the "insiders" know. Success-sellers inform the gullible that they need only visualize what it is they want (the fancy car, the mansion, the celebrity lifestyle) and perhaps *affirm* it to themselves a few times a day, perhaps while frying potatoes at a fast food franchise, and the universe itself will deliver it. As if the universe had nothing better to do than, like FedEx and UPS, make deliveries to us. Or the promoters, recognizing our deep frustration with our unenlightened path, promise to assuage our suffering by offering an escape from humanity and its obvious limitations into a world of magical powers and extra-sensory perception, union with a godhead, or endless reincarnations (or, oddly, the end to reincarnation). Unwilling to actually face the marvelous universe we have inherited, instead we opt to delude ourselves as we grope for a way to break free of our circumstances in this life, and perhaps somehow vault into an *uber-life*, when in fact all we need to do is to break free from are the judgments, narrow thoughts and delusions we have ourselves created. Once we have accomplished this rather simple sounding but sometimes difficult feat, our life can reveal itself as the incredible miracle which it is.

So, when we look at ourselves, do we see someone who is stronger, smarter and better than all his family and peers, someone whose judgment is always correct and who should be able to tell others what to do? Or do we see someone weaker, socially inept, a person undeserving of love and success? Or do we see clearly, a miraculous person by birth, do we perceive an attractive, competent person full of potential, someone who has faced and will face obstacles and challenges and setbacks, but who is resilient and resourceful?

Let us turn now to our incredible senses.

*　　*　　*

Seeing

(For now we see through a glass, darkly). 1
Corinthians 13:12

It is commonplace to say something like, "we only use ten percent of
our brains," and it may or may not be true. I hope I use more than
ten percent of my brain, but I have certainly run across some people
who seem to be saving their entire thinking organ for some time
later, the next lifetime, or possibly never. Maybe if we average out
usage over the world population, even that ten percent figure might
be a little bit high.

But what of our eyes? It seems almost more likely that we use only
ten percent, or less, of our eyes, that is, our visual perception. We
can walk by the most amazing things every day, and never see them
at all. Saint Paul, above, is pessimistic about our visual acuity or
visual potential, telling us that we are limited in our human lives,
that we can only *see* through (into) the glass (mirror) darkly, that we
are all in a somewhat benighted state, and there is nothing we can do
about it. Can't we do better during our time on earth?

First of all, let's take a better look at our eyes. We normally think of
"perfect" vision as "20/20," that is, the ability without lenses to see a
certain level of detail at 20 feet away, which we equate to the
"norm" for seeing at that distance. Usually this is determined by
reading lines of letters and numbers on an eye chart. You can,
however, have better vision than 20/20. For example if you can see
a finer level of detail at 20 feet away, you might have vision as good
as 20/10, which is thought to be the limit of human visual acuity.
But our eyes are tremendous things. We know that, if we stand on
the top of a significant rise or promontory, we might see something
10, 50 or even 100 miles away on a clear day, but routinely we see
things which are a quarter million miles away (the moon), 93 million
miles away (the sun), 570 million miles away (Jupiter), and even
farther. Sirius, the brightest star in the sky, is 8.6 light years away,
and the Andromeda Galaxy is 2,500,000 light years away. And if

we add our brains to the mix, we find that, like some superhero, we can actually see back in time. In fact, whenever we see the sun rise or set, we are actually looking back in time about eight minutes, since that is the time it takes for the sun's light to reach us. When we look at Sirius, we are looking 8.6 years back in time and when we see Andromeda we are looking back 2.5 million years. As I write this, scientists using the Hubble Space Telescope have managed to look back in time, over 13 billion years ago; it is a faint galaxy in the Fornax constellation known by the catchy moniker, UDFy-38135539. We can see pictures of it, and what we see is the light *actually generated* over 13 billion years ago and presented in a photograph. Without the additional knowledge of how the image was retrieved, of course, it merely looks like one white dot in a group of bright and semi bright dots set against a field of black.

We also know that our eyes, aided by electronics and lenses, can see across town (a security camera at our house, or the office) or across the planet (a World Cup game or a disaster on the subcontinent). Of course, it is our brains and our knowledge which provide the context and the subtext for what we see.

Let's return now to our lives and our perceptions. How do we see correctly, how do we defog *our* doors of perception? Can't we just open our eyes and see clearly? If we wake up on a Tuesday morning and it's raining, and we see that it's raining, and we see clearly the drops quivering on the gutters and leaves and watch them as they form and drip in rivulets down the windows and the tree trunks, then are we not seeing clearly already?

It all depends. Before we perceive clearly, we might *believe* that we see the rain when in fact our brains immediately begin to focus instead on which shoes to wear and whether or not the umbrella is in the car or in the closet. We're already seeing the mud splattering the fenders of our clean car as we drive into town, resenting the rain because we will not want to ride our road bikes in this slop this afternoon when we are free (there, we've already renamed it as "slop," labeling it, judging it), and we are wondering if we are even willing to go for a soggy jog in it. Our mood sinks; *if only it gets sunny, if only it clears up by three, or four this afternoon . . .*

However, when we see, clearly, we will see that all there is out there is a Tuesday morning, cool, with rain falling. Everything else is *not* what we are perceiving, but already labels, meanings and thoughts we are choosing to assign to our perceptions.

Whether we like it or not, the only world we have is the one we perceive, or rather, the one we choose to perceive. This particular rain, which may drop our mood and sink our hopes of late afternoon exercise, might make someone else react quite differently. A farmer hoping to get his crop off to a good start might see the rain as a great gift from the sky above, as long as there's not too much of it, but couldn't ordinary citizens like us see it the same way? Couldn't we just as easily wake up to the gentle splash of rain and watch it lovingly as it drips along rooftops and tree boughs, following its beautiful chaotic pathways—no two the same, down into the soil to nourish our earth? I would never want to live in a world without rain.

And, speaking of the biosphere again, have you ever turned over a rock in your garden and seen the wild variety of tiny monsters who live there? I mean "monsters" lovingly, but what else can you call things with 20 or 30 legs, no visible eyes or faces, and lives spent dining on and defecating the moist rotting detritus of the upper world? Most people recoil from those creatures but, look again, closely. They are a key part of what make life possible. Without the potato bugs, spiders and millipedes and the tinier things and creatures they eat—and the bacteria and fungi which process everything from every fallen petal and leaf and stem and insect carcass to every bird and mammal feces and urine and corpse— without them, there is no life. There is no us. They chew it all up and excrete it to enrich our soil and their bodies feed other animals and birds or simply die and compost into the soil, and this mulch in turn nourishes every plant and, in turn, every edible animal we know. Yes, we know, the rain helps them to do their job.

So, dreary, rainy Tuesdays are things of beauty, as are the black and gray, scampering weevils and bugs under rocks and all their leavings.

But correct perceiving is much more than simply seeing the natural world as the complex and beautiful thing it is, like some beautifully photographed National Geographic Special on television. To have a truly awakened experience, a rich and enlightened encounter with the universe, we *really* need to open our eyes. It takes time to fully perceive, even when we completely believe that we are ready to perceive. Sometimes, when we go into a new landscape it may take days to begin to perceive its basic elements, simply because everything is so different. I recently spent four days camping in the high desert region of Oregon's Steen Mountains, a rugged and very dry landscape, a sage and mesquite range populated by prairie dogs and field mice, coyotes and wild horses and great horned owls. It took me all of the first day and evening to adjust to the dry air, the rugged roads and desolate beauty of the place. For the long drive out and the first night I couldn't help comparing this setting unfavorably with the moist, gothic woods of the Coastal Range, all damp and mossy, or the majestic Cascade volcanoes, and the thought occurred to me, "This Steens landscape probably isn't my kind of scenery." By the second day, however, I was entranced by the great distances and clarity, the silences and the immensity of the heavens in the desert sky. By the fourth day I did not want to leave, and now look forward to returning as soon as I get the chance.

If we try, some of us can see through the glass clearly now, through the fogged doors of perception. But others, like Tom, will remain blind to the very world they live in every day for years, their town, its streets and roads, its little shops and parks and ponds and rivers. Walk onto a beach with me now. We have just come through a short stretch of trees and the water's edge stretches in a vast semicircle for about a mile, disappearing into a blend of sand and mist and air. We see the blue sea, the blue sky and the golden sand. But look closer. Our bare feet are half-buried in the sand and there is sea-wrack a few paces off, some rotting mussels, and a piece of driftwood. We look even closer and the sand grains are not golden at all, but some are a translucent white and others are black, and others almost gray, but the light reflecting off and refracting a little through them creates the golden glow. Wriggle your toes and your feet begin to disappear beneath the infinite grains. Walking closer to the water now, we see it is not all blue, but green here at the water's edge and now, with a wave, suddenly a sudsy white, and as the wave recedes it is clear, showing the golden sand below while out there the water is blue and bluer.

Correct perceiving will, of course, involve all the senses. What we are really talking about is not just the correct use of the eyes, but the correct operation of our sensory input capabilities, because it is only when we have turned all of our "receivers" to ON that we can begin to gather the important data being streamed to us nonstop from the cosmos. The problem is, most of us will go through our entire lives with our receivers set to OFF. Occasionally, something terrible will happen (cancer, a horrible accident, the sudden death of a loved one) which will make us suddenly turn our devices to ON. The scales fall from our eyes, and we utter phrases like, "Before the accident / the cancer happened, I never realized how important life is, how precious every day is, the beauty of a small garden or the grace of the river which winds through our town." But for many, if not most, of us this epiphany will happen too late if at all (as my friendly doctor tells me, "The presenting symptom in eighty percent of all heart attacks is death.") and, instead of living in a world of incredible diversity, abundance and beauty, we live a haunted, empty life with ever increasing pain. And then it ends.

*   *   *

An Exercise

I will not propose exercises for each of the seven steps—my experience with books, even good books, is that I skip the part that lists the valuable exercise ("Now, get a piece of paper and for the next twenty minutes . . ."). Maybe if I only propose one exercise for this, the first practice of perception through the five senses, you might do it. Adjust as you wish; after all, this is your do-it-yourself enlightenment. In any event, here goes.

Try to focus, one by one, on five successive days, on each of the five senses. Take the first day and, in a notebook or on a piece of paper, write down one single thing you see, even if you can't name it, and write about your perceptions of it. It can be anything, a tree, a tube of toothpaste by the bathroom sink, a spider web in the corner of your garage or a pair of rubber slippers you left out in the rain last night.

Just by way of example, a page I wrote, "On my run today I saw a beautiful tree—not sure what species, some sort of maple, perhaps—today on 43rd Street, soaked with rain, half of its leaves were still green the other half bright yellow, but they had not turned colors in any pattern that I could understand, not top to bottom or bottom to top, or north to south . . . some branches were yellow, others stubbornly green. I don't know if the healthier branches were turning last, or turning first. And not a single leaf had fallen yet." For a time I practice being grateful for having seen this colorful tree at this particular moment. After all, a blind man couldn't see it, and people here commuting on different routes or after dark will never get to see it, and even most people who look right at it won't actually *see it*. I have been blessed, in a sense, with the gift of seeing this one tree in this one, particular moment.

You are right, this little observation is not much, but this is all you have to do: for one moment on one day really *choose* to see one thing, focus on it as intently as you can for a minute or two, and write what you see, and feel, and finally find some sort of gratitude for the experience. There need be nothing big, or grand, about it; in fact, the smaller or more mundane, the better.

The following day, choose one thing which has some sort of fragrance or smell and really inhale it. Think about what you smell—maybe it is a piece of toast hot from the oven or the damp smell of a laundry load as you transfer it from washer to dryer, or the smell of the newspaper if you hold the pages close to your nose. Be at least momentarily grateful for your unique perception of that object. And the next day focus on touching one object—a ceramic bowl, a silk scarf, wool socks—describe it and again express some gratitude. Finally on the last two days do the same with something you can hear and, next, with something you can taste.

Just from doing this simple exercise (a form of focused meditation, actually) I guarantee that, no matter where you are, your life will be enriched because you will begin to put the brakes on your "busy" but shallow life and your understanding of the individual attributes of things, and their interconnectedness, will begin to increase. The things themselves have not changed, but you, through your perceptions, have changed and enriched them. Once you do this, you will be reconnecting, relating to the universe. It may also amaze you, once you try this for a while, how you will begin to see everyone you know quite differently, especially your family. Instead of seeing a recalcitrant child who needs discipline and harsh words, you may see into a child, hurt and confused who needs nothing more than your eyes looking into his, and the silence of your listening as he explains his day at school or something that happened. You won't have to worry about *what step you should take, how you should advise or admonish him.* He needs you to be there, to be present, and nothing more. It is miraculous how this simple practice can change—create—wonderful relationships. Instead of rushing about before dinner, you might see your spouse's shoulders sagging with the weight of some yet unspoken burden from the day's activities. And from that one moment of perception, your relationship will deepen as well.

*   *   *

Listening

Sweet is every sound,
Sweeter thy voice, but every sound is sweet;
Myriads of rivulets hurrying through the lawn,
The moan of doves in immemorial elms,
And murmuring of innumerable bees.
~Alfred, Lord Tennyson

The spring of 1970 I was sixteen and getting ready for the next season of football and wrestling. My friend Mark was similarly situated—a couple of high school jocks—but we also were interested in the arts, he in painting and I in words but, perhaps surprisingly for football players, we both were interested in classical music. After dinner on warm spring evenings in Drexel Hill we'd meet in his garage (his house had a detached garage) to lift weights, but also to drink beer he purloined from his father's stash, a couple of cans each, and to listen to Mozart. We liked Bach as well, but for some reason the sounds I clearly recall from those spring and summer evenings were Mozart piano pieces and symphonies, labored bicep curls and grunting military presses, and the pop-top sound and quiet sipping noise as we quaffed whatever beer Mark's father was drinking. Exquisite music, at an exquisite time of life.

How disturbing it may be to find, after realizing that we have spent most of our lives blind, or at least purblind, to find out that we might have also been deaf, or half-deaf, as well, to the sounds of the cosmos.

Yet, to open our ears, all we have to do is listen, really listen. There are sounds which are audible every day, and which we never hear. When we awake in the morning, there is a particular sound our pajamas make as we begin to move in bed, and an odd breathing noise we all make as we snuggle back under the bedcovers to try to regain that last warm moment of perfect sleep. But it's no good, we know because we hear every breath, and every move brings the pajama noise, a soft *shhhhhh-shhhhh*. As we swing our legs over the side of the bed, the bed makes a different, creaking noise and we most likely make a medium sigh, or a yawn, or both together: *hmm-yawh~hawh~mmmmhhmmm*.

Those are sounds we make, but the world is making sounds as well, maybe rain is pattering on the roof and windows, a car or truck is rumbling by, myriad birds are singing about their territory in the new light of day, and various kitchen noises percolate around the house from downstairs spouse, alarm clocks, buzzers or beeps. We have the various water sounds from the first morning trip to the bathroom, toilet and sink, and the soft ruffling sound as we dry our faces and hands on the towel from the rack. In our house we have a CD clock radio which plays Chopin's nocturnes—I know it's a bit idiosyncratic to wake up to songs designated as evening songs—and every morning our day begins with No. 1, Opus 9 in B flat, Adam Harasiewicz, and he plays until I have gotten dressed and am ready to leave the bedroom and adventure out into the day. I always regret that it takes an abrupt click on the device to turn off Chopin mid-performance; it seems rude, somehow.

Okay, let's not go nuts about listening, but there is no reason to save all of our *hi-fidelity* listening for the occasional classical music concert or learned lecture. Instead of listening with half an ear, or none at all, your world is transmitting right now on multiple channels and bandwidths. Are you listening? You can hear the keys on your computer keyboard doing their interesting click and clack perhaps and maybe the hard drive backing things up every once in a while, or the soft purr of the refrigerator, the ticking of a clock, or the low, rising rumble of a distant car. Rub your hand gently across your forehead. Hear that? Rub your palms together, hear that? Now, gently, palms open, rub down and then up on your ears—it's like a symphony. As Yogi Berra might have said, "It's amazing what you can hear just by listening."

Once we attune ourselves to listening, it *is* amazing how much we can hear now that we have never heard before. I'm a bit prejudiced, but the things I most like to hear are the sounds of the forest, the faint rustle of a squirrel out of eyeshot but scurrying off the path in advance of my arrival, the wind in the trees, the impact my feet make as I run, different each time depending on whether I'm landing on soft trail duff, dried leaves, wet leaves, an exposed root, or a bit of gravelly scree. The other day I was running in the forest in a windy rainstorm and I heard several of the giant Douglas firs moaning and groaning—almost crying —and at one point I heard a distant crash. I stopped to listen more closely, trying to find the fallen tree's location, but it was of no use. The moment had passed. As far as I know, that tree fell in the forest and nobody heard it, except for me. It made a sound, a *crash-thump* of sorts.

Other nice sounds—of course there's the stereo with the high quality speakers and Bach, Mozart, Brubeck—all the classics! Music, of course, is the simplest and most pleasant method of training or practicing the discipline of correct perceiving. Why is this? Mostly it is because of time, and timing. For almost everything else which we can perceive, we are more or less in control of the duration of the sensory experience. If we pause on a rugged trail to drink in the sounds of a forest scene, a meadow or a glade, or we stop on the spine of a high mountain to hear the wind roaring by, we can control whether we stay there ten seconds or ten minutes, or even longer. If we have a glass of cold water on hot day, we can swirl and swish the refreshment in our mouths for as long as we wish, and similarly, if we touch a silk carpet, it's pretty much up to us how many iterations of the texture we can enjoy. But when listening to music, although we are of course free to replay the music as much as we want, *while* we are listening to it the rhythm of the music and the duration of the notes last only so long and then they vanish and the music moves to the next musical phrase. Like a miniature recap of life itself, musical sounds appear and dissolve; nothing is permanent. Music puts us literally *in the moment* every time we elect to hear it, and like anything in the moment, we must seize that very moment to listen to it and then immediately let it go as we accept the new note, the new moment. Putting aside its fantastic aesthetic and social aspects, perceiving music completely is an excellent exercise in present moment awareness and immediate detachment.

And human speech! I like the muffled sound of the ladies' voices downstairs—right now two are visiting and having tea with my wife, discussing events in the sonorous rhythms of Korean. The Korean language has an even syllabic sound which, from a distance, sounds very close to the sound of Japanese, but extremely different from English. English is an intoned, stressed language, quite distinct itself from the nasal French and Portuguese and the almost baroque musicality of Spanish and Italian, and worlds away from the tonal Chinese. We might paraphrase the hoary Zen comment, "When the student is ready, the Master will appear," to "When the ear is ready, the sound will appear." Outside the concert and lecture halls, prepare your ears, since it is truly amazing what you can hear just by listening.

* * *

Smell

*Odors have an altogether peculiar force, in affecting
us through association; a force differing essentially
from that of objects addressing the touch, the taste,
the sight or the hearing.*~ Edgar Allan Poe

Helen Keller lost her sight and hearing at the age of 19 months, entered into a dark and silent world, accessible only though smell, touch and taste. Yet she lived an enlightened and fully aware life and when she died at age 88, she had written 12 books and touched the lives of millions, and continues to inspire us all today.

Human beings have hundreds of olfactory receptors, each of which binds to a particular molecular odorant. Scientifically speaking, olfaction is an incredibly complex and interesting process. Right now, however, we can simply stipulate that things smell, and we can smell them. Some smell bad, some smell awful, some just smell, some smell good and some smell wonderful. Smells also vary by intensity; it is at those times that we use words like the "faint aroma" or the "reek".

In 1974 Fabio was one of my roommates while I attended the University of Madrid. Fabio was a Colombian and he liked to cook. Since he was a decent cook, and the rest of us were not, he would cook and we would clean up; it was a system which seemed to work. So, every evening, Fabio would first cut onions and cloves of garlic and fry them in olive oil while he played the only cassette tape he owned, *Roberto Carlos Canta en Español*. Later he would coat rice in the hot, flavored oil, and then water to make a Spanish rice to accompany the pork cutlet or fried fish which was to be the meal, or perhaps extend it into a fully fledged *paella*. As November turned into December and the edge of the Castilian winter sharpened, every evening after classes I would enter our little apartment in the Quintana neighborhood, absorb the bright yellow light of the apartment, hear the strains of Roberto Carlos singing his own songs translated from fluent Portuguese into a slightly awkward version of Spanish ("Usted ya me olvidó " for example), and smell the delightful savory smell of garlic and onions frying in olive oil. To this day, 36 years later, if I smell garlic and onions frying in olive oil, I immediately hear Roberto Carlos singing *La Ventana* or *Usted es Tan Linda* (and I "see" the yellow light of our Madrid apartment). And, conversely, if I happen to hear Roberto Carlos singing those songs, no matter where I am for a brief moment, I can literally smell the onions and garlic and oil from that tiny kitchen almost four decades ago.

It is good to smell things in isolation—the fresh cut garlic, the opened rose, the salt sea breeze, the pine sap wafting through the afternoon mountain air, but realistically we smell better in tandem, associating a smell with a touch (the first girl friend, the first kiss, the smell of teen perfume at the time, I think she wore something called *Chantilly* in February, 1969), or with a sight (wood smoke and sea wrack at a late afternoon shoreside clambake), and most often with its chemical sense confrère, taste. Although we can smell certain things and enjoy them greatly without tasting them, it appears we cannot quite so readily do the reverse. Eat a meal (see "Taste" next) while suffering a cold or the flu and see how tasteless the food has become, or just hold your nose for a couple of bites of gingery, garlicky *pulgogi paekpan*. Nada, zilch, nothing.

Imagine now you are with me on a climb in Washington's North Cascades just to the south of majestic Mt. Baker, with Mt. Shuksan as our destination to the east, and we have just finished a rugged, two-hour approach hike to get to this point, and we are resting at the tree line. The path ahead climbs a steep, serpentine, goat trail into a notch, and above that notch our maps say the path enters the talus and gets even steeper. Our shirts and backpacks are soaked with sweat, as are our headbands, everything. The sun is bright and brilliant and we catch our first really good view of snow-capped Mt. Baker in the distance. We listen to birds singing and the wind is blowing gently, enough to begin to cool off our overheated bodies, and we hear not only the voices of the two people next to us, but the indistinct bits of conversation from two others several yards away. The air here in the North Cascades is about as clean as air can be, having blown over the North Pacific Ocean and down through the coastal islands of western Canada. It smells cool and clean but now the hot sun is releasing the fir and pine sap smells, as well as the earthy smell of the crumbling and rotting needles and cones underfoot. We can also detect the faint plastic smell of our water reservoir tube and valve and the slightly savory fragrance of the food we have unwrapped—peanuts, raisins, wedge of cheese, energy bar, and the salty, semi-sweet smell of our own perspiration. All in our group have gone quiet now for some reason and a bird alights on a near branch, making a *shh-fft* sound as she folds her wings underneath her and cocks her head. The silence is barely perturbed by the faintest possible rustle which accompanies a stealthy chipmunk who approaches and pokes his head over a rotting log. We can hear our own breathing. Finally, someone breaks the reverie with a soft, "Should we get moving?"

We need not be out in nature, however, inhaling the pristine wilderness in order to exercise our sense of smell. Every waking moment of every day has some smell associated with it, the smell of the fresh-washed towel drying our faces at the bathroom sink, the smell of tea leaves giving up their taste and fragrance into the boiling water, the smell of vegetables frying for breakfast or the newspaper as we unfold it, the fragrance of damp, rotting yard leaves in late October or new mown grass at the elementary school. Is there any smell as delightful as fresh cinnamon? Is there anything that rivals the smell of porcini or Portobello or chanterelle mushrooms sautéing in olive oil? Basil, rosemary, dill, parsley, thyme, sage, bayleaf, coriander—what a delight. Boiling hot sesame oil with soy sauce dripped over a steamed fish, curry powder infused into a hot lamb curry, taco spice cooking up with beef! And garden smells, the new cut grass, fresh cedar bark spread around as mulch on a sunny August day, the earthy smell as I turn the compost bin. Smell, smell everyday what the world is offering us. We may not be able to smell with the perceptivity of a bloodhound or a scavenger, but the world is revealing its suchness to us every moment, and one of the paths of perception is through its odors and fragrances. Part of this enlightenment puzzle has been under our noses, all long.

* * *

Taste

*He who distinguishes the true savor of his food can
never be a glutton; he who does not cannot be
otherwise.* ~Henry David Thoreau

Taste is the easiest of the senses to focus on; the recent explosion in food interest (our country seems transformed into a Foodie Nation during the last two decades) and the proliferation of cable shows and even entire networks devoted to cooking and eating, and traveling the world seemingly in order to eat, would seem to leave no gustatory stone unturned. The cookbook section of any large bookstore is huge, absolutely massive. And since we eat a few times a day, even if we often are not really that hungry, we taste things. The problem is, we tend to taste the same things with tired taste buds and without our perceptors being even halfway engaged. The solution is simple: taste more and taste more consciously.

The perception of tastes (actually, flavor detection) is the only perception which is not a single sense, such as seeing or hearing, or smelling, but actually a combination of senses. To begin with there is pure taste, that is, the detective work performed solely by taste buds, the tongue's chemical receptors, which are concentrated on the tongue's upper layer. Unfortunately, the taste buds, alone, are simply not up to the task. In order to really taste something, we must at the same time smell it, and also perceive its texture through the tongue's mechanoreceptors, and perceive its temperature through thermoreceptors. Thus, to taste anything, we must engage at least four connected senses.

We taste things every day. For example when we lick a finger to turn the page, we taste a residue of our own dried electrolytes and skin oil, as well as anything else that has lodged itself inside the whorls of the fingerprint. Usually a finger tastes like nothing, or perhaps the tiniest bit salty. Near the ocean you can taste the salt air, but mostly you are smelling the sea wrack, the seaweed and dead sea animals baking and rotting on the sand, releasing microscopic particles into the breeze.

When we talk about taste, though, usually we are talking about the flavor of food or drink, that is, what something tastes *like*. There are five flavors we can sense: sweet, salt, bitter, sour and savory (umami). We can probably add a sixth flavor, hot spice or piquance.

We humans don't like bitter things; apparently, before we had supermarkets, most of the things which could make us sick or dead tasted bitter. We have a limited appetite for sour things as well, probably for similar reasons. Our taste (and desire) for salt comes from our need to keep our electrolytes and minerals at an acceptable level, and our delight in sweets clearly has to do with the ability of stolen honey and sweet fruits (the only original sweets, one supposes) to energize us for life and fatten us up in preparation for a winter of deprivation, a winter of forced fasting.

Most of us go through days, weeks, months and years barely noticing the flavor of anything. It's not that what we eat and drink doesn't have flavor, it's that we rarely have our taste buds fully engaged or we are not often hungry enough to truly taste anything. However, it is an irony of hunger that, while it enhances the pre-fantasy of eating (A hungry hiker says, "Wow, I am really jonesing for waffles and bacon, I can actually taste the melting butter and hot syrup now."), that same hunger will cause the eater to literally wolf down his food, bypassing his taste buds almost entirely, without tasting anything once the waitress finally brings his plate.

One time, on a trail in Montana, I underestimated the length and ruggedness of the hike (16 miles, and perhaps 5,000 feet of elevation gain) and the heat of the day (well into the nineties), and the amount of water I would need. At about the three quarters mark, I had less than half a liter of water left of the original two liters I had started with. I was already parched but needed to nurse that remaining water for four more miles on the steep trail, almost two hours, until I could get back to the car. We came upon a tiny, shallow, slime-covered pond but I had no filter. Fortunately another hiker did and he slowly pumped out enough water for the two of us to sip. I don't know if I have ever tasted anything as sweet as that lukewarm and slightly bitter, mucky water. Back at the cars I had left a gallon of water in the back and sun had really cooked it, but it was so cool and sweet to the taste. We emptied it in record time.

When there is plenty to eat and drink we scarcely notice what we put in our mouths. "What should we have for lunch?" is a common question and usually the answer is some combination of whatever is on the shelves of the pantry, in the refrigerator or in the bread box. We prepare it, we eat it and we clean up the kitchen. We rarely give it another thought. We should give it, however, if not more thought, then at least more perception. What does the first spoonful of steamed rice taste like, what is the combination of vegetables, herbs and meat stock which gives the stew its savory deliciousness, how sweet is that fresh carrot, and what exactly is that strange, unique flavor of celery? How many subtle flavors are there in a dab of mustard?

But again, turning our taste perception to ON may be the easiest of these first tasks. We should simply taste everything more, and be aware and awakened when we taste

*   *   *

The Trouble with Taste

Reason should direct and appetite obey. ~ Cicero

There will always be exceptions in life, and although the five (and other) senses must be elevated and generally trusted first, and above our powers of ratiocination, the sense of taste presents one life threatening exception to this rule. We should try to surrender and see, hear, smell and touch as fully and profoundly as we can. But not taste, at least not always. The trouble with taste is that, given the way mankind has evolved over millennia filled with annual famines and all kinds of dangers, our taste and our appetite display a predilection for things which, if readily available, will do the opposite of what we mean them to. To a pre-agricultural human in 30,000 B. C. Spain, gorging oneself for days on a serendipitous find of ripe berries and honey in late September, larding on as many pounds as humanly possible, was never a bad thing to do. Winter in the cave was coming. Our bodies were created to crave these quick, delicious sweets whenever they became available, and it never did us any harm because at best they might be available for a few short weeks a year. At the time we always had a need for the extra and stored energy from carbo-loaded sweets, and January's starvation would come soon enough. Those extra pounds would keep a body warm for a few more weeks and quite probably save a life. Now, however, that same life-saving appetite will act as a slow poison. If you were to eat sweets whenever they were available (now, always) and for as long as your body would create a craving for them (for hours, each and every day), you could be dead in a matter of years.

The only solution is to engage the mind and make certain rules governing your appetite. In a sense you have to reason backwards, that is, decide on goals (fitness, mental acuity, energy, generalized health and longevity) and create rules for the consumption of what is meant to be your sustenance and fuel for a long and enlightened life, while maintaining full perception of what you finally do consume.

One problem with eating habits is that we too often integrate them (incorrectly) with our soul. *We are what we eat* is an old adage, often taken lightly as though it were only a half-truth. But it may be a whole truth. It may seem almost impossible to believe, but some people actually *are* what they eat, in the sense that "Eating sweet cereal is just what I do," or "I couldn't give up my ice cream treat while I watch Jeopardy," or "Orange juice, jelly on a buttered bagel and a mocha latte is my daily breakfast," become not only descriptions of food preferences, but fixed ideas in their minds. *It's just who I am.* Even people who are involved in the health professions ignore (to their peril) this truth, and may be visiting these bad habits on their children. I have seen overweight nurses setting out meals for their families of sweet jellies and breads, sugary sodas and starchy sweet desserts. It is absurd; if anyone should have witnessed the devastation the obesity epidemic is visiting on the world, it would be the nurses who might need to call extra aides to turn over a 400-pound, bedridden type II diabetic. Yet they may simply be repeating eating practices from their own childhood, practices which have been so imprinted in their psyches and ingrained in their souls that it seems impossible to them to change their ideas of "food" and "sustenance". I will discuss this further in a later chapter (in "Taking Action"). We often think of difficult tasks as something physical, like swimming a mile or running a marathon, but realistically those are easy compared to changing one's mind and mindset, and divesting oneself of dangerous core beliefs.

We wish to taste food in order to sample it for nourishment; from a physiological (think of the human body as a car and the food as the fuel) point of view we now only need to consume enough food to keep us aware, awake, energetic and alive for the tasks at hand. The problem is, the consumption of starchy sweets will create an unending craving for them, along with a sluggishness and slothfulness which only compounds the problem. We generally have a similar problem with alcoholic beverages and, apparently, a host of drugs which can be eaten, inhaled or injected. It is here that our senses can and will betray us, and where we must bring thought and intention to the fore. Reason must rule our appetites, whether for sweet cookies and cinnamon buns, craft beer or *mojitos*, prescription drugs or recreational substances.

* * *

Touch and Texture

I search for the realness, the real feeling of a subject, all the texture around it ... I always want to see the third dimension of something ... I want to come alive with the object. ~ Andrew Wyeth

To me a lush carpet of pine needles or spongy grass is more welcome than the most luxurious Persian rug. ~ Helen Keller

The final perceptor we need to turn on more fully is our sense of touch. Scientifically, touch is mechanoreception or tactition, and is activated by neural receptors we have in our skin, tongue and throat. In touch, we sense pressure, itching, temperature and vasodilation (such as when we blush). The truth is, there are so many textures and so little time. There are so many things to feel: the smooth surface of a desk, the ribbed rubber grip on a gel point pen, a cashmere sweater, the smooth and cool outer shell to a down sleeping bag, fresh cotton sheets on the bed, a warm bath or a hot shower, flannel pajamas, the stubble on my neck where I haven't shaved yet, the smooth skin of my forehead, the liquid softness of yogurt on the tongue, the cool wind moving the tiny hairs on my legs, the cold iron of the dumbbells sitting by a writing desk, the silk Chinese carpets downstairs, the rough stone face of a Buddha's head I bought in Tokyo some nineteen years ago, the jigsaw puzzle-like bark of a mature Ponderosa Pine tree or the rough, almost gothic bark of a big Douglas Fir.

We can taste hot spice tea but we can also feel it in the back of our mouths, warming our throats, and then our stomachs, and then our very core. If we have a big cuppa, soon we are looking to lose the fleece sweater we were so comfortable in only a few minutes before.

When we eat, we not only sense flavor through smell and taste, but we complete our perception of flavor through touch: the numbing sweetness of a gelato, freshly scooped, the warmth of soup, the hot of tea, the cool touch of fresh lettuce leaves and cool, firm peppers as our teeth crush them and release water into the mouth, the slide of the dressing off the vegetables and onto the tongue, and the tongue's easy glide off the tines of the smooth, silver fork.

Touch, however, is not just extending your hand to caress with fingertips some smoothed stone or fabric swatch, or simply testing soup to see if it is cool enough to start eating. Lower yourself into a hot spring (or simply a hot tub) in the early evening, as the night begins to overwhelm the dusk, trees which have been visible all day now turn inky black against the darkening sky. Your blood vessels dilate, increasing the blood flow and quickening the cleaning process of carrying away waste products. Your body, at peace, relaxes its full length and breadth as your now rising body temperature circulates more blood to the extremes, and this is why in a hot spring or a spa you actually *feel more*, down to the very tips of your fingers and toes and up through your scalp. This is a relatively rare feeling for you, it is a chain reaction of tactition, and the sky, the breeze, the air itself seem more present than you can remember. You are more closely connected to the universe through your whole body because your entire body is actually feeling more.

Or you may hold a child's tiny hand and feel something, but the real gift is to hold a baby close to you and nuzzle its head with your nose. You will smell the fresh baby smell and feel the gossamer hair with your nose and lips. Now you are connected to not only another person, but the next generation. And everyone knows, or should know, the sweet touch of a lover's hand, a kiss, an embrace.

So, these are the five senses of sight, listening, smell, taste and touch, our gateways and connections to the universe.

*   *   *

Or, a Simpler Exercise

I have promised simplicity and offer this alternative exercise to awaken the senses. If you wish, instead of spending five days as I suggested above, let's shoot for ten minutes or so. When the season is right, go to the store and buy an apple. My suggestion is to buy a Fuji apple, a largish, almost softball-sized fruit. Take it home and put it in the refrigerator. Now, do your favorite exercise for an hour or so; it doesn't matter what it is, tennis or jogging or golf. Return home, take a hot shower, change and take the Fuji out of the fridge. Don't eat or drink anything. Don't turn on any music or the television. Just wash the apple, gently, as if you were rinsing the shampoo out of a baby's hair, and pat it dry.

Cup the apple for a moment in both hands, as if both weighing it and considering it as an offering of sorts. Note its almost perfect spherical shape and the way at the top and the base the skin curves up into the axis, its core. Feel the cool of the refrigerated fruit now radiating out into your hands, and the smooth but not slippery skin, the heft of the fruit, and bring it to your nostrils and smell it. Place the apple on a cutting board and cut out a small wedge, listening to the knife as it pierces the protective skin and carves into the meat. Now, smell the inner fruit of the apple and taste it while listening to the sound your teeth and the apple make. Slowly and deliberately eat the entire apple, trying to sense everything about it, its weight, its different textures, its fragrance and taste, the various sounds it makes as you devour it. Think about where the apple came from, how it traveled from its American origins (the Red Delicious and Rawls Jennet varieties) to apple growers in northern Honshu, Japan in the 1960s, who crossed the varieties and developed it into the form we know today. The Fuji "returned" to the U.S. in the 1980s and has grown in popularity. Depending on where you are, your apple was most likely grown in the U.S. (mine are grown in Washington State). Be grateful for your health and your ability to exercise, your warm shower and clean clothes, this bright day and this cool, sweet, fresh fruit which has just nourished you and made you conscious of a sweet moment of life. Now that you have done this simple exercise, you have engaged all of your perceptive powers as well as your thoughts and intentions. You are, in a word, aware.

* * *

Other Perceptions

There are other, lesser perceptions, too, and it is probably worth mentioning them, although we have touched upon some of them already. The first is the sense of balance which we rarely notice unless we lose it. But we do lose our balance from time to time in life, since that happens quite frequently, either in childhood or as we get older. Observe a young man and an old man getting dressed in the locker room at your health club; the young man easily balances on one foot, flamingo-style, while putting a second leg into his exercise shorts, while the old man either maintains his balance by grasping the locker door or a nearby counter top, or sits. This sense is called equilibrioception.

Another physical sense, proprioception, is our kinesthetic sense, the sense of where our body and all of our limbs are at any one time. When we wish to reach out and touch something, it helps to know where our hands, arms and legs are. We also have specialized receptors for heat (and its lack, cold), called thermoreceptors, which we have seen not only in the sense of touch but also in the sense of taste. Our pain receptors, nociceptors, are of three types and they warn us of impending or existing damage to our skin, our joints and bones, or our internal organs. Because our internal organ nociceptors follow the same neural line as our skeletal muscle nociceptors, sometimes damage to an internal organ manifests itself as muscle pain; this is the "referred" pain a heart attack patient feels in his arm, for example, when having a coronary. We also have a list of internal sensors, or interoceptors which sense certain internal activities such as how much we stretch our lungs and at what rate (pulmonary stretch), a chemical trigger receptor which may trigger vomiting, gastrointestinal stretch receptors, and others.

*   *   *

The Thing Perceived

Now, after reading this chapter to this point, the reader may (wrongly) believe that perception is only about walks in the woods or listening to bird calls or observing the sunset sky, or drinking an iced drink, or tasting a savory and piquant curry or caressing an old growth tree—that is, big inputs from the natural world or the kitchen. That is not at all the case. We are—in physical terms—perceiving machines, and we can utilize our powers of perception to sense everything which exists in our world. If a person is interested in collecting buttons (I know someone who does this), playing golf or hunting elk, each will invariably find a universe which is as rich in perceptions as any Pacific Crest Trail hiker's. A student walking through the library or an office worker grabbing a quick sandwich in the corporate lunchroom has the same practical perceptive richness as any climber in the Andes.

At first this might seem impossible, but only because we have prejudged and labeled what is *worthwhile* or what is *beautiful* in terms of aiding us to get to enlightenment. Labeling is the enemy of true perception. We associate enlightenment with the Buddhist temple deep in the mountains or the hermit guru in a cave in the Himalayas. But enlightenment is a process, and the act of perception simply requires a perceiver and something to be perceived, and no specific place or kind of place. Contemplating the design of a soup can sitting on the pantry shelf, next to a plastic bottle of olive oil and some candles for the dinner table is as much correct perception as viewing the Sierras at sunrise. Focusing on the lighted parking lot of your local high school on the night of the school musical as the final bows are taken, the applause fades and the first doors begin to open, is as rich to a correct perceiver as watching and listening the breakers on the rocky coast of Maine at dawn.

*　　*　　*

A Word About Koans

Question: Without words and without silence, how can you be one with the universe?
Answer: I think of March in Konan (Southern China). Birds sing among many fragrant flowers. ~
Zen Koan

Practically everyone knows the famous Zen koan: "What is the sound of one hand clapping?" In what begins like a logical question (think of other questions that sound similar: "What is the sound of the wind blowing? What is the sound of a bassoon?"), by creating a question which is impossible to answer (obviously, it takes two hands to clap and make a sound), the koan becomes a seemingly logical question with no logical answer, other than: "You can't answer that, because the question doesn't make any sense."

But koans are simply educational aids which either help the student to question the way she is thinking about perception, or ask the student to stop "thinking about" perception and to start simply perceiving. In the case of the single hand clapping, as we go through our everyday life we know about sounds and how to make them. Since we were small children we knew that, in order to make a clapping sound, we had to use both of our hands. We know what we will hear every time when two hands are brought together with enough force, and in close enough proximity to where we are. We will hear the sound of a clap. But if we look only at the one hand, then we know it has the potential to make a sound, but only if we have another hand nearby. Anyway, the one-hand-clapping question is the easiest of the koans. Many others are non-sequiturs, simply designed to get us to stop thinking discursively.

For example, another famous koan, one that comes with an answer, is: "Question: What is the Buddha nature? Answer: Three pounds of flax." What does this mean? It is not actually a deep or difficult puzzle for us to solve now. The answer is to stop asking questions like "What is the Buddha nature?" ("What is suchness?") in a philosophical, intellectual way, and to start grasping that whatever is in front of us at the time— three pounds of flax or a felt tip pen or a tennis racquet which needs to be restrung—all have the "Buddha nature." This is another way of saying every thing has "suchness," and it is the active realization of that truth which is the whole point of full perception.

Koans arose in a time at temples in China, Korea and Japan when resources were scarce, and traditional teaching materials, such as written sutras, fell short of teaching some of the metaphysical and "ineffable" aspects of awakening which the monks were aiming for. Words and thoughts are limited, after all. Discourse led to more discourse, and theories led to more theories. Awareness was evaporating in a tangle of thoughts. These koans in the form of questions with no answer, and questions with seemingly non-sequitur answers, simply redirect the wandering, discursive mind back to the suchness of life. In that sense they function much like the highly imagistic poetry we discussed earlier. Think about them if you wish, study them if you want, but if you are already fully

120

perceiving the suchness of the world, it is unlikely they will be of much additional use to you.

Another puzzling practice in Zen is the hitting or striking of meditating monks during their *zazen*, their sitting meditation. The idea is, at the correct moment (which somehow the more senior monks know), a sharp crack across the back with a bamboo stick may be just the thing to awaken or enlighten the student. It is a form of physical/metaphysical shock therapy, to force the student to let go of his beliefs and preconceptions and to return to the physical and metaphysical *now* moment. It is not considered punishment, and the student bows and thanks the master for the lesson. You may have experienced this if you have ever done something where you had an assumption ("I bet this lake water must be *warm*," or "That innocent looking vegetable must be a *mild* green pepper") which turns out to be wrong, and you realize the absolute now moment when you either jump into the glacier-fed lake, temperature a shocking 41 degrees Fahrenheit, or pop the entire *habanero* pepper into your mouth and experience a burst of capsaicin inside your oral cavity.

With our comfortable daily lives in a developed country, that often and sometimes for decades at a time, we live in material comfort but we paradoxically lose touch with the material world. We are anesthetized. We float from bed to breakfast table to automobile to desk to lunch to desk to automobile to dinner table to sofa to bed, cocooned in climate controlled atmospheres, and with a musical or entertainment soundtrack (our own MP3 player, news gossip, comedy shows) softly playing in the background. It sometimes takes an intrusion from the physical world, and often a frightening one, to shock us into the *now*. It might be a tree crashing into our roof during a storm, or a house fire, or a personal injury or a deadly disease. Faced with this intrusion, we can't just change the channel to a "new house" or somehow buy a new body, we are forced to confront the physical world, reconfigure what we perceive as reality, and perhaps take action. By confronting it, though, we are forced to return to the *now*, and to the *suchness* of things. We often call it "learning to really appreciate" something we have, perhaps only temporarily, lost, such as how wonderful life was with an intact roof or how good it felt to be without broken bones or cancer. Or

121

perhaps, in that moment of clarity, we truly see the kindness of medical providers, or comprehend the sweetness and shortness of life. We are amazed at how our lives can be changed by such moments. What these instances do is force us out of these soft cocoons we have enveloped ourselves in, our self-administered anesthesia, out into the sun and the wind and the rain of real existence, where we find ourselves no longer insulated by artificial means but directly connected to the suchness of all things. In passing, we note that this is part of the primal attraction of entering into the wilderness to climb a mountain or to raft a river. Leaving our vehicles and suburban bedrooms behind to experience the wild forces us to shed some of the buffering we have layered on for so long and reconnects us with the suchness we all instinctively crave.

*   *   *

Perceptions and Relationships

Perceiving is not just about smelling a few flowers or gazing at an admittedly astounding sunset, or listening to some cello suites or tasting a curry. If that were the entirety of the exercise, then this book could end right here. It might be nice to become a sensory gourmet, an epicure, but the power of perception can take us much farther and lead us to much, much more. It really is the key which unlocks the magic door. Let's take the concept of perception beyond simply connecting to external stimuli and posit that every single perception actually creates a relationship with something outside of ourselves. At first, it may sound odd to say it, but anytime we perceive anything at all, we are creating a relationship to that thing. It may make us laugh to think we could have a relationship with a rock, but many mountain climbers have a deep and respectful relationship with particular mountains, which are simply large piles of rocks. Skiers have a loving relationship with snow. Sailors love the sea. Stop and perceive a moss-covered stone wall on a New Hampshire farm, and you are relating to it. Inhale the hot aroma of beef stew, and you are relating to it. We now can take this relationship concept of perception and apply it to what we more normally think of as relationships. Adopt an animal from a shelter, bring it home and observe it, feed it, bathe it and pet its fur; you are beginning what you hope will be a long and mutually beneficial relationship.

When our children were quite young and I was working very long hours, they were almost always asleep when I returned home, sometimes for weeks on end. While my wife warmed up something for me to eat, I went into each child's room and sat quietly for a long moment on the bedside. I observed them carefully, noting the miracle of their breaths going in and out, the shape of their noses and slightly parted lips and the completely relaxed expression on their angelic faces, which were bathed in the light from the hallway. I kept very still and as I leaned nearer I could sense the warmth of their bodies radiating out through the flannel pajamas and cotton bedcovers, and smell the faint scent of the shampoo my wife used on their hair, and the after-fragrance of the laundry detergent she used to wash the sheets as well. Very gently, I smoothed their pajamas and bedclothes, taking care not to wake them, sending them with each caress the love I felt. I remember feeling such a longing at that time, wishing them to grow up strong and happy in their lives, hoping for a good future for them, and I remember, too, feeling a kind of joy at the mere privilege of watching them asleep at this moment, stealing all these moments and holding them inside me then and, as it turns out, forever.

Through the daily practice of perceiving, of being awake and aware in *this* moment, we hone our senses and take this power to a new level. We can begin to contemplate ourselves and our own consciousness. As we perceive our own suchness, we can now take it to another level, gaze at another person, and perceive the suchness of the other as well. It always strikes me that grandparents, when I can see them in a park with their grandchildren, understand this almost intuitively. They sit with their wrinkled faces and oversized ears and baggy clothing and watch their darling pink grandchildren tumble and roll on the lawn. They do it almost without any reaction at all. I mean this in a good way. They watch their grandchildren as if they were simply absorbing every single detail about them, as if they knew that time was running out of their hourglass. By their gestures and expressions, they seem to know that their opportunity to witness this generation may soon be over, and so they sit and seldom do anything other than nod or perhaps rise and, holding hands, walk their future to the water fountain or the ice cream stand. This is wonderful to me. I don't often get that same feeling watching parents with their own children, far too often they busy themselves instructing, judging, correcting, yelling, disciplining, and herding their wards. But when grandparents sit with their grandchildren, well, it's then that I can witness pure and good perception.

*   *   *

SIX

Thought and Intentions

Always aim at complete harmony of thought and word and deed. Always aim at purifying your thoughts and everything will be well. ~ Gandhi

Skeptics say, "The road to hell is paved with good intentions," and I have probably muttered that phrase more than once. We know from experience, however, that if any path is paved with good thoughts, it is the road to understanding and enlightenment. Hell's cobblestones? Those would be selfish and unenlightened thoughts, anesthetized living and misperceptions; of that there can be no doubt.

What is a thought? Quite simply, it is the most elemental creation you can fashion from your perceptions. It is an act, but one so quiet and shadowy that you often don't even realize that you are taking any action. Thoughts can be roughly divided into wonder, opinion and intention.

Let's say you come into the house after a jog and, tired and a little thirsty, you peel the lone orange in the fruit bowl and begin to eat its segments. You perceive the bright orange sphere, you feel and smell the oil as it sprays from the twisting peel, you hear the peel coming off and then the segments separate and then dissolve in your mouth, and you taste the tart-sweet juice and pulp as you swallow it. So far, so good, all perceptions. Now come the thoughts. "Mmm, this one is really tart. I wonder what type of orange it is. Valencia, I think. I like that tart flavor, and the sweetness, no other fruit seems to have that so perfectly. And what a beautiful package Nature wraps it in, too. I should eat more oranges. I'm really grateful that some farmer, back in ancient times, domesticated and then perfected the orange. This summer, I am going to eat more oranges after I exercise. I'd like to find out more about oranges, I think I'll read McPhee's book on them again. Remember to put oranges on the shopping list."

Eating an orange and then, for a few nano-seconds, generating some thoughts about it, is the most natural thing in the world. You can see the questioning or wondering thoughts (type of orange, is any other fruit as tart, ancient farmer), the opinions (how tart, I like this tart-sweet taste and texture, I'm grateful) and intentions (I should eat more oranges, I am going to eat more after exercise, I want to find out more about oranges, I'm going to look for that book again, I'm going to put oranges on the shopping list.). You do this—perceive and generate thoughts—thousands of times each day.

But sometimes you are not dealing with something as innocuous as an orange. You might be passing by a co-worker or a neighbor, or a stranger or a police officer, or a school building or the fire station. Each time, you pull in perceptions and then your mind begins to generate thoughts. These can be harmless and these can be harmful, it depends on you.

If you drive by a school and see children running in the playground and then, in one corner, observe two boys circling and squaring off against each other, what types of thoughts does your mind generate? You can wonder where the teachers or supervisors are, you can wonder at the ages of the children, or whether the boys are just *being* boys, play-acting from some video game, or getting ready to really fight. You might remember your own elementary school days with fondness or loathing. You can form negative opinions of the children (savages, really) or their teachers (lazy, unfocused), or the entire school system (waste of money), or you can do the opposite. You can form intentions, such as to avoid these school blocks during school hours, or to volunteer at the school to help out in some way. And, after you have driven off, these various thoughts will stay with you for a while, to your betterment or to your detriment. All of this is a way of saying that you need to be careful what you manufacture via your thoughts, since you will carry them with you for quite a while. But how can we do this, how do we control these thoughts which just seem to bubble up on their own?

*   *   *

Your Code of Conduct

When we speak of developing or having correct thoughts and intentions, in a very basic sense what we are saying is, let's choose an internal code of conduct, a set of rules which we will follow, or try to follow, so that our daily thoughts and intentions will be correct. Ever since we were little we knew that thoughts and desires could get us into trouble, sometimes big trouble. The world knows this, too. A twisted, frustrated artist, Adolph Hitler, gave birth to thoughts which ended up in true nightmares such as Dachau and Auschwitz and a worldwide conflagration. A daydreaming Chairman Mao decided that China could leapfrog its way into modernity in 1958, utilize a "great leap forward" which caused the estimated deaths of between 30 and 45 million Chinese from starvation, torture and suicide, all in peacetime.

Perhaps surprisingly, one of the simplest codes we could examine is from the Boy Scouts. The Boy Scout Law says to be "...trustworthy, loyal, helpful, friendly, courteous, kind, obedient, cheerful, thrifty, brave, clean, and reverent." Let's think about that for a moment. Imagine that we have a slate of candidates applying for the position of Our Friend. We will have to select a person to trust, not only to be "friendly" to us, but to keep our confidences, to be honest with us, to be a positive influence on our life and, when potentially harmful situations arise, to stand with us so we can face them together with courage. Now look again at the Boy Scout Law. Maybe we can get rid of "obedient," since we will rarely ask Our Friend to be obedient, but wouldn't we want Our Friend, or any friend, on a daily basis to be trustworthy, helpful, friendly and courteous? In the face of trouble, wouldn't it be valuable for Our Friend to stay composed and to be cheerful and brave? How long would we keep any friend who was not loyal, or not kind?

We might think we could do away with *thrift*, but a spendthrift friend will always be in need, if not trying to borrow our money, then in need of constant advice (which he will never take) of how to right his financial boat and in need of long, late night calls to tell us of his plight. This will be a needy, high-maintenance friend, indeed. High maintenance friends have another label: users.

And, as for clean and reverent, do we really need those attributes in Our Friend? Well, would we prefer dirty and profane? I think not.

When we look at this basic code in this way, we can see that these are all fundamental values which we would want, or perhaps even require, in a good friend. A good friend will not only be a companion but also a trusted advisor. We want those same values even more in ourselves and, particularly, in our own thoughts and intentions. We should require that the way we wonder, opine and intend be trustworthy, loyal, helpful, friendly, courteous, kind, cheerful, thrifty, brave, clean, and reverent. Since our intentions are going to be aligned with this simple code, we can now include *obedient*, because we want our thoughts to be obedient to our higher self. (Later we will go into how to divide our mind, but for now we will simply note that obedience is a good thing to have in our code). We want to be in command of our self at all times, to be able to order the self to not even think or intend something hurtful when our pride has been bruised or as payback to an insult, to be able to order the self to stay calm instead of giving in to peer pressure or anger, and to order the self to step away from unsavory or dangerous intentions.

Now, you may look at this list of twelve adjectives and decide that you want to add some (*harmonious with nature*, or *peaceful*) or delete some. You already know that you are free to do so; this is your enlightenment. At its core, however, we want the self to have internalized a code of conduct so deeply that it will not question any order from the higher mind. I'm not saying this is easy, I'm just saying this is necessary.

*   *   *

The Information Filter

Let's start again from the beginning. The first step we must take in order to get our thoughts correct is to get our perceptions correct. We must first perceive fully and clearly. We cannot be thinking right if we are seeing wrong, we cannot be thinking expansively and beautifully if we are perceiving small and ugly, and we cannot be thinking positively and optimistically if we are mired in negative and pessimistic perceptions. Our first thought cannot be to believe what is wrong, to delight in the shortcomings of other places and other people. This will never elevate or enlighten us. This business of correct thinking will be much easier if we are, on a daily basis, perceiving the suchness of the universe. Recall that each of us is a miracle, and that the planet and every place on it is a miracle, as well. Negative thoughts, such as "That country is the worst dump I've ever been to," or "She's a seriously stupid person," flow readily out of negative people.

There is a word for negative people: toxic. And it is easy to put a universal toxin in our mind, the universal poison, gossip and malicious rumors. Of course, the world runs on gossip, it is difficult to find thirty minutes of television without watching essentially pure gossip. The celebrity news is, of course, gossip, but so are the sports news broadcasts. Apparently the actions on the fields or playing courts are insufficient, so the "analysts" must go on interminably about which player is unhappy with his pro football contract and is going public with his spat, or who made a wolf whistle at a female news reporter, or a fan had a baby out of wedlock with a top basketball star. And the *news* news is equally gossipy: a politician's wife uses $$$ of public funds to take a vacation in Spain, a senator from Massachusetts appeared almost nude in a magazine decades ago, a candidate for governor used to play professional basketball and had a poor free throw shooting percentage. Of what use, at this present moment, or at any moment, will any of this be to us?

So, the next step to getting our thoughts correct is to install a very fine filter on the pipe which allows information into our minds. We already perceive things clearly, since we have implemented the first vital step or practice, full perception. But news intake is different from perception. The flood of news has already been selected and edited and broadcast based on criteria which may be irrelevant to us. Our filter asks a simple question: is this information likely to be somehow useful, important or valuable to us now? Is it true, is it helpful, will it help us to perceive more clearly and will it make us a better person? This may sound silly and so basic as to be self-evident, but our goal in life is to make ourselves into better people, because better people live better lives, they live enlightened lives. It is amazing how often people forget this one thing. There is nothing like an ugly thought to quickly derail us. So we need to filter our information and let pass to us only that which we need to sustain our life, and let the rest drain off somewhere else.

Anyone who wants to understand the scientific basis for positive thinking and positive living may wish to read more about that subject in the various books listed in "Further Reading." Martin Seligman of the University of Pennsylvania has spearheaded the Positive Psychology movement by essentially turning the tables on standard psychological inquiry. Instead of focusing on the worst two or three percent, the pathological "basket cases" of humanity suffering from neuroses and psychoses, and trying to bring them up to a "low normal" level, he decided to study the top five percent or so, truly successful people, the outperformers, to try to see what they had, or did, which made them *super-competent*. If he could find out what their secret was, he could then prescribe these "positive psychological" practices so that people at all levels could raise their own performance in life. This is what we want to do with our thoughts and intentions. Now that we are connected to—plugged into—the universe, we want to have only positive and super-competent thoughts and intentions.

*　　*　　*

Enthusiasm

Enthusiasm is the mother of effort, and without it nothing great was ever achieved. ~Ralph Waldo Emerson.

Once we have trained our perceptors to really perceive, adopted a basic "code of conduct" for our thoughts and intentions, and turned on certain filters to keep toxic substances out, the next step to getting our thoughts correct is to find our enthusiasm. Enthusiasm actually comes from a Greek word meaning "possessed by a god," sometimes for good and sometimes for not so good ends, but the term has grown to simply mean "passionate" or "extremely excited". One thing we know is that we should be enthusiastic; we should be enthusiastic almost to the point of parody. Enthusiasm is a beautiful thing. And we should be incredibly enthusiastic about our lives, our families, what we do, what we are reading or eating, and how we are exercising. I call this "the Rule of Emily," which I named after one of Daughter's friends.

Emily is a grown-up young lady today, but in high school she was a giggly teenager, a teammate on Daughter's swim team. If you have any involvement with teenagers, then you have seen Emily or her facsimile: relentlessly energetic, positive and bubbly, like a puppy. Her giggle fairly erupts and is totally infectious. Emily is a year older than Daughter and so she went off to college first. When she came back to visit us during her first Thanksgiving break, I asked her how college was going.

"Oh, Mr. McCarty, it is SO great. My college is SO fun, and the *people* are SO great. I know *anyone* would love it there, because it is SO great." She turned to Daughter and gushed, "You HAVE to come to my college, it is SO cool. It's really fantastic."

I have truncated her actual reply; as I recall it was at least twice as long. And thus was born the *Rule of Emily*: wherever we are and whatever we are doing, we should feel so positively about it that we think everyone we know, and perhaps even those we don't know, would love to do it and would benefit from it. We have to constantly seek out that which is *vital*. Of course it doesn't have to be exactly true: Daughter might not like Emily's college as much as Emily did—in fact, Daughter chose a different university 3,000 miles away and loved it, every minute of her four years there, and felt about her own school the very same way Emily felt about hers. But for the true *enthusiast*, her enthusiasm must absolutely *feel* true. "You must taste this cake." "You have to get a coat just like mine." "These are the best skis."

We must learn to make our thoughts and intentions enthusiastic. Actually, we must re-learn to be enthusiastic, because enthusiasm is something we were all born with, but many of us have lost it along the way. Life has a way of driving the enthusiasm out of us. The *Rule of Emily* contains its own corollary: if we are reading a book and it's just not very good—let's put it down, let's send it back to the library or leave it on a bus seat. Time is all we have. By reading a mediocre book we are allowing that substandard, sub-optimal book to occupy the place where an absolutely life-changing book might be. Let's *find* that life-changing book, that thrilling activity, that fascinating course of study which *will* fill us with enthusiasm. Now. We can't afford to have a sub-optimal experience with our life today—this might be the last day, or the last week, of our lives.

This *Corollary of the Rule of Emily* says to discard, to the extent we can at this point, all which is non-vital. We have an obligation to really look at what we do with our time and, if it is something which fails to ignite a fire within, and it is not a required act (like a job or other obligation), then to discard it. Immediately. We have a high moral obligation to seek out that which is vital, that which makes us enthusiastic; we must actively invite the "gods" to come in and take over. These are not the capital letter God or Gods, but the lower case gods who will lead us to do something physically adventurous or spiritually exciting, or start to study an absolutely new field of learning, or practice a musical instrument with renewed delight. If what we are doing does not possess us with enthusiasm, let's get rid of it. Let's move on. Life is short enough, let's not shorten it further.

I try to be this way with everything I do, some of which I will discuss in later chapters. For music, I really want to listen to music which I am enthusiastic about, and not listen to anything which seems less than terrific. I realize that my friends may not share my enthusiasm for Bach's *Cello Suites* or Mozart's *Quintet for Winds and Piano* or the *Jupiter Symphony*, or artists like Pink Martini, or Paulo Moura or Toquinho or Sadao Watanabe or Dave Brubeck's *Jazz Impressions of Japan*. That is fine with me. I need to be in love with what I listen to, but I do not need anyone else to validate my taste. For food, I want to eat delicious food which is also wonderful for my body's maintenance and performance; I have searched for two decades for food's holy grail, the "Wonder Diet," the one which will fuel all my needs and keep me healthy—and at last I have found it, I think, or at least the best one so far. For physical activities, I am slowly evolving to the point where I want to continue to improve at a somewhat limited set of activities, to see what I can do with my body as it nears the end of its sixth decade: expedition-style mountain climbing, front-, slack- and back-country skiing, ultramarathon and endurance running, triathlon training, and tennis. These are activities where I never have to gin up enthusiasm—if I could, I would be doing one of them every single day of my life. I will discuss all of these activities and others in more detail in the next chapter, "Taking Action".

It is not important that others wax enthusiastic about your stuff; it is only vital that you wax and stay very waxed about your owntastes and interests. Enthusiasm in our thoughts is the one critical key to knowing that we are vibrant, alive and experiencing a rich life in a sense so much more important than money or property.

*   *   *

Robustness and Authenticity

Because thought and intention lead to words and actions, two important watchwords for our thoughts are *robustness* and *authenticity*. When I contemplate doing something, such as making the commitment to run an ultramarathon or to join the ski patrol or to buy and learn to use more advanced equipment to ski-climb mountains, I have to use two further questions as filters. Is this thought or intention itself robust, and is it also authentic? *Robust* means that the thought will, of its own, fill me with enthusiasm for the task at hand. It will excite me; it will "light my fire." Something which is robust promises to challenge me either physically, mentally or spiritually, or all three at once, and will present a challenge which I not only look forward to, but *look forward* looking forward to. It should quicken my pulse, literally or perhaps figuratively. *Authentic* means that it will present me with something which is true to me, and it means that I will not derive pleasure or value from the activity because of what others or society might think about it. For example, being named ambassador to a foreign country holds no interest for me, nor does making the Hollywood A-list. However, both reading about training methods for, and actually training for, a triathlon, or a 50-mile or 100-kilometer trail race are activities which are both robust and authentic. Buying season tickets to the local sports team's events, tailgating at the big game, or maybe following the team around the region to "support" them is neither robust nor authentic for me. It might be robust and authentic for someone else; that is not for me to say. Again, life is short, and I can't afford to waste any of mine. I don't even want to go down the path of *thinking* about something if it does not promise to be both robust and authentic when it comes time to act.

*   *   *

Gratitude and Generosity

Gratitude bestows reverence, allowing us to encounter everyday epiphanies, those transcendent moments of awe that change forever how we experience life and the world. ~John Milton

So far, we have seen that we can keep our thoughts and intentions guided by a code of quality adjectives (courteous, kind, helpful, and friendly). We are lighting the fuse with enthusiasm. We also filter the news and information we receive by testing to see if those flows are positive and non-toxic, and we further test our thoughts and intentions to make sure that they are robust and authentic.

We can also test our thoughts to see if these thoughts contain two other two key aspects: gratitude and generosity. A person whose thoughts and intentions lack a sense of gratitude is an ingrate, and one whose thoughts are without generosity is a cheapskate. Life without gratitude and without generosity will at best be life as a sub-human experience. When a person's intentions are guided by gratitude and generosity, however, he will not only be highly evolved, but will have a super-human experience. When my mother was in a nursing home, on my visits I would notice the various residents, some of whom were spending their last months in relative harmony and grace, and others who were spending their last months in bitterness, depression and general turmoil. The difference between the two groups of residents was so simple it was shocking, and the staff confirmed it to me. It was not health or wealth which determined the difference. Two basically identical eighty-five year old women staying in adjacent rooms, isolated and failing physically, would have completely different realities. One, Grace, would be thankful to the staff and to a grandson who came to see her, grateful for the little potted flower the staff placed by her bedside, thankful to see the sun in the morning and the moon at night, grateful for the memory of her late husband and their 43 years together, and generous with her thoughts and her stories of how her life had been. Another, Bella, would be bitter at the staff who was always late and the granddaughter who almost never came to see her anyway, depressed by this tiny room when once she had lived in a big house on three acres, resentful of the tiny flower pot when she had once had a huge garden, and even a gardener, angry that her husband was no longer alive and there to do her bidding, and selfish with whatever lessons she had learned from life.

We have already seen, in the alternative exercise for perception where we spent a short amount of time with an apple, how to practice seeing, feeling, smelling, hearing and tasting. Surprise—all the while we were doing that exercise we were also exercising our gratitude. Gratitude is nothing more, once you boil it down, than spending some amount of time actually perceiving something or someone. Now, some "sophisticated" people may find it silly to be grateful for a piece of fruit. Imagine, however, that you were shipwrecked on a desert isle with no food at all, or imprisoned in a Mexican jail and being fed a mystery stew once a day, or marooned deep in the wilderness on a Forest Service road when your fuel line began to leak and your vehicle stopped dead. How would you view an apple then? Why must we lose something before we can value it? Are we that dense, that unconscious, or just that arrogant? The electricity in your house which lights your lights, runs your refrigerator, microwave, toaster oven, computers, televisions and perhaps part or all of your heating systems—do you have to live without electricity for a day or two before you can appreciate it and be grateful for it? Look at all the conveniences you have, each of which started out as a marvelous invention—and before that, a thought—at some time in human history. Glass for your windows, insulation, planed lumber for your walls and floors, composite shingles on the roof, hinged doors, concrete sidewalks, macadam streets and driveways, bicycles, cars and city buses, inexpensive machine-made fabrics for cotton sheets and shirts, wool sweaters and suits, silk ties, supermarkets with refrigerated meats and vegetables, fruits from thousands of miles away, soap for washing your body, your clothes and your dishes and kitchen surfaces, running hot and cold water—imagine your life for just one week without these. We should be thankful every day for this very short list of things without which we would struggle just to get by. Don't believe it? Go out to the garage and throw the circuit breaker on your electricity and keep it off for just forty-eight hours. While you are there, let the air out of your tires (car and bicycle). And, instead of living in your house (modern marvel that it is), set up a tarp shelter in your backyard and live there in just the clothes you have on your back until you decide to re-electrify your life.

Imagine two weeks in a man's life. The first week finds Richard, suburbanite, floating along with his wife and two children, working at his mid-level job; he starts the week off by going to church on Sunday and ends it watching a movie with his family, eating popcorn in the den. The second week finds Richard, arrested in his driveway on Sunday morning, his computer and cell phone confiscated, handcuffed in front of news cameras and taken to jail to be arraigned on a conspiracy to commit murder charge, as part of a terrorist organization. He is the lead story in all the papers, and not just locally. Certain of his colleagues are interviewed and a few state that, yes, there was always something a bit quiet and a bit mysterious about Richard. Something not quite right. His family is isolated, the children stay home from school. Helicopters fly overhead and news vans and reporters line the streets. Several of Richard's friends and a few colleagues, however, stop by to show support. One friend, a lawyer, offers to defend him in the initial proceedings, for free. He spends the week in jail, focusing on every inch of the concrete wall, the disgusting toilet, the almost intolerable sounds and smells of the place, unable to sleep, depressed, worried about his wife and children. The only light in the jail is fluorescent light, and he thinks longingly of the sky and clouds and the sun. The first night in jail, he lies down in his orange jumpsuit and weeps until he has no more tears. On Friday, though, the investigators discover that they have been "played" by the real terrorists, and conned into arresting and charging an innocent man based on planted evidence. Richard is released, with apologies, and he spends Saturday at home, not wanting to go anywhere, walking through his back yard, seeing the skies, the trees, the flowers, listening to the wind and the lovely free sound of cars driving by and distant house doors opening and closing. He sits down on a swing in the backyard and begins to weep, again, only now his tears flow at the absolute beauty and poignancy of his existence, which he never realized before. Just thinking about Richard for a moment, we can see which week would be more memorable and important in his life, which week focused him on each breath, each instant?

Fortunately, we don't need to be arrested on false charges and spend a week in jail to understand what we have, the suchness of everything. Scientists have discovered that the brain can't really differentiate between a remembered fact and a remembered "imagined fact." An athlete who has run a great race, say a sub-four minute mile, can draw on this true fact through memory in future races to instill confidence before and during the competition. An athlete who has not (yet) achieved this actual result will not be able to draw on this extra edge. As a consequence, he may become more nervous before the gun sounds or lose confidence during key points in the race, and will run at a disadvantage to the first athlete. There is a *however*, however. If the second athlete can visualize vividly (the crowd, the colors, the track, the sun, his heart pounding) a race where, during each step of the way, at each turn, he wills himself to run a sub-four minute mile to victory, and repeats this visualization process several times in order to imprint it indelibly in his memory, then he will be able to draw on this "imagined fact" as fully as though it were in truth an *actual* fact, an actual sub-four minute mile he had run, and so he will be on an even psychological par with his competitor. Of course, his physical performance in the race will be up to him, as this sport imaging technique only creates an equal *psychological* footing for our competitor, it destroys psychological impediments to performance, but it cannot build muscle or endurance. The power of *imagined facts* is the basis for sports imaging (see Maxwell Maltz' book, The New Psycho-Cybernetics in "Further Reading"): if you imagine yourself running faster or jumping higher and do it enough times so the imagination becomes a "memory," then in competition you can draw on this memory during your performance. Personal performance coaches know that, in addition to sports competition, we can also use this imaging technique, the creation of "imagined facts" to help us overcome almost any serious psychological obstacle which may be panicking us, whether it is a difficult exam, a public speaking engagement or work-related obstacles.

And so it is also true that, to appreciate what you have as fully and as richly as possible right now, you can also close your eyes and imagine that, Job-like, you have lost everything. Perhaps you are marooned on a deserted island, or lost in a wilderness as night falls without any shelter or food, or stricken by a deadly illness. Feel what it would be like to have everything taken from you, understand the loss as fully as you can. You live in a world of pain and want. Now open your eyes and see with new eyes (and the memory of "imagined facts") you, your family, and everything that is yours, now magically restored to you, to see, hear, smell, taste and touch.

Once we truly appreciate what we have, then it also becomes much easier to be generous with our thoughts and deeds. After all, what it really takes to be generous is a full understanding of how wealthy we truly are.

This is one reason to respect those who regularly attend religious ceremonies, and to contemplate doing so yourself. During religious rites and ceremonies, people congregate and practice gratitude by giving thanks, meditating on their blessings and praying for their needs (not their wants, but their needs) to be met with mercy and justice. They also practice generosity in giving time and energy to the religious community's activities of education and charity and by giving money so that the religious community may continue. Of course, people can practice, and should practice, gratitude and generosity without a religious affiliation, but sometimes that is a difficult thing to do. People get busy, forget, and so many things get in the way.

If you have any doubt about your thoughts and intentions, ask yourself: is what I am thinking gracious (grateful), and is it generous? If it is not one or the other or both, lose it immediately.

*   *   *

The Courage of Your Perceptions

Although perceptions are paramount in this enlightenment puzzle we are attempting to solve, and indeed are a high percentage of the whole gig (I say it's 70%, but that's just me), these steps or practices are connected. Well, this first connection, between perception and thought, is the most important connection of them all. Perceptions, fully and "honestly" received, will inform and infuse our thinking. Eventually, this influence, this slanting, will draw us to our bliss. It is popular to say, "You must have the courage of your convictions," but I think that is completely wrong. The "courage of your convictions" has brought us all kinds of saintly and creative people—Buddha, Jesus, Confucius, Saint Francis, Mother Teresa, Da Vinci, Michelangelo, Rembrandt, Abraham Lincoln—while it has also brought us all kinds of equally "convicted" (and eventually convicted, if not by courts of the time then, later, by the "court" of history) sinners and destroyers—the Qin Emperor, Nero, Hitler, Stalin, Mao, and a host of criminal names all too familiar. It is unlikely that Hitler had more doubts about his actions than Lincoln did about his, in fact, it is pretty clear from history that Lincoln was a lot more conflicted and a lot less convicted about his tasks during the Civil War than Hitler was about the purpose of the Third Reich. If anything, Hitler clearly had more conviction about how he intended to lead his people to their "destiny." What you must have and here is where you must have it, is the courage of your perceptions.

I like stories of people who persevere against obstacles and odds and stay true to themselves, and one of my favorite stories is that of the comparative mythologist, Joseph Campbell. He was born to an upper class family in New York City around the turn of the 20th century. As he grew up his family and influential friends wanted him to follow a high powered career, one in the investment world at one of the staid banking houses. Joe was not interested. As a child he had absorbed (perceived) wonderful tales of American Indians and was drawn to that. Fine, his family then believed that, since Joe liked "stories," then he could salvage some sort of *respectable career* by getting a PhD in English literature and teaching at some ivy infested ivory tower. It wasn't investment banking, but at least one need not be ashamed of that sort of bookishness. This time, Joe tried, but found the entire PhD process stultifying; it wasn't for him.

Joe exited Columbia with a master's degree in English literature in 1927 and for the next seven years did little except continue privately to search into the tales of the Indians and general mythology. He failed utterly as a fiction writer. In 1934 he found work, not in the ivy but at a ladies' college, Sarah Lawrence. It took him fifteen more years before he would publish his first solo authored book, at the age of forty-five. At Sarah Lawrence, Campbell was able to teach and to follow his bliss (a recurring theme in his talks and writing) and delve into human cultures around the world, and their storytelling and their mythologies. Out of this bliss grew books such as The Hero with a Thousand Faces (1949) and The Masks of God (1959 – 1968) and a wide ranging understanding not only of cultures and their mythologies, but how each individual can be informed and enlightened by understanding his own hero's journey.

You may be thinking, wait a minute, we don't need perceptions to discover what we should be doing, because there are now all sorts of computerized methods where we answer a bunch of questions and get the "right" result. We might use the "gold standard," the Myers-Briggs test, to determine our personality and our aptitudes, *scientifically*, or perhaps delve into enneagrams to discover which of the nine personalities we possess and which passions, temptations, fears, desires and virtues accompany that particular personality.

The problem with going about it in this *scientific* or *quasi-scientific* way is that these questions have been created with thoughts and we can only answer these questions with thoughts. The computerized method skips perceptions completely. If a computerized career test asks us, "Do you prefer to work practically, or do you prefer to work theoretically?" how do we answer that? As for me, I like both, so apparently I cannot go on to "Step Three" because the test can't decide whether I am a "sensor" or an "intuitor." Also, since we are human, when we are asked a question, not only do we bring all of our judgments, prejudices and labels in with us, we also, as innate puzzle-solvers, will be trying very hard to get the "right" answer. The problem with using thoughts to decide these things is that thoughts are already corrupted. If we use bad data, then we know that *GIGO, garbage in garbage out,* will be the result. Fortunately, we also know that our world is incredibly rich and complex, and that our interface with it will provide us with correct and true perceptions, and that those perceptions will, eventually, lead us to the rest of the steps to enlightenment.

How does the connection between perception and thought, and eventually intentions, expressions and actions occur? Quite simply, as we perceive the manifestations of the universe, again, not labeling things, simply absorbing them through our five senses, we will be drawn in certain directions. The universe will guide and inspire us.

Are we drawn to the sunrise, to bright sunny days, to sandy beaches and blazing deserts, to bright sunlight flashing down through canyons? If so, this heliophilia does not necessarily mean we need to take up astronomy or heliology, but it will provide input as to our choices of residence, vocation and avocation. Our sun lover would likely be unhappy living in Seattle or Vancouver, B.C., and certainly be unhappy in Juneau, yet whether she would enjoy Florida, Colorado, New Mexico, California or Texas will depend on other perceptual inputs. If she is not only drawn to the sun, but also to "big" Nature of the sort that has rushing rivers or snow capped mountains, then perhaps the southern California coast or the Sierras would be more attractive than, say, central Florida. But let's also assume that our sun- and nature-lover is also delighted by language. Words just somehow trigger all kinds of delight in her, and she has loved, since childhood, the adventure of learning new words, using them, writing poems and in her journal, and that delight just never seems to quit. A love of words could lead her to linguistics, the study of various foreign languages, a career as a journalist or writer, a path leading to literature, or the study and use of words in theology, law or business. When the sun-, nature- and word-lover is offered positions in Colorado and in Iowa, perhaps she will favor Colorado.

We don't know where these true perceptions will lead our protagonist, who simply started out delighting in the sun, but we do know that ignoring these perceptions will most likely lead her down a path to relative unhappiness and unblissfulness. If you are delighted by plants and the magic things they do in the spring and summer, then you might be happy living in the Pacific Northwest where plants never go brown, and where they stay green even under the occasional dump of snow in the valleys and along the coasts, even though the sun often hides behind clouds during the long, cool winter. Plant delight will probably lead you at least into the garden, and perhaps to not only create a backyard Eden but also to study, either as a vocation or an avocation, flowers and vegetables, trees and shrubs. This in turn may lead you to harvesting fresh plants for your table, or preserving them for later. If you are delighted by the taste of things, as Julia Child was, it may lead you into the art and science of cooking. If health and physical activity and sports give you joy, then you may look for your career and hobbies in the world of sports training, coaching, or physical therapy, or sports medicine, and of course in individual sports themselves. If there is a nexus in your perceptions with sports and nature, then perhaps you will discover your calling in nature sports, such as hiking, climbing, trail running, skiing, kayaking, or paragliding.

Perhaps it is people who fascinate you, the trials and obstacles they face, their stories and their humanity. The human dilemma is the puzzle you are endlessly fascinated with, so you might study psychology or become a daytime talk show host, like Oprah (and be perfectly happy to live in a city like Chicago without the weather and nature of Colorado to enjoy). No one could have given Oprah a computer test or assigned her an enneagram when she was, say, eighteen or twenty, and come up with her trajectory into television production, business entrepreneurship, philanthropy and celebrity. Perhaps the computer test would have printed out: *extrovert / intuitive / feeling /perceiver*, and determined that she was a "spontaneous idealist," who would work well as a team member, but what good would that have done?

If nothing is quite so pleasant to you as euphonious and harmonious sounds, you may be drawn toward music, and become an ardent fan or a musical scholar, a composer or a performer. If you love story-telling, then you might be best suited to a career and a life associated with the arts, perhaps in writing or acting in plays or film, or in some sort of teaching (which is, in fact, a kind of story-telling). Are you entranced by the feel and texture of things, then maybe you will find your bliss in interior design, putting that Oriental rug with the perfect Swedish chair. Perhaps you are mesmerized by creation and engineering, then you might like to design computers or buildings or intricate gear. Or your senses may, over time, resonate with history or other social sciences, or the physical sciences.

The point is, unless you open up your senses, *sans* judgment and *sans* thought, to the universe, you won't know what the connection may tell you about *you*, or how it will guide you to your bliss.

*   *   *

Gratitude and Death

Perhaps the best cure for the fear of death is to reflect
that life has a beginning as well as an end. There was
a time when you were not: that gives us no concern.
Why then should it trouble us that a time will come
when we shall cease to be? To die is only to be as we
were before we were born. ~William Hazlitt

Several times in the previous sections I have mentioned death. I said that we need to be enthusiastic and vital—today— because this might be the last day of our lives. Life is short, I said, let's not shorten it further. But I don't feel much of a need to think or talk about death, and don't feel you should, either. As Yeats famously noted, man creates "death," that is, the dreaded mega-event which often overshadows life, by "dreading and hoping all." When we dread and hope, we project ourselves senselessly into the future and lose track of what is really important, which is *now*. If we can live each moment enthusiastically, and be present each day, hour and minute as each unfolds, then man-created death will never actually arrive, but eventually the natural phenomenon of death will arrive, quietly, in its own "now" moment. And death will truly have no dominion over us during our lives.

When our time is finished and death finally arrives, this wonderful experience which we are having—this banquet—will give way to whatever follows. You may choose to believe whatever you wish about what follows *this*, but don't let your efforts to deal with *that* obscure the kaleidoscopic marvel that is *this* life, *this* consciousness and *this* awareness. *That* would be most ungrateful, and a tremendous sin against the gift of *this*.

*   *   *

The Rule for Rule Making

One decision has made a tremendous day-to-day upgrade in the quality of my life, a boost to my happiness. This rule doesn't exactly fit into this structure, but I put it here because it is a thought and an intention, one which people get wrong for so long. It is, simply put: "Don't make rules for other people which you do not have the authority to enforce, and even if you have the authority to enforce rules for other people (for example, for your children while they are young), think long and hard about it and only make (and enforce) really important rules." If you want to make yourself and your family miserable, sit around and dream up a long list of rules (sometimes we call them "expectations" or "judgments") that others are *supposed* to agree with or to follow. If you want to be truly unhappy in your community, wherever it is, start off ten sentences in a row with "People should never . . ." or "No one has the right to . . ." and finish them with actions you have *no* authority over: "No one should ever get paid more than X$$ for playing baseball," "People just shouldn't color their hair purple," "Nobody should ride noisy motorcycles," "Only idiots use leaf blowers," "A man is a fool to drink hard liquor," "No one should ever vote Republican (or Democrat)," etc.

The essence of making rules for others is judging others, and the Bible, in Matthew 7:1, "Judge not that ye be not judged," wisely warns against it. No one is more unpleasant to be around than someone always making judgments, your crackpot uncle who sits and yells at cable news all day, for instance. We may find our own judgmental thoughts (and expressions) hard to eradicate, though, especially if we were brought up in a judgmental household. Remember that we are really only meant to judge ourselves, to make rules for ourselves, to keep our internal code, and to live by our own correct thoughts and intentions.

When our children were teenagers, the era of great conflict, I found that if I reduced the number of rules and expectations I had for the two of them, life improved greatly. When they were younger they needed more rules and structure, and even in the teen years (the

145

"danger years," really) we still were obliged to set rules and expectations so that the kids could get through that turbulent time and be on schedule to move forward into life. However, I decided early in their teenage years that it would be counterproductive to respond to every bit of sass and lip they might present, and that certain things like curfews and study times might need some adjusting. It is not that they would *not* have been better off coming home early and studying more—they would, indeed—but I had to balance my desires for them with what was really going on in their world. Also, I felt it would be important one day for them to look back at their childhoods and remember more than just one long string of arguments and conflicts with their dad. So I tried to set only important rules, and only enter the fray when something was afoot which might endanger their well-being.

More mundanely (let's face it, 99% of life is mundane, miraculous, but mundane), when someone cuts us off in traffic, it is counterproductive to allow the self to get mad and say, "You shouldn't drive like that," throwing in a few expletives. Remember, we have no authority and we're not police officers; we will be best served by watching the bad driver get well ahead of us and out of sight. Eventually he will cut it too close, cause an accident and have his property damaged and his rates raised, and without our participation. Unless we can enforce whatever rule it is ("You aren't allowed to cut me off," "Well, I didn't."), then let's relax and let it go. It's a small thing, unless we choose to inflate it.

Finally, creating correct thoughts and intentions also touches on a later topic which I will only mention briefly now: meditation. It doesn't matter whether we are sitting in a Zen priory and counting our breaths, sitting in a church praying to Saint Theresa and counting our blessings, or meeting with a small focus group and praying for world peace and other wonderful goals; all meditation, well-practiced, is not only correct intention, but is also correct action, as well as correct mindfulness. While meditation is not, alone, more important than the initial step of full perceptions, because meditation practice combines three of these seven vital steps, it is the second keystone to enlightenment. At its base, meditation settles us and centers us so that we may have a foundation on which to think correctly, to intend correctly and both to speak and act correctly, while at the same time we are practicing staying calm, super calm, in the face of all circumstances. If we build this foundation properly, then we can understand what is correct (and what is not correct) and proceed accordingly.

*   *   *

The Parable of the Car

Mike was an elderly widower who, several years ago, had retired from his job working for the city. He had one son, John, who lived in the same city and worked nearby. One thing that Mike had always regretted, on his limited income and limited resources, was that he had never sampled any of the finer things in life: he had always saved for a rainy day, and he had never taken an expensive (or even inexpensive) trip overseas; he had never eaten in a fine restaurant in a big city; he had never driven an expensive car. Old Mike had always been a bit careful in his life, in fact, he had been timid. There was nothing he could do about that now, but he recognized that shortcoming in his life. He loved his son, John, deeply, and since his wife had died he realized more and more that John was the only thing left of him. So, one day, he went to the Mercedes Benz dealer and bought a brand new car for his son.

The car was perfect, jet black with beige leather seats, a fit and finish suitable for movie stars and celebrities. When John visited him the next day, and noted the fancy car parked out front, Mike asked him if he'd like to take it for a drive.

"Sure, Dad, who wouldn't? Wait, that's yours?"

"Oh no, Johnny, it's yours."

John took the car home and parked it in front of his house. It drove, and rode, beautifully, at least for the first two years. However, John was not very caring where cars were concerned, especially when it came to maintenance. Even though the dealer would maintain it for four years for free, under the warranty, John tended to let things slip, and missed oil changes and routine maintenance. By the time John was experiencing real problems with the car, it had gone out of warranty and would now cost serious money to repair. John used a friend to try to maintain it, with less than mixed results. Also, the beautiful finish of the car, after sitting in the elements and under messy trees for so many years without any care, was now faded and scratched. The leather seats had dried out and begun to crack last summer. Now, with the Mercedes a little over five years old, it looked and sounded like a fifteen-year old vehicle. Each time Mike saw the car it disheartened him, but he said nothing for a long time.

Finally, one day, John came to his father's house, but he was driving another car, a Korean car, one that belonged to his girl friend.

"What's the matter with *your* car?" Mike asked.

"Oh, it's got some problems, so I'm using Gail's car for now."

"What are the problems?"

"Well, the guy at the garage says the engine needs a lot of work, and I don't really have the kind of bucks it takes to repair a Benz. It's more than two thousand dollars, just to get it "road-worthy," whatever that means. And then he said there's probably much more that needs to be done."

"Geez," Mike said. "How many miles are on it now?"

"About eighty thousand, I think. Maybe that's all it's good for."

"You know, I gave you that car, for free. All you had to do was take care of it, and you would have had a great car for a long time. A Benz can run for two-, three-hundred thousand miles. Easy."

"Dad, look. I appreciate the gift, but I didn't ask you for a car. Let's face it; it just may not be the kind of car you're thinking of. Maybe they're not making them as good as they used to, you know, back in your day. Who knows?"

Who knows? Well, everyone reading this, especially those who are parents, know what I am talking about, and it's not cars. The gift is the greatest gift a person can give, that of life itself, and it is not only comprised of the determination and generosity of the ancestors, but tremendous luck in avoiding diseases, accidents and wars. And, yet, like Mike the widower, once the present is given, the donor must relinquish rights and responsibilities for the care of that precious gift to the donee. Whether you want to limit the idea of the "donor" to biological parents and grandparents, or expand it out to the cosmos, to Dylan Thomas' "force that through the green fuse drives the flower," to Chinese *qi*, to Brahma or God, it matters little. The recipient, like John, all too often ignores not only the sacrifice the giver has undergone in order to make the gift, but disregards the preciousness of the gift, and fails to take even minimum care of it. Soon it sits, scratched and dented and rusting on a side street.

*   *   *

SEVEN

Correct Expression

Speech is the mirror of the soul; as a man speaks, so is he. .~Publilius Syrus

Remember not only to say the right thing in the right place, but far more difficult still, to leave unsaid the wrong thing at the tempting moment.~ Benjamin Franklin.

After comprehending the great gift and miracle of our own lives, and appreciating the incredible prize it is to be able to perceive the universe through our senses, perhaps the next most astounding capability we have is our ability to express ourselves in speech and writing. We are just beginning to understand the complexity of human language, which is an amazing cognitive ability to learn and use complex communication systems. We acquire speech as infants, and have more or less mastered it by the age of three or four, although we generally expand and refine our language at least until young adulthood. We are given one language freely, our mother tongue, and actually can scarcely be termed "normal" without mastery of our native language. We may even decide to learn other languages.

Yet our verbal communication is not merely the words we use, but an incredibly complex system utilizing several parts of the brain, and it is a system which relies upon our ability to discern certain verbal and non-verbal clues, and to time and modulate our responses, in order to communicate effectively. We can say the same words in a single sentence with differing emphasis to imply different things:

I thought you were going to bring the potato salad. (maybe it's my fault, but I was clearly under the impression that . . .)

I **thought** you were going to bring the potato salad. (you led me to believe . . .)

I thought **you** were going to bring the potato salad. (and not someone else, and certainly not me . . .)

I thought you **were going** to bring the potato salad. (did you change your mind at the last minute?)

I thought you were going to **bring** the potato salad. (we were counting on you . . .)

I thought you were going to bring the **potato salad.** (and now we have 3 coleslaws!)

Mastering the spoken language is one thing, but we are also given a tremendous gift, a legacy, really, in our written language. For English speakers, each of us has received the incredibly rich inheritance of what was once simply a local Germanic language spoken in Anglia, and which is now the world's *lingua franca* or de facto "Esperanto," the common tongue not only of 500 million or so native speakers (from more than 30 countries, including America, Canada, Australia, England, Ireland, Scotland, New Zealand, Jamaica, etc.) but also up to a billion more who learn the language as one of their national languages (India, Pakistan, Philippines, Ghana, South Africa, etc.) or acquire it as the required second language to be learned in schools (China, Japan, Korea, Brazil, etc.) or, later, struggle to master it for academic and business purposes. English has a vocabulary of perhaps 600,000 words, but it is a mixed marriage, since we get our words (not our grammar, but our words) from Norman French, native (Germanic) English, Latin, Greek, Old Norse, Dutch, and others. There are thousands of books you might read in your lifetime if you are diligent, and you can get the best ideas and stories of writers and thinkers both dead and alive to increase your knowledge and fuel your imagination.

Of course you have a similar inheritance if your language is Chinese, or Spanish, or German. If you want to use any of the words in the dictionary to write a letter, an editorial, a poem, a novel or an essay upon the history of zippers, there is no charge, no fee, and no requirement of footnoting or attribution. Every single word and all of the language is free for the taking, by anyone. This is yet one more thing to be incredibly grateful for.

So far, we have seen that each of us is a tremendous perception collector for data from this miraculous world which we are blessed to live in. We have also seen that, using that rich lode of data, we can apply a simple "software" comprised of a code of positive adjectives to test our thoughts and intentions. We must make sure that we are positive and enthusiastic, use filters of appropriateness, robustness and authenticity, and focus on generosity and gratitude to create correct thoughts and correct intentions. Perceptions and intentions are the seeds of words and then deeds, which is why it is so critical at this point to control anything noxious before it can take root as a thought, then possibly sprout as speech, and eventually spread as an epidemic action.

Now, correct expression, the natural extension of our perceptions and our intentions, may be the first step we take which can have an impact on others. What we perceive and what we intend will stay private until we express ourselves outwardly, or take an action. (There are those who are completely irresponsible and speak without thinking, but since we have already taken the first two steps, that could never be us.) Correct expression means we should only speak or write after we perceived the world fully and have created correct thoughts and intentions.

Speech is powerful; after all, it is almost the only way we have of knowing and relating to other people. Unless we have the gift of telepathic mind reading, we will never understand others' intentions and motives and thoughts, and we are rarely in others' company long enough to observe their actions for any meaningful period of time.

And *vice versa*. And actions can often mean different things. A man in a suit runs into the hospital almost knocking over a school child? Is he being rude, or unconscious, or is he rushing to a dying relative's bedside? Our main interface with others in the world will be through speech and writing, and only secondarily through actions.

For a rich and full life, we are well advised to take care in our expression and, at times, not speak, not express ourselves. This isn't because we want to hide something, but rather because we understand how powerful words are, not only in defining and possibly limiting how we will be perceived and, by extension, who we will be in the world, but also because our words can work to define and limit others in ways which may not be enriching to anyone.

Of course, it is not only through speech and writing that we can express ourselves. We can paint, compose music, design buildings (architecture) and machines (engineering), but now we are crossing over from expression into action (the next chapter). Clearly when we sing, dance, act dramatically, or create movies, we are moving beyond mere expression.

*   *   *

EIGHT

Taking Action

The superior man is modest in his speech, but excels in his actions. ~ Confucius.

Many struggle through life trying to do the right thing. Doing the right thing, though, and taking the right action, become easier if we have been practicing the first three steps of sustainable enlightenment: full perceptions, correct thinking and correct expression. In fact, if we have done these three things assiduously, it becomes much more difficult to do the wrong thing, or the weak thing, or to take the easy way out when it comes to taking action. Instead of setting ourselves up for failure and disappointment, we have set ourselves up for success and happiness, and for awakening and enlightenment.

What is an action, anyway? Put very simply, an action is any physical step you take based on a conscious decision to do so. A sneeze is not an action in this sense since the decision to sneeze is not generally up to you; it is merely an involuntary reaction to dust, pollen or some internal invader. When you see that the rain has stopped and then decide to ride your bicycle the six mile round trip to the gym, and then actually do so, you are taking an action. Given the health benefits and perceptual aesthetics of regular bicycle riding, it is most likely a correct action. When you open the cupboard in the kitchen one morning and select one tea among the teas on the shelf, brew it and savor it, you are taking a correct action. The vast majority of the actions we take are small actions in the great scheme of things; often we have taken some actions so frequently (morning tea, Saturday swim) that they have become habits. If the action—now a habit—arises from what we might call "correct consciousness," that is, the result of full perception and correct thinking, then it is a good or correct habit. Regular—we can say habitual—exercise can be a beneficial habit. Still, it is a good idea from time to time to remember *why* we are swimming on Saturday morning (rather than surfing the internet) or riding a bicycle in the sunshine (rather than driving the car), and to take a moment to consciously savor (sense) the physical and mental rewards from such beneficial habits.

Successful military and business operations often refer to the "OODA" concept or loop. OODA stands for "observe-orient-decide-act." Originally invented for fighter pilots to use as a combat decision making framework, OODA has been utilized in all types of combat operations and now even in business. But this is nothing new to us now, since these are merely three of the steps of enlightenment. Observing and orienting are nothing more than fully perceiving. Deciding is thinking and intending. And acting is, well, taking action. The military understands this as a continual loop in a hot fight, and we can use the same concept, the steps of perception, intention and action in a continual loop in our own "hot" action, that of living fully aware.

As is the case with speech and other expressions, the actions we should be taking, since they arise from the now *correct* thoughts and intentions which we have formed, will mirror those thoughts and intentions. Our actions must obey our inner code of conduct (helpful, friendly, courteous, kind, etc., to the extent each applies), and our actions will be positive, robust and authentic, and be executed with enthusiasm, graciousness and generosity. We will never resent or regret any actions which follow this template, although we will want to review our actions and re-measure them against our code from time to time. Perhaps an action did not turn out to be as kind or as courteous as we had intended; it is possible that, in our enthusiastic rush to start a new course of study, we might not have noticed the person behind us at the library door, for whom we could have paused a second longer to hold it open. In general, however, except for some minor tweaking, actions which flow out of the first three steps, properly taken, will be beyond critique.

Correct actions also ask us to re-exercise our perceptive powers while executing the actions themselves. My neighbor Paul introduced me several years ago to the pleasures of road cycling and we try to find the time, nine months of the year, to go for regular rides two or three times a week. We have standard routes which take us out into the farmlands and vineyards of Lane County, and we usually select one of two rides for either 23 miles or 37 miles, and occasionally longer rides. Although this sort of riding has become a custom or a habit, and I never need to summon much will power to hop on the bike and go, I always remember—always—to pause my mind along the way and savor the views of the little farms and vine fields, the fresh air and country smells, the sound and feel of the breeze cutting through the thin suit material and onto my damp skin, the pressure of my stiff road bike shoes as my legs power through the cycle and the kinetic joy of moving forward with the gyroscopic motion of a two-wheeled, finely-engineered and geared vehicle. In this way, I try to make sure I stay as conscious and in the present moment as I can, even while partaking in a customary ride, a habitual action I may have done three or four hundred times already.

If we look at our actions, we can roughly divide them into actions of working, eating, learning, enjoyment (mental expansion and somewhat more passive entertainment), exercising and recreating (health and active entertainment), and resting. At this point in the process, it should not be complicated to keep all of these actions in line with whatever code we have settled on, our filters and our guidelines. We will look in slightly more detail at the big or macro-picture of working or livelihood in Chapter Ten. Suffice it for now to note that livelihood itself is nothing more than perceiving, thinking, expressing and taking actions, and all should be done consciously.

Although taking correct actions is listed as the fourth step here, in fact, it was also the first step we took. The instant we turn our perceptors to ON, we are taking the first and most necessary *correct* action we ever can. Opening up to the universe without having to judge any part of it, connecting to the world in the only way we can, through our senses, is the key step in attaining awareness and enlightenment. And, although I have described it as an "ON" switch, it may be something more like an iterative switch. Or we may even wish to think of it as a faulty or questionable switch, in the sense that we must frequently monitor it. Am I really seeing, am I really hearing all that the world is offering me at this moment?

And, after mining the world for perceptive minerals, we now manufacture thoughts, expressions and actions. These actions, all actions, will not only lead to further awareness and awakening, but also arise from awareness and awakening. If we have practiced seeing the world and ourselves clearly, and have begun to think with enthusiasm, gratitude and generosity, and made sure our speech follows in this same path, we may now more easily take the actions we need to take to carry out our intentions.

Let's return to the example from before. We wake up in the morning and it's cold and raining. We see that clearly, but instead of being depressed we elect to be fascinated by the fractal geometric and chaotic patterns we see, we are delighted by the smooth sheen of the botanical softscape and the architecture-like hardscape of our environment, all rinsed clean and still dripping and damp. We are not "faking" enthusiasm, somehow "priming the pump" in order to feel this way, our enthusiasm is authentic now. We also absorb the rhythmic sound of the rain on the roof and windows of our home. We rise and, while retrieving the paper from the front step, we inhale the wet leaf and earth smell of fresh rain. We set a kettle of water on the stove, noting the metallic *clap* as the kettle rests on the grate and the *shoompff* sound as the pilot light ignites the burner. We hear the water begin to heat up inside the kettle—a peculiar, rumbling and rolling sound—and we smell the slight fragrance of dry tea as we extract it from its container and put it in the waiting teapot. We pause for a half a second, remembering that this tea has come a long way for this next step, harvested by some farmer's hands in India or Sri Lanka, bought and sold in sunny, dusty market towns and transported across the world, and each tea leaf now awaits its real purpose, the moment when the scalding water drenches it and it releases its pent up flavors and oils. As we glance over the paper we quickly absorb (while noticing the feel and sound of the paper) only *that* news which is of value to us, and discard the rest. Our tea is ready to pour and as we raise our cup we notice the caramel colors of the tea and actually see the milk still swirling and blending with the dark brown liquid, like some slow motion explosion. Finally, we engage our taste and other sensors as we sip the hot drink and let its warmth percolate down our throats and into our bodies. We are grateful for the day, the sunrise behind the cloud cover, the rain and its glisten and its fragrance, our comfortable shelter, the newspaper, our kitchen and our tea. Simple pleasures, but rich pleasures. We have already perceived the world correctly; we are functioning with proper intentions and have even taken several small but correct actions. Thus today, through these modest actions we repeat each and every day, we have continued the process of sustaining ourselves and sustaining our enlightenment.

All of our actions this morning, even though the day has barely begun, have been correct and wholesome, both for our bodies and our minds. We have also, so far, abstained from any action which might be unwholesome. In other words, we have been building, even in this small way, a beautiful and awakened life, and we have taken no actions which would work against this awareness. It is still early in the morning; we probably have some time to take more action. Our stomach is warm but not filled yet, so it would be an easy step to sit and stretch for a while (yoga), or to sit quietly in focused concentration (meditation).

*   *   *

Concerning things which are *imperfect, good, better, perfect,* and *good enough*

Dans ses écrits, un sàge Italien
Dit que le mieux est l'ennemi du bien.
(In his writings, an Italian sage
Says that perfect is the enemy of the good) ~ Voltaire

What keeps us from taking certain actions (and, later, embarking on certain quests) is rarely fear or doubt about the outcome, or lack of confidence in our prospects. It is most often a damaging criterion our egos inflict on our selves: the requirement that we execute perfectly and achieve a perfect result, and dissatisfaction with anything less. We think that *perfect* is the only standard worth striving for, and that *imperfection* is akin to shame. I'm not sure where this comes from, perhaps from parents or teachers, or simply from an internal source tapping its toe and wagging its finger at us. For example, once you reach a certain age it becomes very difficult to learn another language. This phenomenon is not because the vocal chords have diminished (they have not) or because the part of the brain which can acquire language has had its power cut (it has not).

The difficulty in learning a foreign language after the age of, say, twenty, is an ego-imposed disability, and it arises from a supposedly "mature" self-image. *I am now an adult, I am dignified and I have left behind me the clumsiness and childishness of youth. My speech is sophisticated and wise, I am worthy of respect and admiration. I make no errors, ever.* Just remember how embarrassing it might have been for you as a teenager, using your native English and mispronouncing a word in public (one which you had only seen in print and never heard, perhaps *debacle* or *aegis* or *vehement)*. But to learn anything, to do anything, is not only to accept imperfection but to embrace it. If you cannot embrace the certainty that, when speaking in Spanish you will, within two or three sentences, almost invariably fumble a verb tense (perhaps not even knowing that the past pluperfect subjunctive even existed), mispronounce words with a heavy, foreign accent and choose the wrong word to begin with (perhaps saying you were completely *embarazado* by something, only to learn that it means you were "impregnated" by it), you will never communicate in Spanish. So you have a choice, do you want to learn to speak Spanish or not?

There are, however, many more ego-imposed disabilities than simply foreign languages. Think of all the things "adults" say about activities and actions. Start with "I can't" and end with things like ski, swim, ballroom dance, surf, rock climb, learn a musical instrument, start a new career, run a marathon, learn to sail, ride a bicycle across the country, etc.

To an enlightened person, however, these ineluctable imperfections and errors present no hurdle whatsoever. What could it possibly matter if, after receiving accurate information in Japanese from a clerk in Karuizawa about boarding time and platform for your train, you thank him by saying, *Dozo arigato gozaimasu,* ("Please thank you very much") instead of the correct *Domo arigato gozaimasu* ("Thank you, thank you very much)"? No harm has been done. We already know that during the course of a single morning, even with all of our sensory tools on high alert, we will fail to perceive more than half that the universe is offering us: we savor our morning tea on the patio and smell a faint woodsmoke in the air but fail to notice the junco sparrow hopping beneath the brush or feel the light breeze lifting from the west. Our perceptions will always be imperfect and somehow incomplete, but that imperfection will more than suffice to reach awareness and enlightenment. Our actions, similarly, will never result in perfection—frankly, we are much too busy to be bothered with such a nonsensical goal, anyway.

We can accept that our actions and even our existence will be imperfect, but enlightened nonetheless. As for the question of setting goals, however, what should we aim for, what is the standard we should set for ourselves? It cannot be imperfection—we may settle for imperfection but we will never set our course for it. It cannot be perfection, either, because that may simply paralyze us. After all, if we have to do it perfectly, then each step, beginning with the very first, must be the very model of perfection. Who would dare to dip a toe in those waters now?

The solution, however, is simple: we should search for excellence as a model (and not perfection) and imitate it as closely as we can, and be satisfied if, on a regular basis, we are simply getting better. A standard of excellence is more than sufficient, we can leave perfection to the angels. You ask yourself a simple question: what would an excellent student, or athlete, or outdoorsman, or parent, do? If you wish to be successful in your studies so that you may enter into a career which seems promising, you must consider what the "hypothetical" excellent student is doing, and ape that. To be healthy, study what people in excellent physical condition do, and adjust your habits and diet accordingly. Even if your parents were not excellent, some of the things they did worked out, so keep those, and you must have known friends who had excellent parenting. What was the nature of that, the basis for excellent parents? Were the parents involved, interested in their children's ideas and values, in attendance at back-to-school nights and recitals and events? Did they bully their children, or cooperate with them, or even let them plan and decide certain things for themselves?

If you wish to learn a language, you were already at one time an excellent student of languages yourself—in your childhood. Remember the sense of relaxation, music and play that accompanied language? Apply those actions to the language you wish to learn today. Relax. Be playful. Sing out its rhythms in nonsense syllables. Do you like opera? Then read the libretto to *Madame Butterfly* and sing along, "Un bel di vedremo / levarsi un fil di fumo / sul estremo confin del mare . . ." If you favor more modern songs, then buy a Boccelli cd, read and translate the lyrics in the liner notes, and sing along.

Remember, however, that it is *good* and *better* which we are aiming for, not *perfect*. But it is also not *good enough*. *Good enough* is possibly the worst standard anyone could accept. Recall our discussion of enthusiasm. *Good enough* is a cramped little vessel, never containing enough space to hold any true enthusiasm.

Do you like that book you are reading? Well, I dunno, I guess it's good enough. Toss the book.

Do you like working as an attorney? Not really, but I'm stuck with it. I suppose it's good enough. It's time to start looking for a new career, a segue into something *good* and away from just *good enough*.

Good enough is a half-measure for, frankly, half-wits. Little Reginald, doing his piano practice in preparation for a recital, is tempted by the sound of other children playing outside to cut short his work and join them. After all, his effort is probably *good enough*. In all events, he's seen the other kids at these recitals, even if Reginald makes a few mistakes he'll still be better than most of them. This is a disaster in the happening.

Good enough almost never is any good at all. And *good enough* contains no enthusiasm, and never has enough traction to get to *better*, which is where we are really aiming with our actions. The truth is, *good enough* is simply another way of saying half-hearted or even lousy.

*   *   *

Diet

Clogged with yesterday's excess, the body drags the mind down with it. ~Horace

In general, mankind, since the improvement of cookery, eats twice as much as nature requires. ~Benjamin Franklin

Republic of Korea, Kangwon Province, Weon Tong Village, March, 1977. The village market was busy, and wide, tightly woven straw baskets were filled with an assortment of grains harvested the previous fall and a rather depleted selection of vegetables. My co-teacher, Mr. Kim, was pointing at one particular basket filled with something that looked like dark, green weeds plucked from a suburban lawn somewhere.

"Those are *san namul*, which means "sprouts from the mountain-side." We gather them from the mountains in the early spring, it is for now when we run low on vegetables and *kimch'i*. Good for health, good for stamina."

Good for stamina. Those words, and ones similar to them, would be repeated to me frequently over the first three years I lived in Korea. As a 22-year old Peace Corps Volunteer, assigned to a middle school in a village just a few miles south of the DMZ, I remember the old teachers (for me at the time, the "old teachers" could have been anywhere from thirty years old and up) were strangely focused on eating for reasons other than the reasons I ate for. They ate a number of things—ginseng root, raw ginger, garlic, honey, as well as selected Chinese medicines such as deer antler powder—for stamina. Of course, in those days I rarely thought much about eating, and never about cooking or ingredients, and absolutely never about stamina. My rationale for food was simple: I was hungry, so I wanted something to remedy that situation. It did not matter too much what. If possible, I wanted the food to taste good, and absolutely I wanted the food to cost as little as possible. This whole concept of eating for energy or stamina seemed silly. I was twenty-two; I had way too much energy and way too much stamina.

There is probably no action we take as often, with as many potentially beneficial as well as dire consequences, as what we choose to eat. In order to survive, we know we must breathe, drink a sufficient amount of water, and eat, as well as keep a reasonable body temperature by using clothing and shelter, but the choices we make at the supermarket and in the pantry are paramount in determining whether or not we will have the mental and physical capacity—the stamina—to take all other actions. All of us are born with the potential to be fit, healthy, robust and active human beings during our entire lives, but if we look at any main street or shopping mall in America, what do we see? Three hundred pound plus thirty- and forty-year olds barely able to waddle from bench to bench, a phalanx of people so prematurely decrepit that some must motor from shop to shop in specially designed mobility scooters emblazoned with names like the *Pride*, the *Gusto*, and the *Sunrunner*, because they can no longer ambulate on their own, and others who, as if perpetual denizens of an airport terminal, must walk with oxygen tanks rolling behind them like carry-on luggage. Now a few, very few, are in this sad situation through no fault of their own, but the vast majority have eaten, smoked and sofa-sat their way there. (Sadly, as I was preparing the final edit, newspapers reported that 12 states have adult obesity rates over 30%, and our "best" state, Colorado, sported a 19.8% rate.)

I won't tell you what to eat, but I will say that what you eat is probably limiting your life right now, limiting your energy and how you feel, what you can do, how much confidence you have, and what decisions you can make. Without energy and confidence it is very unlikely that you can be aware and enlightened in any meaningful sense. The American diet, and by that I mean eighty percent or more of what is stocked and sold in the aisles of Safeway, Albertsons,

Stop 'N Shop and the rest of the supermarkets, is simply not acceptable food. Take the entire soft drink aisle and blow it up. Gone. Take the cookies and candies aisle, the chips and dips aisle, the breads and muffins aisle, the canned vegetables and canned soups, the jellies and jams and preserves aisle, and the bakery and cakery section. *Kaboom. Blam. Pow.* Gone. What do those sections stock that you (your body) can really use? And, what is hidden in those stacks of cans and boxes and plastic-wrapped packages which is slowly killing you?

For me, the usable portion of the modern supermarket is almost limited to the periphery aisles selling fresh vegetables, fresh fruits, fresh fish, meat, dairy and dried legumes. Add in a few canned goods (tomatoes and beans) and fresh corn tortillas, and I'm done.

Our bodies are like cars. When they are new, they run perfectly, at least for a while. No matter how you take care or don't take care of them, they just seem to hum along. Now I view of my "car" as a 1954 Douglas, which ran pretty well on little to no maintenance or care until about 1994, but around then I, too, began to look for better foods, a fuel which would make my '54 model run better, something good for *stamina*. I began to read diet books and experiment with various methods. Some worked better than others. Eventually, restricting my intake of carbohydrates seemed to work best, as did upping the intake of vegetables. I tried the Adkins diet for a few months and lost weight but it was a difficult diet to maintain. I generally felt lousy most of the time, and my breath came out sweet and sickly smelling, even if I looked better.

Luckily, I have had the good fortune of eating a heavily Asian diet straight from 1976 through to today, about thirty five years. It wasn't until I went gluten-free this past year, however, that I returned to the vim and vigor of my twenties. The result of going G-free is very odd, very odd to me, and it's not anything I expected. But, considering that the human species in more or less its present form—certainly its present general metabolism—has been running around the planet for several hundred thousand years, and that wheat agriculture has only been here for ten thousand years, then it's not surprising to find that, at least for some of us (and I believe, a lot of us), wheat is not the staff of life, but rather one obstacle to a rich and healthy life.

In any event, I'm not suggesting that you go gluten-free right now, although you may want to try it (it's fairly easy to do). What you need to do in terms of your diet, however, is try to scrape away all the information that you have received from family, friends and the food manufacturers and purveyors, and try to figure out, based on your perceptions and your own enlightenment, what things you should be eating to further your own cause. You won't regret getting serious about eating, of that you can be sure.

*   *   *

The Reluctant Runner

Stadiums are for spectators. We runners have nature and that is much better. ~Juha Vaatainen

Misery is a relative thing. ~ Lance Armstrong

Share a little run with me. On a typical late Oregon fall day, I ran out the side door (elevation, 500 feet) and up the road into the trails. During the next few hours I ran about 13 miles up and down the Ridgeline Trail, gaining perhaps a total of 2,000 feet on the various rises and ridges which lead to the summit of Spencer Butte (2,055 feet) and, on the way, passed through four separate squalls. It was sunny at the top for the moment (and cool with the breeze pressing my now sweat-drenched clothing against my skin), but I could see a new set of clouds scudding toward me, dark and roiling, from the Pacific Ocean, 70 miles to the west. During the time I was out I ran through a typical suburban development, into a secondary growth forest of firs, yews and pines, up into a fern forest topped by old growth Douglas Fir, Ponderosa Pine and Big Leaf Maples, and scrambled over the bald basalt rocks on the summit of the butte, home to a few relatively retiring rattlesnakes and a generous collection of poison oak. All the while my heart was pumping, my legs were churning and my core was engaged, my entire being focused on balancing to keep from experiencing an exciting and untoward event.

By running, across time, I was engaging in an action which our species has been doing for hundreds of thousands of years. You can't say that for sitting in a car, fiddling with a computer or MP3 player or watching television. By running in the woods, I had a connection with the prehistoric forest runners of ancient Africa, Europe and Asia. The funny thing is, I have no business running, none whatsoever.

As a child, I remember that some could run like the wind, and others could not. I was among the others, and sadly I could not even qualify for the elementary school sports team (fifth and sixth grade, a pretty low bar) to participate in the annual sports day in Drexel Hill, Pennsylvania. I never really enjoyed running, and never thought I would. I went out for a lot of sports teams in school, and enjoyed the experience, mostly, but never was any great shakes at anything I tried. By the time I was a senior in high school I had dropped football and wrestling and only competed on the track team. Since I lacked speed for the sprints and had no endurance for the distances, I ended up trying to specialize in a single skill event, the high hurdles sprint. In the end I managed to snag a varsity letter in track, but only because they had, for track teams at the end of the season, a special Loser's Meet. Now, understand that to letter in track in our school district you needed to have raced to a first, second or third place in a dual track meet or at the league championship. I never got a single one of those, but all the losers had one last chance to get a first, second or third at the Loser's Meet, competing only against similar inepts. And thus, I was able to come in third place one day in May 1972, received a pity medal in the Loser's Meet, and my high school varsity letter.

In the 1990s I began to jog a little, never for pleasure, always for general health. In 1997, however, I blew out my left knee skiing a run in conditions I should never have been on. After my head-over-keester yard sale on the ski slope, it seemed likely that I would not ski again, and probably not run again. The injury, the surgery and the rehab, however, turned out to be a blessing. It awakened me to the fact that, at 43, I would *not* be active for my entire life, and if I vaguely wanted to do anything, I had better start soon or it might never happen in this lifetime. So, while I was waiting for my reconstructed knee to mend (12 months), I bought some snowshoes for the winter, and started walking in the snow, and took a kayak course in the late spring. Without belaboring the point, within two years I was back to full speed tennis (singles, with a knee brace), hiking and climbing, and returned to skiing the following year. I began to jog some in the good weather a little more regularly, and tried to participate in the local 10K race on the Fourth of July each year. For several years I did the same activities and then, in 2008, for some reason I began to elevate the level of what I was aiming for. I started doing more serious downhill skiing (some tree runs, the black diamonds and heavier powder runs, rather than just the blue groomers), and more technical climbing attempts. In 2009 I joined the local backcountry ski patrol and, the next summer, volunteered with them at an aid station at a 100- kilometer (62-mile) ultramarathon race. When I saw the runners come in to our station at the 50-mile mark I was impressed and immediately knew I wanted to try this. There was a shorter (50-kilometer) ultramarathon just three weeks away.

This is the way awareness works. Because I perceived the world fully and really saw my own potential and nature correctly, I was pushed to an intention I did not think I could or should have. And then I took action. So, the first action I took was to run out the door and down through the cemetery and up some steep roads, and then climb onto the Ridgeline Trail here in town where I had seen trail runners before. To me, these runners had always seemed a little strange; to my mind they were moving way too fast to enjoy the forest scenery and seemed to be tempting injury with every step. I started to jog, slowing to a fast walk on the steepest parts of the trail, but trying to jog the flattish parts and then more or less bounce down the downhill portions.

I noticed that my body, in self-preservation mode no doubt, had begun to make some not so subtle changes without any instructions from my brain. Instead of falling forward and landing on my heels as we are likely to do on the streets and roads, I ran more upright, lifting my trailing foot each time to make sure it cleared any root or rock. I began to run lighter on my feet and at a faster pace or turnover. I lifted my arms slightly as well, as an aerialist would, to balance myself. I imagined that I was somehow floating, as if in a swimming pool, and my arms were helping me to tread water; I was treading air and treading trail. My perceptions were changed, too. I was completely in the moment and focused on the trail about 8 to 10 feet ahead of me, processing all of the important data: slope, rocks, roots, bushes, tree branches, slippery spots, scree or loose gravel areas. This was like no running I had ever done before. It was very, very pleasant and, in a word, beautiful. The sunlight pierced the forest canopy in a constantly changing dappled pattern, and I ran in silence through the alternating rays and shadows. I felt a little like the Terminator, the computer cyborg who collects and analyzes all the data from his environment as he moves through Los Angeles on a search and destroy mission. Everything in that space immediately ahead of me was vital and key, but once I passed it, what had just been important data about the trail behind me was immediately irrelevant and gone. I needed to evaluate *right now* this down slope of the path, a smooth rock to the left, a puddle to the right, a patch of gravel slightly ahead, and a branch at eye level approaching. The process and the feeling also reminded me of white water canoeing or sea kayaking in surf—total focus, mental and physical, on the task and the moment at hand. The risks of not doing so were too great: injury, potentially grave injury.

Finally, there was something primordial about this running. It was as if I had gone back in time and were running with the aboriginal inhabitants of any of the continents, the Calapuya or the Chinook on their mountain ridges and in their forests—there was something incredibly and basically human and natural about this. This primal experience made me feel more natural than I had at any time in memory; I was probably six or seven years old when I last felt this free and this wild.

I contacted the director of the 50K ultramarathon and he kindly gave me one of the last slots. In the buildup to the run, I ran an hour or so on our Ridgeline trail a few more times, and managed on September 11, 2010, despite a rolled ankle and slightly torqued knee, to finish the official run. The last hour of the run was not pretty, but to be honest, it was as good as I have ever felt in my entire life, in a completely fatigued and absurd way.

So we can see that in the chain of chance, my blown knee led to some clear thinking which led back into mountain climbing and skiing, and some limited running, which led to the ski patrol, which led to an aid station in the wilderness, and now finally led to long distance trail running. Oddly, the guy who at eleven years old couldn't run is now at 56 years old running longer than seems possible. I am incredibly grateful for this, as this is a kind of physical enlightenment I had no reason to expect.

Although many runners find that eventually running on hard surfaces is too hard and switch to softer paths or trails, there is a theory out there, based on Daniel Lieberman's research and described in Christopher McDougall's Born to Run, that we actually evolved to be trail-running hunters, and that it is not only something we can do, but something we were specifically designed to do. The theory, based on our unique cooling system—the design of our skulls and noses and our naked skin and easy perspiration—makes us the only creature capable of running for great distances without being forced to stop and cool off. We basically cool off on the go. We are capable of running prey literally into heat stroke and cardiac arrest. Although almost all other land mammals are faster in sprints than we are (go ahead, try to catch your dog sometime, or a squirrel or a mouse), none of them can run continuously for miles and miles as the skin-cooled human can.

There is also something about the body which loves movement and, particularly, running, especially if a manner of running can be found which does not injure us. First, we know that gravity helps the body and that an erect position such as we use while running, aids us not only in circulation but in digestion. Peristalsis, the muscular wave contractions which transport food and drink literally from top to bottom, is greatly aided by gravity. Note how much better our digestion works when we can walk about, and how stopped up we get if we linger on the couch or are bedridden for any significant amount of time. Just notice how bad we begin to feel if we do not

169

get up and move, and how good we feel if we can at least walk a bit while recovering from an illness.

Running also acts to reinvigorate the entire cardiovascular system, strengthening the heart and lungs, strengthening the skeletal muscles which aid in the circulation of the blood, speeding up the metabolism, eliminating toxins and producing those lovely brain chemicals, the endogenous (inner) morphines, a.k.a. endorphins.

Running is also the most efficient of activities and, in a time-sense, the most "moral." Since time is all we have, making the most efficient use of it is a moral good, and wasting time is an immorality. Like many Americans, I have participated in a veritable catalogue of sports exercises: countless children's games, tackle football, wrestling, track, weightlifting, taekwondo, crew, mountain climbing, alpine and nordic skiing, rock climbing, kung fu, rugby, basketball, baseball, golf, squash, tennis, aikido, cycling, kayaking and canoeing. Now that I am running on trails through nature, except for the mountain sports of climbing and skiing, none can compare aesthetically or spiritually with running. All activities have had their merits and attractions at different times, but none on the list was ever as economical or as efficient as running. Look through that list again and check for ease and efficiency: how many people do you need, what kind of facility (lake, tennis court, gym, swimming pool, rugby pitch) is required and its cost, what kind of gear (bicycle, cleats, spikes, football pads and helmet, rowing shell or scull and oars, tennis gear and balls, rock climbing ropes, harness, devices, quick-draws and chocks and caribiners, skis, climbing skins, crampons), and how much time does it take just to get to the mountain, ocean or lake, tennis court, playing field or swimming pool, and compare it to running. What do you need to run? A pair of shoes, and maybe a hat. Facility? Streets, roads, paths, trails. Cost? Next to nothing. Time? Maybe you need some time to get to where you want to start, but you can almost always start from home and you are already into it from your very first step.

What about equipment failure? They might close your pool. Your bicycle can easily have a flat, or break a chain. You can bust a pole or a binding while skiing, foul up an oarlock on a scull, or break your strings or even your racquet on the tennis court. Running? Except for wearing out the bottoms of your shoes, or maybe breaking a lace, nothing ever goes very wrong with your running equipment. Running efficiency? It has to be the highest on the scale.

I confess, however, that I still retain a vestigial love of a sport with a ball, whether large or small. There is something just so much fun (and almost silly) about bouncing and hitting a ball and the way we are hypnotized by it. I will retain tennis, despite its obvious inefficiency.

*   *   *

Other Actions

Of course, there are countless actions other than adventures in nature, proper diet and vigorous exercise which involve taking correct action. If we go back and focus on perceiving things fully as they are, and having correct thoughts which grow out of our perceptions, thoughts which we monitor as to certain specific qualities, then we will find it relatively easy to take the correct actions in our lives. How do we test then for correctness? Well, from the beginning, a correct action will simply feel correct, legitimate, and moral. When I return from a three-hour trail run I feel better, like I have done something which not only makes me a better person but which also makes the world a better place. Literally. And, in a sense, I have. But I also feel better when I discover a new section of the library, or attend a talk about theoretical physics at the university, or take a multi-day course about emergency medical care or avalanche safety, or when I sit down to tea with my wife, or when I straighten up the garden or the garage. *There*, I say to myself after each of them, *that was a good thing to do*.

Every action we take should be a good thing to do, in context.

You may decide to attend a series of lectures on certain arts you were interested in during your youth, or to go back to graduate school or to take clarinet lessons again after a 30-year lapse, or to join the city choir, or to take part in a volunteer organization whose goals resonate with your intentions. You may make a documentary film or really dig in and finally write that novel that wakes you up at 3 a.m. You may seek to reconnect or mend fences with family or friends who have drifted away (or, you may not). You may contact an aging relative or neighbor or retired teacher who meant a lot to you. You may decide, like me, to stop procrastinating and write that book which contains everything important that you ever learned.

I could probably write several chapters, or even an entire book, about possible actions you might like to take, but it would make *no* difference. Only *you* can determine the correct course of action for you. That is the whole point of correct action. You should understand that any correct action may, and probably will, lead to other, connected and correct actions. A lecture on poetry may lead you to take a writing class, which may lead you to write a book of poems or a memoir.

One of the most important actions we can take is to actively seek out and execute proper rest:

> *Sleep that knits up the ravelled sleeve of care*
> *The death of each day's life, sore labour's bath*
> *Balm of hurt minds, great nature's second course,*
> *Chief nourisher in life's feast.* ~ William Shakespeare

We don't normally think of resting or sleeping as an action, and most of our go-go Western culture seems to think of sleeping as idling or wasting time. Just like eating, though, it is probably the one thing so many of us get wrong for so long. The lack of proper rest affects all of our physical and psychological functions and impairs true enlightenment. If you are fatigued and sleep-deprived, then you simply won't be alert enough to perceive the universe fully, or to think and act correctly. You will take fatigue-driven shortcuts, and begin to live on a version of autopilot. If you sleep enough, however, you will restore not only your muscles and your organs as well as allow your brain to defrag and reset, but you will better fight off illness and also give your gland systems (endocrine and exocrine) vital, deep sleep time so that your brigade of glands (hypothalamus, pineal, pituitary, thyroid, pancreas, stomach, kidney, adrenal, parathyroid, sebaceous, mammary, prostate) may produce the legion of vital hormones (somatostatin, melatonin, thyrotropin, beta-endorphin, vasopressin, calcitonin, neuropeptide, histamine, insulin, glucagon, rennin, cortisol, DHEA, testosterone, adrenaline, dopamine, enkephalin) which can keep you a *vigorous* version of you. Scientists appear to be battling it out as to whether it is the slow wave (SW) phase or the rapid eye movement (REM) phase of sleep which restores the glands, but it is clear that when we are deprived of full sleep, and the deeper phases of sleep, our minds and our bodies, and particularly our glands, suffer. Humans have a talent for believing that we can make the rules for many things, and sometimes we are right: we *can* build bridges across raging rivers and design the most amazing equipment to take us into inhospitable places on earth and beyond. However, for our bodies the rules are already written—exercise, proper diet and rest. We can only seek to discover and obey those rules.

*　*　*

Correct Reactions

It's not what happens to you, but how you react to it
that matters. ~ Epictetus

Sometimes, however, we are not acting, but instead we are forced to react. How can we react with generosity to someone who is ungenerous or even aggressive toward us? If we are generous in our thoughts, then when someone is aggressive toward us or rude to us (whether by negligence or on purpose) we know we should not rise and take the bait. We should not react (that is, allow someone else to seize control, to incite us to some sort of action); rather we will act, always under our own control, and with generosity. This is a hard task, because to accomplish it we may need to work against a lot of our own history, a history which may want to bypass what we know to do and, instead, simply react without proper consciousness.

Let's propose that, because we can now see a bigger picture more clearly, we realize that perhaps that particular aggressive person is having a bad day, he is under unusual stress, he is going through a bad time, or maybe he has not been given, up to this point, the same gifts and generosity and patience we have been given in our lives so far. We can enumerate many reasons why that person might act in an unpleasant way and, thus, with a generous heart forgive him or, at least, refuse to react in kind, refuse to escalate. Perhaps, just the thought, "I guess Steve just isn't having as good a day as I am," will be enough to let us glide onto other matters, rather than getting stuck in a downward spiral not of our design. Even if what that person says is needlessly unkind or cruel, and it is directed at us or someone we care about, remember that we are not responsible for anyone else's education, ignorance or faults. That, we know, is their journey, not ours.

Once at an art show in town, a guy I did not know very well, who had had a glass of wine or two, for some reason yanked his thumb in my direction and finished his sentence with "just an jerk, like this guy." Conversation stopped, and the people in that immediate group looked more than a bit uncomfortable. I didn't know what to make of it since there had been no prologue, no preview and no link to anything earlier in the conversation. Except to say hello, I was not even part of the conversation; in fact, I didn't even know what the first half was about. Was it art? Was it politics? Was it a joke, was that the *punchline*? Was I the punchline? Or was the guy *that* drunk? In the end I made nothing of it. I think I might have said, "Hmmm," which is a very easy thing to say when you really have nothing to say. You just put your lips together and hum. I did not feel the need to pursue it or to confront him. In fact, I simply accepted that, for some reason in his life at that moment, he felt the need to burp out this unkind thought and I was the recipient. I will discuss Karma later (which is quite different from the popular Western understanding of Karma) but, for now, let me say that I even accepted responsibility for his expression in accordance with Karma, since it was directed at me; I accepted the responsibility that somehow I had not earned his respect. Maybe I could do better in the future, but perhaps not. To the extent that his insult coming out of the blue had any effect on me, how I chose to react to it was my responsibility, not his. And I chose not to react, at all.

Later I learned that at the specific time he was under tremendous stress, that he had some very real family problems. Maybe he resented my happy family, I really don't know. I never asked, and I never was told. Perhaps by being there and being the target of his outburst I had alleviated some of his personal pain. It is possible, of course, that he immediately regretted what he said (certainly there have been times when I have immediately regretted what I have said) and that he came to a sort of knowledge, self-knowledge, about his situation which aided him in the future. I really don't know. And, whether any of that happened or not, *that* part of it remained on *his* journey and *his* responsibility, not *mine*. As it turned out, my only role was to be there and to choose to have no reaction. In any event, other than remembering it for the oddness of it, nothing else ever came of it. I never pursued it, and he never explained or apologized.

Further to the discussion of confrontations, sometimes we find it hard not to react, because the situation itself seems to back us into a corner. At the same time, we realize calmly that reacting to someone else's actions or words is likely the worst possible thing to do. As we saw earlier, somebody cuts us off in traffic, nearly causing damage to our brand new car. What do we do? Tailgate his twenty-year old pickup truck? Try to re-cut him off to teach him a lesson? Is it *our* job to teach him a lesson? Should we floor it in order to pull up alongside him and give him the universal sign of disdain and disrespect? When did it become *our* responsibility to answer insult with insult, to try to keep the cosmic score even? If we react at all, we know we will be doubling down with a losing hand. We must instead *act*, rather than react, and we must act correctly. What is the correct action in the face of a traffic cutoff? It is simple, isn't it? We simply send him on with our blessing, hoping that his unevolved state of mind and reckless attitude toward driving won't cause any harm. Unless we are willing to call the authorities and try to make the case against him (good luck with that), we are best advised to let him drive on and, as he drives out of our sight, to actively remove him from our minds.

What if someone says something which asks us for a judgment, or something which simply makes us uncomfortable, and we are likely to be stuck in the situation at least for a while? What can we do? We can say, "Hmmm," as I noted above. One skilled potter I know has an excellent response. He fires pieces which sell for relatively high price tags (for potters), and his creations are real works of art suitable for the serious collector. On occasion, someone will show him a recent purchase, often a piece poorly crafted and rather kitschy, and ask the potter's opinion. "What do you think of this super nice bowl I just bought?"

The potter is in a spot. If he says it's good or nice, that will be untruthful and against the standards of his life's work. The skilled potter is an expert, after all, and he is uncomfortable looking at kitsch and declaring it art. But if he disparages it, he might appear small and petty, or jealous, or arrogant. So, his response is, "That is very interesting, but it's not my aesthetic. I'm glad you like it." He doesn't lie ("very interesting" can mean almost anything), he tells the truth ("not my aesthetic" which is a gentler way of saying, "to me it's ugly") and sends the person away with a good wish ("I'm glad you like it").

What do you do when someone asks you an uncomfortable question, such as "You're a lawyer (or trader, or writer), do you make a lot of money doing what you do?" "Yes" or "no" seem inappropriate, and yet "none of your business" may be difficult to say in certain circumstances (such as at a dinner party) when you are more or less captive *in situ*. There's always "Hmmm," but that may not deter an aggressive inquisitor for long, if at all.

I have conditioned myself to say, "That's a very interesting question, *why* do you ask?" The questioner will rarely answer honestly and say, "Because I am so nosy," or "Because I make other people's business my own," but he might not let the matter drop. He might press you with, "Oh, come on, it can't be that big a secret. I just want to know."

"Very interesting, fascinating, in fact. And *why* do you want to know? Are you thinking of going into law (or writing a book)?"

"I don't know, I remember reading about lawyer's fees and wanted to know."

"Oh, very interesting. *Where* did you read that, was it a good article?"

"I don't remember, it might have been in <u>The Economist</u>, or in <u>Forbes</u>."

"Oh, I love <u>The Economist</u>, but I rarely find the time to read it through. Funny, I always find time to read the <u>New Yorker</u>, though. Where *does* the time go? I heard once, and I thought it made a lot of sense, that our lives seem to go at an increasing pace as we grow older, as if we measured life in miles per hour. So when we are little kids, life drags by at maybe eight miles per hour—it's like we're stuck in a shopping mall parking lot, but when we get to be seventy or eighty, everything zips by as if we're on the Autobahn. Certainly my life seems to be speeding up. Is everyone else in the same boat?"

By this time the original question is deflected, and most likely forgotten. This is the type of deflection which has worked perfectly for me for many years, and its magic comes from its sincerity. First, you declare the uncomfortable question to be "very interesting," which indeed it is. It is *always* fascinating how unthoughtful and prying people can be. Second, you ask a sincere question of the questioner: "Why do you ask?" You are sincerely interested, at least for the moment, in finding out why this person who barely knows you wants to know some sort of personal information which is perhaps known only to you, your spouse and the IRS. You are much more interested in asking that question than answering his. And, then, as in any good conversation, one topic leads into another, perhaps to a more interesting topic for everyone to talk about.

Of course, this method is easier to describe and write about than it is to put into practice sometimes. In the next chapter, "Splitting the Mind," we will go into the efficient uses of meditation, but for now it will suffice to know that, with meditation we will, over time, achieve the proper distance from our reactive self, that is, what we normally think of as our undifferentiated self. We will discover that, in fact, there is a part of us above the reactive "self" and, by training ourselves to observe the reactive self, we can not only control it but actively command it. For our purposes now, let's take a moment to prove that there is a split mind, with one partition "above," and potentially in charge of, the normal self, below.

Try this: summon all of your powers of imagination to envision that you are driving along a familiar rural road. You see a doe lying on the shoulder, horribly twisted and lying in a pool of now drying blood, lifeless and dead. A quarter mile further up the road you slow down and stop to see, peering out from the trees, two beautiful fawns, still wearing the dappled fur of youth. They appear to be waiting for someone—their mother—a someone you now know will never arrive. How does that scene make you feel? Empathetic? Sad? Would you want to do something to ease the fawns' despair, even though you know it would be close to impossible? When you think about the fawns and their next few days, which will almost certainly be their last days on earth, do you sense the tragedy?

Since you are a fully functioning, highly-evolved human being, of course you feel sad for the orphan fawns and, as you think about their impending doom, you probably feel a certain heaviness. And it is you who feels it? Am I correct?

But isn't there another you, a controller or commander who agreed to read the words I wrote, and who ordered your mind (the lower "self," the "order receiver" or, simply, the "reactor") how it should paint the colors and shapes of the particular scene? Isn't there a commander who instructed your reactor to select from certain stored memories of deer to use for the characters in this "deer drama" and it is the reactor who displayed those in some sort of order? There has to be an entity, like a film director (commander), sitting above your mind (reactor) who gave the instructions to manipulate these few written words into a dramatic scene, amplifying the description until your emotions kicked in and then modulating them so that you did not break down and cry while you were imagining and creating this scene. The *you* up there, the commander, is still in control, right, giving orders? And isn't there also a differentiated *you* below, the reactor, not only receiving the orders but also executing them and experiencing the emotional effects of the deer drama, as well? The commander is always there, watching you react, and capable of stepping in at any time. We can easily see that you are *bifurcated* into a commander above and a reactor below.

Let me pose another, real life test, one you may have participated in. You have not had a good day at work, you are worried about certain aspects of your job and perhaps the health of one of your parents; it has just *not* been a good day, stress-wise. At home, when you are looking to de-stress and just have a peaceful dinner, your teenager begins to whine and vent on a subject which has been brewing for several weeks: "Why can't I get my own car? I'm sixteen. Jill got a car when she turned sixteen, but I never get what I want. Her parents are no way as rich as we are. You and Mom have cars but I don't get one and when I need to borrow one you want me to drive that old minivan which is so lame and my friends make fun of and life just so sucks around here. . "

You tell yourself to count to ten, and you count, "One, two, three, four . . ."

Fine, stop the scene right there. Tell me, who is the *you* who is counting, the counter, and who is the *you* who is telling the counter to count? And now, at the end of your count, you relax because you feel yourself calming down, but who can relax now and who is actually calming down? It is a dialogue between two entities across a partition of sorts, taking place inside your head. In your world, as long as the *commander* commands the *reactor*, life will be good. As soon as the commander loses control of the reactor, you can almost guarantee that the wheels will come off and chaos will prevail. Meditation practice, and correct concentration, will help us develop the strength of the commander.

*   *   *

Wu Wei—No Action

*One of the lessons of history is that nothing is often
a good thing to do and always a clever thing to say.*
~ Will Durant

We sometimes forget that no action is also a form of action. The Catholic Church categorizes transgressions into sins of action (sins of commission) and sins of inaction (sins of omission). However, we are dealing not with sins but with virtuous practices, and there must not only be correct actions (meritorious commissions) but also correct inactions (meritorious omissions). Sometimes the correct action to take is no action. Cool Hand Luke has the famous tag line: "Sometimes nuthin' is a real cool hand,." And sometimes it is. Securities and commodities traders know that, in addition to "long" and "short," "flat" (no position) is also a position. The previous chapter already noted that refraining from saying something is a form of speech. Now we will see that refraining from doing something, especially when others are encouraging or inciting you to do something, is also a form of action. Often it can be the only correct action. In climbing expeditions, sometimes when we ascend a mountain and establish a high camp, bad weather rolls in, or the snow has melted off more dangerously than we supposed. Our best course of action may be no action, and eventually retreat; taking any other action in such a circumstance can end in tragedy.

Chinese thought and martial arts have the concept, largely absent in traditional Western thought, of "wu wei" or doing nothing. Now, of course, *doing nothing* in the West has been a tradition for centuries, but it is generally called idling or sloth or laziness. As sloth, it is considered one of the seven deadly sins. But Taoism recognizes that *wu wei* or doing nothing can, in certain circumstances, be the goal which is to be desired. Chapter Two of the *Tao Te Ching* says, "The Sage deals with things by doing nothing, and teaches without words." Think of it as the opposite of multitasking. When we do nothing, or *wu wei*, we are permitting the world to unfold without our efforts, struggle or interference. We are, as they say, going with the flow.

In the next chapter, "Splitting the Mind," we will see that the essence of meditation, where we strengthen the commander in our consciousness, is to sit and not do anything; it is, in fact, making the effort to do nothing, to think nothing, for periods of time, and to train ourselves to do so without, in the end, even making *that* effort to do nothing. *To do nothing effortlessly* is, literally, the essence of correct meditative practice.

Even in the West we sometimes call it "stopping to smell the coffee." Although what we are proposing now is not stopping to smell the coffee, but stopping to smell the coffee and then stopping smelling the coffee, at least for a short while. Only fools or the over-caffeinated feel the need when relaxing at the beach in the presence of a perfect sunset to run about, check their phone messages, texts or Blackberry. Life is so precious, that merely from an aesthetic point of view, when confronted by natural beauty, we absolutely need to stop what we are doing and do nothing for a while. For true enlightenment, though, let's take it a step further and, even when we are *not* confronted by natural beauty, at regular intervals for a short period of time, let's stop contemplating everything, and stop doing every little thing which our busy reactive mind keeps proposing. We do nothing and sit quietly and allow the world to keep doing everything that it is doing.

While I consider myself, at best, an adequate parent (my wife is the great parent in our house), perhaps my greatest moment as a parent presented itself when Son was living in Japan on a Rotary Fellowship and I seized the opportunity to do nothing. One of the reasons he decided to go to Japan was to revisit where he had spent almost six years of his childhood, when our family lived in Tokyo in the 1980s and 1990s. His Tokyo friends and their parents were anxious to see him, and he had many invitations. He had graduated from high school in Eugene and was spending a "gap" year overseas in a very small Japanese town on the main island of Honshu, about 600 miles west of Tokyo, living with a family and attending an extra year of high school. In the late spring of 2002, toward the end of the year, Son, nineteen-years old, fluent in Japanese and with many friends in the Tokyo area, was informed by his local Rotary board that he would *not* be permitted to travel outside of his school district. He asked me to telephone, and during the call told me that he felt he was being treated like a child, that Japan was safe and that he could easily take the Shinkansen to Tokyo on his own time and with his own money to visit his friends. To him, it had escalated to the point that, if nothing changed, he thought he might just flout their rules and go anyway.

I asked what could happen if he openly disobeyed the local Rotary's rules. Son said that they might send him home early, a month or so ahead of his scheduled return. There would be a Rotarian hubbub about it, no doubt, on both sides of the Pacific. Now, I agreed on all of his points; in fact, there is almost no country on earth as safe as Japan, and few of the millions of travelers to Japan every decade have even one percent of the language or cultural preparation that Son had at that time, even at nineteen. He certainly had *our* consent to travel up and down Japan. I was tempted to call Son's sponsoring Rotary here in Eugene and begin to get some wheels working. Then I thought, maybe I should simply call the head of the Japanese Rotary Club in Son's town. I spoke Japanese and I thought I could reason with him, and get Son his furlough. A good father would get involved and do that to help his kid, right?,

As we were talking, however, I remembered how at certain key moments my father had not stepped into my life either to help me out or to influence me to decide something the way he thought it should be decided. He stepped back, instead. Dad couldn't understand why I was interested in languages and poetry, and thought I should be studying business or law, but except for a few muted suggestions ("Ever thought about taking an accounting course?" "Nah."), he never interfered. He let me have my own path. And, remembering that, I simply said, "Well, Son, you're a smart lad. You might go back one more time to the Rotary and see if they will see it your way. Or you might see if your host father (also a Rotarian) would go with you to help you make your case. Or you might decide just to do what you want to do. I'm fine with your decision, however you make it. If you get in trouble with them and they send you home early, I certainly won't view it as a disgrace. Mom and I miss you anyway, and would be happy to have you home four or five weeks early. You've already gotten most of the benefit out of your year there, and you might be able to pick up some work here at your old job, get a little more spending money for college. Anyway, it's up to you, I'm sure you'll end up with a decision you're happy with."

As I hung up the phone, I wondered just a little about whether or not I had made the right decision, and hoped I had. Son had grown up into a fine and bright young man who had always exercised and demonstrated good judgment, and I thought he would benefit more by taking on the full responsibility for himself at this point than by having his dad step in. If it was a mistake, it would be a tolerable mistake, a learnable moment. If it worked out, it would be his achievement. Either way, instinctively I thought doing nothing on my part was the best course of (in)action.

As it turned out, Son worked out his own compromise with the local Rotary. It was really a matter of letting them save face and keep harmony, as they also did not want the turmoil of having to send someone home under a cloud. If anything, the Japanese are all about harmony. The deal ended up that the host father would be responsible to the local Rotary Club to confirm Son's safe arrival at the Tokyo home he was visiting, and would also confirm on Son's return day that he had left Tokyo and was headed back on the Shinkansen line across the bottom of Honshu. In the end, my recusal worked out perfectly, much much better than any actions I could have taken. *Wu Wei.*

Now, maybe this is too many words about doing nothing. In fact, it must be. In order to practice "doing nothing" in a situation when "something" seems required, however, we need to think it through a few times to see why it is we might wish to do nothing. *Wu Wei.* Often it takes effort, and some practice, to restrain ourselves, to fight against this Western urge to constantly be in motion, taking action, stirring up something. The next time we feel pressured to do something, let's ask what would happen if we did nothing immediately, and maybe nothing at all. We don't always have to be doing something; sometimes nothing is a real cool hand.

*   *   *

NINE

Splitting the Mind

Concentration exercises makes the mind stronger. Meditation does not make the mind strong but it takes us beyond the mind. Meditation is all about dis-identifying with the mind. Meditation is to be alert about our thoughts and witnessing our desires rather than indulging in them. ~ Unknown

As a time commitment in this enlightenment enterprise, mindfulness—meditation—is, as we have seen, almost negligible. It is not unimportant, however, it just doesn't take very much time. Correct mindfulness is comprised of a few important concepts: basic meditative practice, bifurcating the mind, and a proper understanding of Karma (taking responsibility), all of which lead to a higher, or enhanced, understanding of the suchness of things

*   *   *

Basic Meditation

It sometimes seems that the step of meditation and mindfulness is the hardest or the most complicated one for people to practice and master, although, in fact, it should be the easiest of all, since it requires almost nothing to achieve it. The reason why we may find it so hard is that we come at meditation from the wrong angle; we have a number of expectations which have nothing to do with the actual practice of meditation. In one case, many people I've spoken with try meditation once or twice and come to the conclusion that it just *doesn't work*. People in this first group sit there in the correct posture, count a few breaths, try to keep random thoughts at bay, and at the end of ten minutes or so stand up. "Look, I gave it a shot, I did what I was supposed to do, but it didn't work. It doesn't work for me. What did I get from it? Nothing, nothing at all. I guess meditation isn't the thing. Or, at least, I can't do it." They followed the instructions to the letter, but nothing happened.

But what are we to expect from correct meditative practice? Bells? A heraldic trumpeting? Scales to fall from our eyes?

A second group really *likes* meditation, really *enjoys* it, but needs a proper setting, or a meditation group. They like to have incense burning in a candlelit temple or "Zen Center," with images of either Zen art or the Buddha, or both, and a leader who starts the "practice" with a chime and then ends it with a chime twenty or thirty minutes later. Afterward, they will often sit, respectfully, and talk about the experience or a selected sutra or a koan, generally being led in the discussion by the guy in the official looking robes, who may or may not be called "roshi" or "rinpoche" or something else. Green tea is the contemplative drink of choice at these sessions. I asked a woman I knew who went to these things how often she simply meditated at home.

"Not ever, not really. I don't really have the right space set up for it. And I can't always get to the Center, so sometimes it just slips by. I just like every thing about the service, the incense, the teaching. Even that little chime. I try to get there as often as I can. But I basically never meditate on my own."

A third type views meditation as some sort of spiritual marathon, and wants to build up his meditational "endurance" in order to go deeper into the ether and closer to Nirvana. Meditating for 30 minutes? "Why, that's nothing," he says, "I regularly meditate for two hours, and then do at least 45 minutes of *tai chi* before lunch. In the afternoon I am often doing hot yoga." His expression all but shouts, "Top that, if you can!"

In my view, the first two viewpoints are missing something fundamental, and the third is simply laughable. Those in the first group are actually getting the beginning benefits out of meditation, they just don't realize it. They are looking for something more, something which makes a bigger splash, an epiphany, a revelation. Mathematically speaking, they are like algebra students solving an equation, but they keep getting "zero" as the solution; and they won't accept that zero is the correct solution. They want *something*. But, in the deepest sense, zero *is* the solution.

And the second group is confusing a set of Asian aesthetics with the practice of meditation. For them, the rich ambience is what brings about the meditation, it's a vague set of feelings they get from images and idols, the solitary chime, the incense and the green tea. I wonder whether anyone in the second group gets any benefits from meditation other than a shared sense of spiritual tourism. And it is this second group that is so vulnerable to the kinds of "enlightenment" products, programs, seminars and cruises noted in the first chapter.

The third type, the truly *holier than thou* or *more must be better* type, absolutely misses the point of meditation from the beginning. Meditation is a simple training tool, a simple practice, which leads to identifiable results. It is not an end in itself or an athletic or endurance activity. It makes no more sense to meditate for an hour than it does to floss your teeth for an hour, yet it makes as much sense to meditate for ten minutes as it does to floss your teeth for ten minutes (see *Davich* in the Appendix).

Meditation can be done at any time and in almost any place, although to be sure it is best focused in the beginning in a quiet place at home. After all these years, I still prefer to meditate at home when no one else is there. I like the knowledge that no one will interrupt me. I use Son's room, which has been empty for ten years now. The other place I can meditate as freely is in an airplane terminal when I have ample time to wait for boarding.

Meditation is so simple, and yet it is rarely taught as such. We sit quietly and comfortably in soft, loose clothes (at home, pajamas are perfect) with our backs straight and our stomachs forward and relaxed. We keep our eyes open, or we close them; it can work either way. We inhale, expanding our stomach, not our chests. We exhale. We count our breaths to begin and spend ten minutes or so controlling and clearing our reactor, what some call the "monkey mind," by means of our commander, then rise and go about our business. It is really as simple as that. There will be no incredible breakthroughs or cascades of "enlightenment," sudden blinding lights or rainbows across the heavens. In fact, after our first session or our 10,000[th] session, there will be no noticeable difference in our lives preceding the session versus our lives immediately after. The difference will accumulate and occur throughout our days, weeks and years. We will notice more and more that this simple practice aids and augments the higher understanding of ourselves, and of every thing in the world. This simple practice helps to recharge the batteries and refocus the light in this great flashlight—enlightenment—we can now use.

For the second group, the meditation center people, it is important to remember that the kingdom—that is, the awakening and the enlightenment— truly *is* within us, and is not reliant on Asian architecture, fragrances or decoration. Now, since I lived in Asia for more than twelve years, our house is decorated with Asian touches and artifacts, of course, and I appreciate them, but I never confuse them with the meditative practice —which takes place entirely within my mind.

*　　*　　*

Splitting the Mind

Schizophrenia, a split mind, is a strange affliction, a mental disorder manifested in a number of symptoms—asociality, hallucinations, delusions, paranoia, disorganized mental functions—and may be caused by many factors or combinations of factors. A person could be born with it in his genes, get it in the womb, or acquire it through childhood experiences or via substance abuse.

We are not interested in this sort of *split mind*, the pathology or part of a slide into destruction, a condition which would require counseling and treatment. We are interested in splitting our minds on purpose, or rather training our already split minds in order to become calmer and better people.

As noted in Chapter Eight, the existence of our bifurcated mind is a given. Have you ever heard or said, or can you understand, something like the following statement: "The next time Joe tries to rile me up, I'm not going to let myself get involved with his game."? It makes perfect sense: Joe likes to wind you up, get you going, and get your goat. And you promise yourself that you won't let yourself get involved in Joe's shenanigans.

Clearly there are at least three minds at work in this, if not more. We'll stick with three. There is the instigator, the agent-provocateur, Joe. There is also the mind which is the commander, the one who has decided to limit the reactions to the instigator, Joe. Finally, there is the mind which is identified as "myself" in the initial statement, the reactor who is clearly the everyday *you* who is going about, perceiving and sampling the world 24/7, and reacting to it. You have a commander and a reactor. Metaphorically, the two of you are like a driver and a vehicle, or a jockey and a horse.

In the world of horse racing, if a jockey never practiced controlling his horse and putting him through his paces, how would things go on race night once the starting gate clanged open? Not very well, we can be reasonably sure. The jockey would not know or trust his horse, and his horse would not know or trust him. To the horse in particular, nothing would be familiar in this moment of high anxiety at the race track, the lights, the noisy din, the sight of all those people screaming and the smell of cigarettes and beer wafting across the oval track—all of this could certainly disorient or frighten the horse. The jockey might not be able to calm the horse sufficiently, since he had never practiced working the horse and gaining his trust. Similarly, the jockey would not be able to trust the horse's reactions or performance, and it is probable that he would feel physically in danger during the entire ride. Without regular practice and preparation, the stage is set for a subpar performance at best. We can easily imagine a situation where the jockey or horse, or both of them, might panic with unfortunate or even disastrous results.

Put simply, why do the jockey and the horse need to practice? So that they may remain calm in the face of all circumstances and challenges. And, just as simply, why do *our* commander and *our* reactor need to practice? *So that we (the two of us) may remain calm in the face of all circumstances and challenges.* If we are truly awakened and enlightened, then, what will be our natural reaction in the face of all circumstances and challenges? Calm.

All of this leads us to the essence of the practice of meditation, which is the fundamental practice session where the commander and the reactor sit quietly together on a regular basis and learn to trust each other. It is a training session, that is all. This is the essence of meditation. We stretch a little, get our backs in line, find a comfortable position on our chair or *seiza*, either close our eyes or focus them on the bare wall and begin to breathe. The two of us are together, commander and reactor, breathing in, breathing out, counting breaths, perceiving sounds and settling down. Sitting, just sitting and breathing. Now our reactor breaks away from our commander, he splits off. Nothing matters, the outside world is irrelevant for this training time, but our reactor remembers an errand which must be done later this morning, and begins to chafe at all the errands he must do, and by such and such time. So our commander deftly steps in and, with a wave of his metaphorical hand, sweeps the disturbance away. We are sitting, just sitting and breathing. Our reactor hears a car door slam outside and a voice, and begins to wonder who that might be; our commander pushes those perceptions and sounds aside for now. Our reactor now conjures a flower he saw yesterday, such a lovely flower, was it an aster or a chrysanthemum? Our commander sweeps the attractive but distracting image away, and now our reactor brings in an old grudge and begins to chew on it, and our commander sweeps that away, too. We are sitting, and breathing, counting our breaths, one, two, three . . .

At some time during the session, our reactor will finally settle down and content himself with sitting, just sitting and breathing. When that happens, our commander has nothing to do but to observe the reactor, sitting and breathing. *Good horse.* In a few minutes the signal to end the session sounds and the commander and the reactor re-form into one mind. We stretch and do a few simple yoga exercises before rising and re-entering the world. The world is no different than it was fifteen or so minutes ago, but the team of commander and reactor are more practiced, more at peace, more integrated, and more settled than before. It is a better world now, or at least a world which will be easier to negotiate for the rest of the day.

Meditation practice is really this simple. We need a place to sit where the commander and the reactor can practice. Just as we do not need to be in a national park or a scenic wonder to perceive all the sights, sounds, smells, tastes and textures of the universe, wherever we are is just fine, the same is true of meditation. We simply do not need a special room or institute or center to meditate. If you are sitting in your minivan, waiting for your child at the elementary school, that moment and that place is perfect, as is the empty office or conference room at work, or inside the cab of the big semi parked at the rest stop. Ten minutes or so, that is all. It's like a game of catch in the backyard, or rallying across the court in tennis with a hitting partner to sharpen your game. Meditation is simply a place and a time when we can practice for a few minutes.

Once we get into this practice, we will find it easier to bifurcate into the commander and reactor at times when it is opportune or advisable to do so. Say a woman jumps ahead of us in the checkout line at Costco or Trader Joe's. We *bifurcate* and notice that the reactor has a small but growing sense of injustice. How sensitive the reactor can be at times, we notice. We decide to let the reactor react, but only appropriately. What does this mean? Well, maybe no reaction is the proper reaction. Wu-wei. Maybe we have plenty of time, and have no feeling one way or the other. If the woman *had actually* turned and asked us politely if she could go first since she had only two things to buy and she was already late to pick up her child at school, the reactor would certainly have reacted with generosity. So why not simply *imply* those motives, expressions and actions *to* her and let her go first without comment or reaction?

Or, perhaps the proper reaction is to say, very quietly, so that only she can hear, so as not to publicly embarrass her: "Excuse me, but I think that I was next." She might apologize and laugh, saying, "Oh my, I don't know where my mind is today. I'm so sorry." On the other hand, she might want to escalate the encounter by staring daggers at us, or by saying, "No, I was here first." So now the commander must determine how the reactor will react, if at all, to this new input. It is clearly not worth it to rise to this challenge, to get caught up in this woman's issues, and perhaps experience spillover and carry it with us all day ("Honey, you won't believe what this dumb lady did at Costco this morning . . ."). We are already having a good day, an enlightened day; it would be foolish—unenlightened—to lose it. Remember, all we have in life is our time, measured in hours and days. Will it ever be worth it to cede control of our day to someone else? What could we possibly gain from that, and what would we be likely to lose?

If the incident at the checkout line is too simple or benign, let's change the scenario to arguments at the workplace, or maybe to what have traditionally been uncomfortable family holidays. If we meditate and train our "race horse," we will most likely be able to ride through those and many more "events" in peace and harmony, rather than risk escalating confrontations. And who has a richer and more beautiful life, the fellow who was cut off by an unevolved driver and was unfazed by it, or the other fellow who determined that *no one* was going to cut him off and raced after the miscreant, and will be talking to the police and his insurance company representative for the next several weeks explaining how and why he caused a six-car accident? Who would you rather be?

Charlie sits down in inner peace to eat turkey at the family holiday table after his brother-in-law, Philip, has spent forty-five minutes trying to wind him up about Charlie's small house, Charlie's current town and his town's lackluster sports team. Charlie has made no reaction other than a bemused, "Hmm, maybe that is true," and, "That's interesting." But Charlie's brother, Johnny, similarly "egged on," has disputed Philip on each and every single jab and jibe with several of his own zingers—some of which were not age-appropriate for the children at the table—about Philip's house, Philip's town and sports team, and would sincerely like to push Philip's face down into the mashed potatoes, and is so angry he can feel his blood pressure rise. Who is having a better experience, Charlie or Johnny?

*   *   *

Advanced Meditation

Although I believe that just ten minutes or so of meditation once a day is sufficient for sustainable enlightenment, you may wish to expand the time spent in meditation if the practice is pleasing to you. Some meditation guides and philosophers, in addition to prescribing long sessions of the practice, state that meditation has no purpose and no meaning, since the entire "goal" of meditation is to separate oneself from concepts such as purpose and meaning. To me, this way of thinking is a confusing game of words and concepts. Life is short, and to awaken to it you must act out of purpose and meaning. I believe that meditation *does* have a clear reason and a clear purpose, and we already know this from our jockey and horse training sessions. When we quiet our reactor mind and "do nothing" we are already achieving meditation's goal, a goal we achieve without striving because the goal itself is achieved when, moment by moment, nothing happens and no striving occurs. However, just as sometimes we may wish to listen to a longer piece of music, a symphony rather than one movement from a concerto or a short song, sometimes we might want to extend our meditation for a longer time, to stay in the "meditative moment" longer than ten or fifteen minutes. This is fine, this is pleasant, and this can be enlightening, too.

However, meditation is not the *only* way, and not even the *best* way, to discover that the point of existence is attained in the immediate moment. Every conscious moment of perception, full perception of the suchness of whatever it is we are perceiving, brings us even more effortlessly into the immediate moment, and it can do it nonstop, all day long. Sitting meditation is, however, along with yoga and other meditative practices, the best way to train the commander and reactor.

Lately, scientists have been studying meditation and discovering interesting scientific results. Meditation is apparently useful in lowering stress levels (but we already know that, since meditation is training specifically to keep us *calm in all circumstances and challenges*), and may be useful as well to fight the aging process and addictions, to control or eliminate depression, and to manage pain. Recent studies have shown that meditation may increase the body's production of something called "telomerase," an enzyme which protects specific parts of our chromosomes which control cell breakdown and aging. Whether any of this science remains the case after a decade or so of further research is anyone's guess, but my guess (for what it's worth) is that science may find even more physiological benefits and applications for meditation. As far as *sustainable enlightenment* is concerned, however, it is enough that short sessions of meditation enhance our serenity and help us to train our minds. The fact that there most likely are extra bonuses to the practice is nice, too.

*   *   *

Karma

To be a man is, precisely, to be responsible. ~Antoine de Saint-Exupéry

It is easy to misunderstand the real meaning and actual use of "Karma," mostly because we want the sound bite of Karma, and are unwilling to spend much time really thinking about it. I am tempted to skip this topic since it is a nest of misunderstandings and potential disagreements, but will risk including it here. Why? First of all because in the West we instinctively gravitate toward a misplaced karmic equation, as when something untoward happens and the first words out of our mouth is "What did I do to deserve this?" This kind of searching for a cause for a current effect is pretty much human nature. Secondly, however, and much more importantly, because understanding Karma in a useful way, as a prescription for approaching the whole of life, rather than as a phenomenological explanation or law, can be very helpful. It is to me, at any rate.

If you ask a reasonably informed person in the West what Karma means you will receive a number of familiar answers:

"The law of cause and effect."

"What goes around comes around, baby."

"You will be punished or rewarded in the next life for what you do in this one, and you are being punished or rewarded now for what you did in your last life."

Although we know that the concept of Karma arose in Hinduism and is currently part of the spiritual understanding of the world in Sikhism, Jainism and Buddhism, for our purposes where or how the concept arose or how it was conceived and interpreted is of little importance. The question we have to ask is simply, can a grounded understanding of Karma help us to sustain our awareness, and in particular, our mindfulness? I believe it can.

Westerners sometimes, with their linear logic and discursive reasoning, and perhaps a little too much misplaced enthusiasm, miss the whole point of Karma. If we believed in Karma as simply the *linear* law of cause and effect in one's life, then a logical response would be to say, in the case of a wife losing a husband in a train wreck, "If I have this terrible misfortune in my life, then I must somehow have caused it. And, what is almost worse, my husband must have done something horrible in his life, something I never knew about." And that grieving person would then do some heavy soul-searching to find out what she had done to cause her husband to be crushed and burned to death on the way to work. Was it the candy she took from her sister's Halloween bag in 1975? Was it the lie she told her parents in high school, or the test she cheated on as a sophomore at Brandeis, or was it that she stopped going to Mass after the string of priest scandals surfaced? Following this absurd road can lead pretty quickly through self-recrimination to self-hatred and destruction, none of which should occur because of a misinterpretation of Karma.

Another "traditional" response might be to look at a current tragic condition, say the same commuter train wreck, and reach this conclusion: "The suffering of the people on the train is simply the cosmic and inter-incarnational account settling known as the karmic law of cause and effect." All of the riders, victims and narrow escapees alike, are participating in some grand cosmic plan which stretches across multiple lifetimes and even life forms. If someone insists that this is true, we would be correct to dismiss Karma as patent nonsense. After all, the various people on the train shared little in common except where they lived, generally. Some boarded at Station One, some at Station Three, some *missed* that particular train because they overslept or spilled coffee on a blouse or had a dentist's appointment or woke up with a headache or hangover, others only took that particular train *because* they had overslept or spilled coffee on a blouse and missed the earlier train, etc. Assume the accident occurred between Station Eight and Station Nine; now, some people got off at Station Seven, unusually for them—one saw an acquaintance and wanted to talk, another was simply confused and erroneously thought it *was already* Station Nine. What is the pattern here? Is the Highest Accountant doing His sums up Above, and putting this immense Rube Goldberg machinery in place to settle all the accounts, giving some of the people narrow escapes, and others horrible deaths, critically injuring and maiming others, while lightly injuring others and letting some others off scratch-free? This interpretation of Karma also makes no sense.

Let's examine a more useful example of how to understand, and apply, Karma. We will use the lives of two fictional boys, identical twins, Bobby and Barry. Bobby is born healthy and robust and, seven minutes later, Barry is born with cerebral palsy. For some reason, at some point during pregnancy, Barry was denied a certain amount of oxygen, a condition called hypoxia. Bobby grows up to be the star quarterback of his high school team, the class valedictorian and a National Merit Scholar. Barry grows up struggling. Now, since Bobby and Barry's separate conditions existed at the moment of birth, and even existed at some time before birth, it would take the cruelest mind imaginable to claim that it was something either of them had done. And let's not even consider that it was payback or debt settling from a prior life, we know that is simply irrational cruelty.

What if we look at Karma, not as a literal, scientific statement about linear cause and effect ("igniting gasoline in a compressed area will cause an explosion which will push the piston and the drive train and eventually the wheels of the automobile"), but rather as a prescriptive statement? Let's try the following. Karma is how we must deal with an uncertain, "unfair" and chaotic world; it is simply the way we must act, if we are to be freed to attain our highest possible experience in life. Karma is shorthand for, "We will take ownership for our lives and all of our circumstances. We must take responsibility for everything which happens in our lives, good, neutral or bad, *as if* we had caused it. And, just as importantly, we are obligated to make the most of it."

As if we had caused it. That's all. *Not because* we had caused it, but *as if* we had caused it. We can look to no one else for our situation.

Let's return to Bobby and Barry for a moment and examine the possibility of *not* taking responsibility, but rather attributing the cause to something or someone else. After all, in the West, science rules and if there is a variety of outcomes, then there must be a cause or causes for those outcomes. It doesn't really matter what we look to in order to find the cause and attribute the blame, we can take our pick. In Bobby's case, here he has the most wonderful life possible while his brother struggles to accomplish even simple tasks. Since Bobby can not possibly *deserve* this good fortune while his twin brother is forced to suffer, Bobby quite naturally begins to feel guilty; he begins to suffer sympathetically with his brother. To put it simply, he does not deserve what he *has*, and he *knows* this; he is some kind of fraud, or worse, some kind of thief or at least the recipient of something which is not, or should not be, his.

And, since Barry also could not possibly deserve *his* fate, he lashes out and blames the cruel world for his situation. Barry did nothing to cause this condition, it dates from before his own birth. Barry grows bitter against the world, his parents and especially his brother, the *perfect one*, and begins to hate him. Who dealt these cards and gave such a winning hand to his brother, and this poor hand to himself? Why isn't it fair, or at least fairer? Because of guilt and blame and hatred, these two lives may be slowly destroyed.

But, what if Bobby takes responsibility for his good fortune, appreciates it and vows to use all of his gifts and capabilities to the highest extent possible? He can do this because he now feels responsible for his life, and all the good that is in it, and is tasked to make the most of it. It has so far been a wonderful life, and he will accept a scholarship to college and do everything he can to maximize his potential. He has been given a great gift and must now honor it with all his actions.

And, what if Barry, instead of descending into blame and bitterness, willingly takes responsibility for his condition? He *owns* it now, and vows to make the most of what he has and who he is. It makes no sense for him to wonder why anything is as it is, it simply is. Barry helps his parents, trying to ease the burden of caring for a disabled young man, he cheers for Bobby and is delighted to see his tall, handsome brother do things on the football field and in the classroom that only a few can. He is now free, by taking full responsibility for *his* condition and *his* life, to love his brother rather than resent and hate him. Now he is freed to fulfill his own destiny. Barry always does his best, and in his struggles he finds meaning and victories of his own, every bit as great as those of his brother on the college football field and in the classroom. People who know Barry are amazed at what he tries to do, and how often he succeeds. Much more than Bobby, Barry inspires everyone he comes in contact with, and literally makes his world a better place.

Both Bobby and Barry are now free to live their lives to the fullest extent possible, because they have taken *responsibility* for who they are and what their situation is, as if they had caused it themselves. It is the utmost irony that, by taking the full responsibility and full burden for our condition and for everything which happens to us, we become free as never before; by tying ourselves to reality, we unshackle ourselves from its power over us. The seeds of guilt and anger are not permitted to take root. Karma doesn't say, in any Western, logical sense, that we are going to get what is coming to us or that if we are blessed in this life then we must have been a saint in the last go-round. As Helen Keller noted, "Self-pity is our worst enemy and if we yield to it, we can never do anything wise in this world." In conclusion, Karma says simply, "Own your condition, take full responsibility for everything that happens to you, good and bad, and take responsibility for your actions and your outcomes. Only by doing this will you find true freedom and realize the richness and fullness of life."

Understanding Karma in this way may have some of the same, beneficial effects which victims of crimes receive when they manage to forgive those who have done them some great injustice. Although victims are not encouraged to "own" the reality of what happened to them, by forgiving the criminal, they in effect release themselves from the deadly hold the crime, and its bitter fruit, the continuing anger and hurt, have on its victim. As Buddha said, "You will not be punished for your anger, you will be punished by your anger." It is terrible to be victimized once, but how much more tragic to perpetuate the crime's effect on oneself for the rest of a life? And yet, when wronged or slighted, how firmly we hold onto our anger and sense of injustice, often for a lifetime.

*   *   *

Infinity in the Palm of Your Hand

*To see the world in a grain of sand, and to see heaven
in a wild flower, hold infinity in the palm of your
hand, and eternity in an hour.* ~William Blake

Up to this point, we have done all in our (growing) powers to do everything through our perceptions, our intentions, our outward expressions and our actions in such a way as will enlighten our lives.

We have learned to meditate simply and correctly, to use each meditation as a training session to split our minds into two and practice together, and we have internalized the true lesson of Karma and begun to take complete ownership of all—merits and demerits, gifts and obstacles—in our lives, and by doing so have set ourselves free. We are now ready to be challenged to raise our awareness even more. This—higher mindfulness—is what will make our lives bountiful and rich, and our minds and souls more at peace with the universe and all within it. When we hear Saint Mark's phrase, "What benefit will it be to you if you gain the whole world but lose your own soul?" it is *this* soul he is speaking about. When we have finally done everything in our power so far to take these first five steps, now comes the final part of step five where we will "amp up" the interplay of our perceptions and our mindfulness and achieve our birthright, a soul which can comprehend instantly in the most commonplace of things both infinity and eternity.

Higher mindfulness is the highest union of correct perception and clarity of vision, a vision which can now perceive heaven in Blake's single wildflower. When we exercise higher mindfulness we begin to unlock all things for what they really are, in their incredible richness and complexity and, instead of simply perceiving something, we are able to bring our focus to it and see it clearly in all its meanings and connections, at once. When we focus this bright light of ours on a thing, any thing, and we can be awakened to the true nature of a simple object, then it becomes easier and easier to see the fullness—the suchness—of everything and everyone. You may think of your computer and its ability to compress files and then unlock them. The world has, through individual manifestations, compressed itself and is ready to do a "file transfer" to you via your senses. It is now, with higher mindfulness, that you can unlock all of these compressed folders and read everything which was heretofore hidden.

> *When we try to pick out anything by itself, we find it hitched to everything else in the universe.* ~ John Muir

Let's take a very simple example of a real chair in my house, although there is no reason why it could not be an old dish, or a sweater or wooden wheelbarrow. We received this particular wooden high chair ("Chair") from my parents' house about twenty eight years ago when Son was born. We used Chair for both of the babies, Son and Daughter, and then put it away in the attic. A few years ago, we retrieved Chair and placed it in one of the children's rooms where it now holds Daughter's *Hello Kitty* plush toy. H. Kitty sits on it now, like a child. Chair was manufactured perhaps seventy years ago and used in my parents' house for each of the five children growing up in the 1940s and 50s. We somehow inherited Chair and used it for our children in the 1980s, but since then it has been either off to the side or somewhere in storage. I have not refinished Chair, although I have thought about it a few times, and it still has its original woven rattan bottom. Chair is not a work of art but rather a functional piece, and it is nothing special from a historical or aesthetic point of view. In truth, by most accounts, Chair is just an unremarkable chair, which somehow found its way out of the attic and back into our lives, as I said, and now takes its place in what was once Daughter's room.

If I see Chair clearly in accordance with the first practice, correct perception, then I see it as a chair, sitting in a space, uneven varnishes and stiffening rattan, layers of dust slowly collecting on it. It has a musty smell. It has a certain "weight" and its textures are interesting in the changing light of day. I don't fool myself about its value, either by potential use or what it could bring in a yard sale or on Craigslist. Chair is simply a chair, although, since our children outgrew it long ago, it has not been used for its "purpose" (seating a baby at a table) in over twenty years.

If I see Chair clearly in accordance with this fifth step, higher mindfulness, however, while it is still a "chair as chair," Chair is also a subject with almost infinite aspects and characteristics; it is, itself, inextricably connected to the universe. On an atomic and molecular level, we know that Chair is a mass of disconnected but somehow connected whirling particles and waves, glued together in some fashion, formed from the detritus of the Big Bang and the subsequent explosions of the galaxies and our own solar system. It's myriad molecules, like all molecules on earth, have traveled billions of miles to get here.

On a biological level, everything which went into the making of Chair, with the exception of the iron nails which hold the framework together, is from some sort of carbon-based life: maple tree for the wood, wood stains and varnish derived from organic pigments and resins, rattan from palm. (The nails themselves are not lifeless alloyed materials, but engineered and crafted, single-purpose, man-made and, therefore, bio-engineered "tools," set in place.) These simple materials have been transformed by another biological input, human culture and its knowledge and tools, to design and fabricate Chair, which means that this chair, inanimate though it is, is part of life on earth. I wonder where the factory was, who the owner was, who the foreman, the factory hands, the helper, and the salesmen were, who in the end were responsible for the creation and sale of Chair. Using the production methods of the time, how many of these chairs did they produce in a week, or in a year? The factory shipped Chair sometime in the late 1940s to Charleston, West Virginia and my parents, probably six or seven years before I was born, bought it at the Coyle & Richardson Department Store in downtown Charleston. They might have bought two, because when I was a baby we had two identical models, necessitated no doubt because I came along 374 days after my brother Don. I'm not sure where Chair's twin has ended up, perhaps it has been sold in a yard sale or even destroyed.

Chair, conceived and perfected according to its own destiny, had an existence several years before I was born, and I assume Chair will "outlive" me, but I cannot be sure. Chair has held the bottoms of at least seven children surnamed McCarty and has been splattered and spattered with juice, milk, pureed vegetables and fruits, melted butter and pancake syrup. Forensics from some laboratory would be able to find traces of much more, I'm sure, but I am also reasonably sure that I don't want to know the details—too many runny-nosed and soggy diaper bottomed infants to contemplate those chemical residues.

In the mornings in the summer, H. Kitty sits on Chair in a bright glow of sunlight. Since we don't really use the space now, every few weeks my wife will go through the room where Daughter once played and studied and dreamed of being a swim champion or the best dancer in school or the prettiest girl at the prom, and vacuum the floor and dust off the surfaces. Chair will receive nominal attention, a perfunctory dusting, and then the door will close on H. Kitty and Chair for another few weeks.

We can see that this single, unremarkable object, Chair, properly observed, has many aspects reflected in physics, biology, anthropology, industry, culture, family history and the baby boom, a variety of uses and almost ancient memories. It also has a space in our home in Daughter's former room, and it still has potential. Perhaps in the future Chair will be kept in our family but taken to a new home and used for another baby's bottom, or maybe Chair will finally be sold at a garage sale to be used by another family. If the latter, then its physical and biological history will remain, but most of its other history will be lost. A new human history for Chair may be started, but it will lose its seven decades of McCarty "family cred." Realistically, I fear that any family who buys Chair at a yard sale for a few dollars will scarcely appreciate it, and Chair may find itself trashed and destroyed within a score of years.

Higher mindfulness, of course, is not simply about writing five or six paragraphs of rumination on any household object. Higher mindfulness means that we are able to witness ourselves and our world in such a way as is rich and true, but neither as a reductionist nor as a sentimentalist would. To a reductionist, the chair is simply a mass of subatomic particles and waves, literally a spatial phenomenon full of quantum "fury" and "signifying nothing". The reductionist sneers at the true bounty of life, the idea of a partial history of the world contained in a banged up chair, and says, "So what?" "Let's move on," and "Get over it."

To the pure sentimentalist, on the other hand, Chair is an almost animated part of family history, a participant in scenes of chaos, laughter, squabbles and joy through the years. The sentimentalist gazes at Chair and coos; he might imagine all the fun scenes Chair has watched, anthropomorphing Chair into a family witness. *If only these walls could talk, and this furniture speak*, he says, wistfully.

With higher mindfulness, however, we can see that Chair is more than mere materiality or sweet sentimentality. Now we might begin to think that higher mindfulness will do nothing for us but clog up our minds with useless trivia and mindless contemplation. We might think that the more efficient way to go about life is to reduce everything to atomic nuclei or subatomic particles. But higher mindfulness is not a clogging mechanism, rather it is a magnifying and clarifying mechanism; higher mindfulness is an ongoing process which enriches our lives and informs our existence. Like William Blake, we begin to see the world in each grain of sand, and experience eternity in an hour. Higher mindfulness destroys obstacles to enlightenment—we can find the entire cosmos in a small garden in Yachats, Oregon or in a city cemetery in Brooklyn. Higher mindfulness levels the cosmic playing field and brings our room, our house, our town and our locality into proper focus; this process is quintessentially Thoreauvian. Seen with higher mindfulness, a church and steeple in Concord, Massachusetts is as full of sublime beauty as a palazzo in Florence, the Fern Ridge Reservoir in Veneta, Oregon is as rich in culture and abundance as the Sea of Galilee, and the North Fork of the Willamette River is equal to the Nile. This is not cultural relativity but rather higher mindfulness. Our powers of perception, properly developed through the five steps so far, no matter where we are, will reward us with an experience of life so rich that it would take a thousand lifetimes to begin to comprehend fully even a modest part of it and will, at the same time, reward us with such a fountain of understanding and peacefulness that it simply overflows the human soul's capacity. This bounty will not overwhelm us but rather enrich us. Immeasurably.

*   *   *

TEN

Making Your Way in the World

*It is the first of all problems for a man to find out
what kind of work he is to do in this universe.*
~Thomas Carlyle

*Vocations which we wanted to pursue, but didn't,
bleed, like colors, on the whole of our existence.*
~Honore de Balzac

Whatever we are doing as a career, we must utilize the first
step to perceive it clearly. What exactly *are* we doing?
What is our job? Is our livelihood a calling, a career, or is
it a trap? Do we stay in our vocation out of love, or because it
confers a sort of status on us, or is it lethargy that keeps us on the
wheel, or do we stay because we fear uncertainty and change? If we
are happy and fulfilled, then it's fine. If not, we have two choices.
We can either change what we are doing, or we can change the way
we understand it and think about it. We cannot have an enlightened
life if, day in and day out, we are miserable.

This does not mean, however, that we have to quit our job and train
to be missionaries, leave our position at the bank and move to Tahiti
to paint, start a charity to erase world hunger or become a Taoist
monk in the misty mountains. Outside criteria cannot define what
our correct livelihoods will be. As always, the analysis will be
highly personal and the decision a do-it-yourself project. The first
five steps we have worked through, perception, intention,
expression, actions, and mindfulness, have led us to this point where

205

we will know how to determine whether what we are doing is the correct livelihood for us.

Let's take an example of someone who works as a university administrator, and let's call him Bob. Bob's position is a job like all jobs with its daily successes and frustrations. People in the work place can be pleasant or unpleasant, cooperative or uncooperative, hard working or not very hard working.

If Bob considers his livelihood, then he might think, "Jeez, my life is passing me by while I toil away year after year in this job. We still owe a lot on the mortgage and that won't be paid off for 15 more years, but for all the money I'm putting into it, it's still the same average house in the same average neighborhood. People say that housing values are going down now. Ours is still worth more than we paid for it 12 years ago, I guess that's some comfort. And we have lived there, so we have *that* benefit. Still, it's not exactly *lifestyles of the rich and famous* for us. And the kids' costs, those keep going up. Orthodontistry, music lessons, sports fees, new clothes all the time. I don't know how we're going to pay for college. We'll get some sort of deal if the kids go to *this* university, that is, if with all the budget cuts and belt tightening they still have that tuition-for-employees program in place by the time Jimmy and Judy get to college. But why should my kids be limited to one university when other kids get to pick among the ones they get into? Now I can really appreciate my parents, what they went through, what an unconscious and ungrateful lout I must have been at times."

As for his specific job, Bob might think, "If I'm honest about it, I'm just a bureaucrat here, a replaceable part. It's the deans and the professors who have all the power. Oh yes, and the president and the big donors. Let's face it, they run the show. With me, it's just, 'Bob do this,' or 'Have Bob do that.' Not much to show for a life. If I dropped dead at my desk they'd have a replacement in a week, maybe sooner. Harry would jump at the chance, so would Jill. I had big dreams, once. Anyone could do this job with a little training and a thick enough skin to put up with Harry's antics and Jill's devious scheming to get ahead."

However, Bob may need to perceive more clearly what he is doing. If he starts to perceive his world and himself fully, then he may also begin to think more clearly. He might begin to act with enthusiasm, generosity and vigor to carry out his functions, where before he has been sometimes admittedly a little slack. He will meditate regularly and not only be aware of the difference between things which bother him and learn how to control his reactions to them, but also grow aware of the greater purpose of the university and how it touches many lives.

By utilizing these steps, Bob might see that he accomplishes at least two important goals through his work. First, Bob provides, in the form of salary and benefits, for his own food and shelter and financial security as well as that of his family. He transforms his energy and his enthusiasm in his job into groceries, clothing, mortgage payments and utility bills, as well as money for occasional doctor's appointments, music lessons and sports fees for his children. His salary also pays the cost of the family's yearly vacation and various home celebrations on birthdays, Christmas and other holidays.

Second, Bob helps the university carry out its educational function, helping students achieve their training and educational goals so that they may go out into the world and pursue a livelihood, much as Bob does now. Not everyone involved in education has a PhD and delivers incredible lectures which change students' lives. In fact, very few do. A university is a complicated operation, where a lot of information must be processed (which courses to offer, how many students will sign up, what lecture halls will handle the capacity, how many dorm rooms will be needed, what kind of maintenance will be required this year, this month, and this week, etc.), tradeoffs negotiated and agreed upon, decisions made, orders and instructions given, and processes and progress monitored and reviewed.

*   *   *

Robustness and Authenticity

Bob knows that he also needs to ask two questions about his livelihood to determine its appropriateness for him. They are the same questions which surfaced in determining the correctness of his thoughts and his actions. Since correct livelihood is really a series of interwoven intentions and actions, here again they are key questions. First, is it robust? Second, is it authentic?

As for robustness, it is certainly easier to gauge robustness when you are comparing actions, say, climbing Mount Shasta versus watching a pro sports game on TV while drinking a beer. But all activities, including livelihood, need to be robust as well. They need to engage our faculties and abilities and, by so doing, improve us over the course of time. Again, Bob can view his job at the university as mere drudgery where he just does the same thing this year with the class of 2012 that he did ten years ago with the class of 2002. Or, if he is engaged in his work, he can use the experiences he gains over time to grow each year in efficacy and wisdom. Here we find that in some ways, robustness is more a choice Bob makes than one with which he is faced; robustness measures, in some sense, the attitude and energy Bob can bring to his job. It is also true that, if Bob is fully engaged in his work and makes it into a *robust situation*, he is more likely to be given more responsibilities and promoted to positions which will carry higher robustness and authenticity in the future.

Authenticity goes to the issue of, is this a correct job for Bob? Is there anything about being a university administrator that forces Bob to be untruthful, dishonest or deceitful either to himself or to others? Can Bob always be authentic to himself and to others while carrying out his duties? I am not talking about the minor adjustments we have to make in order to work smoothly with others or in order not to be cruel or unkind. If a subordinate performs in a substandard way, it is not *inauthentic* for Bob to try to find a positive way to change the subordinate's attitude and performance, rather than reading him the riot act, or "ripping him a new one." Similarly, if Bob's boss acts unreasonably or unkindly toward Bob, it is not untruthful or deceitful for Bob simply to absorb the boss's actions without reacting, even though his reactor wishes to, well, react.

Authenticity requires Bob to see his position as a whole. Does he buy into the mission of the university, despite its hiccups and flaws? Can Bob continue to help the professors and their students, despite the formers' more than occasional arrogance and the latters' more than occasional misbehavior? On balance, can Bob, embracing the bigger picture of the university and the overall good that it does, embrace *his* position in it as authentic to him? If so, then it is an authentic livelihood.

Of course, any job, and by that I mean literally any job—car salesman, waitress, school janitor, senator or barista—can be analyzed this way to judge its validity, robustness and authenticity. And any livelihood can be robust and authentic

*   *   *

ELEVEN

The Quest

*When you are inspired by some great purpose, some
extraordinary project, all your thoughts break their
bonds: Your mind transcends limitations, your
consciousness expands in every direction, and you
find yourself in a new, great, and wonderful world.
Dormant forces, faculties and talents become alive,
and you discover yourself to be a greater person by
far than you ever dreamed yourself to be.* ~
Pantanjali, Yoga Sutras.

*Security is mostly a superstition. It does not exist in
nature, nor do the children of men as a whole
experience it. Avoiding danger is no safer in the long
run than outright exposure. Life is either a daring
adventure, or nothing.*~ Helen Keller

* * *

Extended Effort

The final step in awareness and enlightenment is completely
practical. When we can command the mind and body for an
extended period of time to take several connected actions

with a larger and often daunting goal in mind, we call this extended effort a "quest."

Thousands of youngsters engage in "musical" quests every week, usually without knowing it. These young but serious musicians, each time they receive a new and more challenging piece of music to learn and perform, begin a quest which, once finished, will raise their total musical mastery and leave them ready for more difficult tasks. By "serious musicians," I don't mean those who are eyeing concert hall careers, or even contemplating majoring in music or music education when they arrive at college. *Serious musicians* includes all middle school and high school children who have specialized in an instrument with some private lessons, and who are most likely in their school's band or orchestra or musical ensemble of some sort. These youngsters might receive a complicated piece of music from their instructor, say, a movement from a concerto which has been transcribed for their solo instrument and piano, which they work on for several weeks or even months and then present during a local recital or perhaps as soloist at a school concert. I've seen (and heard) this with my own children as they labored through a new piece, week after week, struggling and sometimes feeling overwhelmed. Like any quest, it doesn't come easy, and requires an extended effort to get through it. Then the moment comes, nerves and all, and they perform it in some setting, quite beautifully to my ear, although they often will say, afterward, "Well, did you hear my stumble?" or "I kind of wobbled on one section there, I can do it better." But they never perform it in the recital venue again. Rather, the piece becomes part of their normal practice repertoire at home, and a new piece, the next level higher, is assigned and the *quest* process begins anew.

Remember, correct action flows naturally out of full perception and correct thinking or intention, and that correct action can be *physical* (running, bicycling, playing a sport, walking to work, eating well, building something, resting), *non physical* (<u>wu wei</u>), or *metaphysical* (deciding to do something or not to do something, acting out of enthusiasm, generosity or gratitude). Correct mindfulness contains as its basic building block correct meditative practice, an efficient way to train your jockey and your horse, and a taking responsibility for our lives and all their merits and demerits, gifts and obstacles. Higher mindfulness leads to an expanded understanding of the suchness of every single thing we experience. Correct livelihood is a series of questions and answers to judge the expressions and actions we must undertake to make our way and earn our living in the world.

The undertaking of a quest, the final step in enlightenment, is a step beyond the simpler, discrete actions described in Chapter Eight. Deciding on and embarking on a quest enables us to accomplish larger goals, goals which might have seemed, up to this point, beyond our abilities. To succeed in a quest , we must first exert correct intentions—*our will*—to command the mind and the body for an extended period of time, perhaps to submit to some level of self-denial or suffering, perhaps to overcome a sense of fear or dread or vague anxiety, keeping a larger goal in mind. As a simple example, it is correct action to be enthusiastic about going for a single trail run today, and to repeat that action two or three days from now. But it becomes a true quest when we decide to work diligently and undertake a one-year training regimen to prepare to run a 100-kilometer run next summer. It is correct livelihood to work with enthusiasm and gratitude at a job which is satisfying to us and helpful to others, but it becomes a true quest when we take the initiative at work and take responsibility for a larger task than we have ever done before, or when we break away and start our own enterprise in line with our personal code of conduct and our understanding and learning from the first six steps. We are aiming, through the quests in our lives, to reach out to our own unique destinies. As Hemingway noted:

> *There is nothing noble in being superior to your fellow man; true nobility is being superior to your former self.*

We will only achieve a completely enlightened life if, after taking all of the steps and practicing diligently at all the levels we have discussed up to now, we take the final step to venture forth to accomplish a bigger goal. And by a bigger goal we mean something from our conscious mind which is more than simply perceiving the world clearly, thinking correctly, speaking correctly, acting correctly and working day to day at a livelihood which is in concert with who we are. These are not inconsequential things, of course; in fact, if a person could achieve all of the first six steps, then he might be truly aware and enlightened. In fact, he certainly would be more awakened and "richer" than the vast majority of people. But there is a step beyond. By deciding to exert this kind of effort, we are undertaking to achieve our own personal suchness through effort and perseverance. We are edging toward our ultimate purpose in life. It is the quest which will, finally, complete us, and enable us to go even farther along our own paths, toward our destiny..

*   *   *

The High Peak Effect

*It is not the critic who counts, nor the man who points
how the strong man stumbled or where the doer of
deeds could have done them better. The credit
belongs to the man who is actually in the arena;
whose face is marred by dust and sweat and blood;
who strives valiantly...who knows the great
enthusiasms, the great devotions, and spends himself
in a worthy cause; who, at best, knows the triumph of
high achievement; and who, at the worst, if he fails,
at least fails while daring greatly, so that his place
shall never be with those cold and timid souls who
know neither victory nor defeat.* - Theodore
Roosevelt

Many of us know that there is true magic in a big goal, a true quest which requires a focus and a concentration beyond what is necessary for every day life, a goal which, if achieved, can grant a bigger meaning to our lives. And, in undertaking a true quest, there is a bigger reward, perhaps the biggest reward a human can achieve, the reward of ultimate self-realization. Most people know that the entire process of preparing for and achieving a big goal is more important and has a longer lasting effect than the single "crowning" moment during which goal is achieved, and that it is also more than any "glory" or "afterglow" of the achievement. It is a commonplace to emphasize the process by saying, "Value the journey, not the destination." The true benefit of completing a quest, however, is *even more* than the process (the "journey") and the glory (the "destination") combined; for us, the true benefit will be not only the journey and the destination (and its afterglow), but also what continues afterward and transforms us, the overall after-effect on the achiever. We can call this the "High Peak Effect," which I first discovered as a teenager.

In July 1970, I attended the North Carolina Outward Bound School and learned the basics of rock climbing and expedition hiking, along with a number of other skills. It was a robust 26 days in the Great Smoky Mountains for this sixteen-year old suburban kid. It was my very first quest, actually, although I did not know it at the time, and I was happy to be able to finish the course, tanned and scratched and slender. But the real lasting effect of attending Outward Bound and finishing a course which included a daily cold morning run through the mountains followed by an icy dip, three separate, multi-day expeditions, several technical days of rock climbing, rappelling, traversing and other skill building, a 3-day "solo," and a final 6-mile trail run up and down a mountain, was the "high peak effect" I retained afterward when I returned to my home outside Philadelphia. Of course, I did not call it by that name at the time; I just knew that somehow things had changed for me. After Outward Bound I was no longer a tight fit with the group of friends I had known since the second grade, although, to be honest, it was the age when most long lasting friendships begin to fracture as their members go in different directions, looking for "who" they are, listening for that different drumbeat. I wanted more. I did not know exactly what I wanted, but I wanted more than just the life of a teenager, and later an adult, in Drexel Hill, Pennsylvania. Having now traveled on my own and had my own adventures at Outward Bound, I knew that I simply wanted more. Despite the fact that the mountains we climbed in North Carolina were never taller than five or six thousand feet, the overall result was a "High Peak Effect," one which gave me the confidence to go farther and climb higher. And, more importantly, it injected me with the burning desire to do so.

As I noted, I did not fully understand this at the time. The High Peak Effect manifested itself more as simply as an urgent desire to find more of the same stuff—adventure, uncertainty, discomfort, risk— which Outward Bound had introduced me to. The following summer, I bummed a ride to Colorado and then hitched north to a job I had written for. After eight weeks of bucking bales on ranches on the famed "Mormon Row" several miles north of Jackson Hole, Wyoming, I found myself, in late-August 1971, climbing the Grand Teton—a true High Peak, at 13,775 feet—with two guys I barely knew. Despite my Outward Bound training, I still had a lot to learn about the mountains, and didn't even own a climbing helmet. The older boys I was with were not the safest climbers you could climb with, and let's just leave it that I was lucky to escape from that climb with my life. After hauling an old climbing rope up to the saddle at 10,000 feet, they made the decision on an exposed and icy rock face not to deploy the rope but rather to simply free-climb to the summit. At a crucial and very dangerous point, I slipped but managed somehow to catch myself. Had I not been able to catch myself, the fall would have no doubt ended my earthly sojourn, in a bloody pulp, several hundred feet below in Idaho.

We made it to the top, however, a true High Peak summit, and then rappelled down using some ropes another group had left there, but no climbing harness, no rope harness, no rappel device, just a pair of gloves and a rope around my back and up through my crotch. Technically this is referred to as "non-mechanical rappelling" and is greatly frowned upon. I would never think of doing this today. In the end, though, I managed to muddle through that time without any disastrous mishap. The Grand Teton was the highest altitude I had ever climbed, and was to remain my highest climb for the next 39 years. The High Peak Effect was still active, but instead of sending me to higher and higher peaks, which it easily could have, instead it sent me farther and farther away. During the twenty three years from 1972 to 1995 while I would attend college, graduate school and law school and begin to work, I would also spend thirteen of those years overseas, living in Spain, Korea, Japan and Hong Kong. The High Peak Effect for me had gone from vertical to horizontal.

On July 7, 2010 I rediscovered the High Peak Effect when I journeyed south on I-5 with Daughter's Boyfriend and climbed Mount Shasta, a 14,180 foot mountain at the bottom of the Cascade Range in northern California. I was easily the oldest guy on the summit that day. It had taken me almost four decades to ascend higher than the Grand Teton, and it took a lot out of me, but almost immediately I felt a renewed confidence to go farther and climb higher. In the car on the way home I began to dream of other, higher peaks. There were, I mused, quite a few 14,000 foot peaks in Colorado, and of course Mt. Whitney in California and Mt Rainier in Washington. Over all of them loomed Denali in Alaska. At 20,320 feet it is "only" some 6,000 feet taller than Shasta, but its geography and high latitude make it one of the most dangerous mountains on the planet. It is actually a "bigger" mountain than Everest, base to peak, since Everest starts atop the Tibetan Plain at 17,000 feet which makes climbing its 29,000 feet a climb of "only" 12,000 feet. Denali sits on a base at 2,000 feet above sea level, and the vertical distance to its summit is 18,000 feet. It is not the height, however, which is so daunting about Denali but rather the weather. Apparently the coldest temperature on earth was recorded by a thermometer left on Denali one winter, more than 100 degrees below zero Fahrenheit. Ferocious winds can lower the technical temperature by tens of degrees.

I don't know if I will ever attempt to climb Denali, or even higher peaks. There is so much pain involved in dragging forty or fifty pounds of gear up a mountain, and even more when the weather is savage. Certainly if I am going to attempt Denali, given my current age, it will have to be relatively soon, and most likely within the next decade at the latest. The fact that I am even thinking about it, however, I now recognize as the High Peak Effect.

A more direct result of Mount Shasta's High Peak Effect on me, as I have mentioned, happened when I decided to run an ultramarathon. The longest organized run I had ever done before was a half marathon, 13.1 miles, fifteen years earlier, but with Shasta behind me it "just made sense" for me to sign up to run a 31-mile ultramarathon trail run along Oregon's McKenzie River. Farther, higher. When we embark on quests, because they are activities which require a great deal more than we are used to, while they daunt us and set our nerves a bit on edge, they also result in a lasting effect to the good on our souls, and help us to perfect and expand our growing awareness and enlightenment.

* * *

The Failure Effect

Failure is instructive. The person who really thinks learns quite as much from his failures as from his successes. ~ John Dewey

When we undertake a quest, whether it's climbing a high mountain, learning a new and difficult skill, attempting to run 31 or 62 or 100 miles in an event, or starting a new business, there is no guarantee that we will finish it, that we will stand on the summit or bask in the thunderous applause of a concert hall. Perhaps the goal is beyond us, beyond our physical and mental powers, or perhaps we don't have the equipment or resources to finish the quest, or maybe our preparation is not up to the task. In Chapter Eight, we discussed how "perfect" is the enemy of the "good," and how learning to live with imperfection and imperfect results will lead to (in fact, is the only path to) excellence and excellent results.

Undertaking a quest is already taking a step toward growth and destiny, and that struggling and persevering in that quest puts us squarely where we should be—in the journey of life. If we succeed we can look forward to the benefits of the "high peak effect." But if we fail? What then, is all lost, is it a failure?

The answer is relatively simple and not so bad: we can learn. We might learn what the outer limits of our physical and mental powers are, we might learn that "success" in a quest is sometimes very dependent on the level of preparation and equipment one can afford. We could learn that what we believed, throughout the entire process of getting ready for the quest, would be sufficient preparation (enough lessons and repetitions of a concerto for piano, enough miles of running on the track and in the mountains, enough planning and thinking about a new market and a new venture into it) turns out to have been well short of what was truly required. So we limp off the race course or the mountain, perform poorly at the recital or file for a bankruptcy liquidation. We limp off having failed to succeed, but not necessarily defeated. It may well be that we have run up against the limits of our talent, brains, strength and endurance, that we simply can't do something which appealed enough to us to make it into our quest in the first place. That would be a good thing to know: our limits. We can learn from our attempt; in fact, if we fail to learn from the quest, whether in the end we "succeed" or "fail," it destroys the entire effort. So, in the end, win or lose, we have to learn from what we have tried, and go on from there.

*　*　*

Struggle and Perseverance

Character cannot be developed in ease and quiet. Only through experience of trial and suffering can the soul be strengthened, ambition inspired, and success achieved. ~ Helen Keller

It may seem strange now, near the end of our discussion, to bring up struggle. After all, isn't enlightenment much simpler, and even easier, than everyone has been saying all along? Why would we wish to set up these prolonged, difficult series of actions called quests?

Perhaps this awakening is, after all, a sort of trap—an enlightenment bait-and-switch? Have we been duped? We started out so simply, just inhaling the fragrance of a cup of tea or the dew on freshly cut grass, we hear the sound of the wind through the trees and see the dark sky surrendering to the day. Perceiving is an action, of course, but of all the actions we ever take, perception has to be the most passive. Smell the roses, taste the coffee, watch the sunrise. We were doing so well, even coasting into thoughts and actions and meditation, why this late and devious chicanery into suffering?

The reason why we must, in the end, struggle and persevere, is because struggle *is* the nature of all Life. The greater part of our world is inanimate matter: rocks, gravel, sand, clay, water and air. We, the living, are formed of a few inanimate elements which, in the end, struggle through consciousness to do a few simple tasks: eat, survive, and reproduce. To accomplish this, we perceive the world and act in ways which, we hope, will be beneficial to ourselves and to our tribe. We are the inheritors of Life's struggle forward, from long before the moment the first limbed fish struggled to find footing on the margin between land and sea, to the moment four decades ago when we witnessed the first biped to step out of his spaceship and onto the surface of the moon. In the end, we only complete ourselves when, having taken compass bearings and, buoyed by hope, set our course. We sally forth into Life, to witness the exquisite pageant of the universe and to ride Life's surge toward our purpose. It is, in fact, the goal of enlightenment to put ourselves in position to see, think and act clearly enough to undertake quests, to struggle, to persevere and to fulfill our destiny. Quests must, of necessity, involve effort and sacrifice and struggle. And, like everything we have discussed, each person's quest will be different, and each will be a do-it-yourself project.

Ironically, it is the struggle which makes us strong—in every area. Subtract struggle at the most basic level and we will die, almost immediately. Astronauts in a weightless environment can, with the flick of a finger, propel several tons of equipment hundreds of yards if they so wish. If they remain without the "burden" of gravity for more than a few days, however, they begin to grow weak, while we, here on earth with our daily physical struggle against gravity and air pressure, stay strong as if by magic. Air pressure at sea level is roughly 15 pounds per square inch, and we must struggle to move against it, swimming as it were, against and through the atmosphere. We don't notice this, any more than a shark notices the 60 pounds per square inch of water pressure against his skin when he is 100 feet below the surface, or the 220 pounds per square inch of pressure when he dives to 500 feet. But if we were suddenly thrust into a pressure-less environment, such as the one we might find outside a space station 250 miles above the earth, the dissolved nitrogen in our blood would gasify into painful bubbles, (the "bends") and the moisture in our mouths and eyes would boil away. Our lungs would shift into reverse, expelling oxygen and we would experience the twin joys of brain asphyxiation and corporeal hypoxia. We would be dead within minutes. (Of course this truth gives the lie to the comic book myth of Superman, whose powers derived from the much greater gravity of his home planet, Krypton. He could never be more, on a planet such as earth, than a "Weakling-Man." His muscles might look bigger, at least momentarily, as all the water in them "boiled" off into a much-expanded vapor, but the vaporizing of water would eviscerate his muscular power and he would collapse into spasms and twitches and a death rattle. And, as would be the case if I were cut loose from the International Space Station, here on earth Superman would suffer from a fatal case of the bends and die. He would, in effect, be a weakling-man and a dying-man from the moment he landed here.)

So, this is the upshot of it all. Life—through consciousness—perceives, thinks, acts, struggles and perseveres. We were born as part of the great caravan of life, therefore we were born to perceive, think, act, struggle and persevere. This is our purpose, here on the green and blue planet. In the end, if we fail to do this, we will fail at everything. But, ultimately, if we endeavor to do this, then we fail at nothing and fulfill our destiny.

*　*　*

TWELVE

FAQ

Can anyone, or everyone, actually reach enlightenment?

Yes. Anyone who can drive a car can reach enlightenment. In fact, many who could never drive a car can reach enlightenment. If you have the tools of perception (sight, hearing, smell, taste and touch), or at least some of them, and you can think and express yourself, then you can reach enlightenment. Remember Helen Keller, who clearly led a fully enlightened life without ever seeing or hearing a thing. Of course, it might help to read this book.

So, an average person can reach enlightenment?

Certainly, and many below average. Average is a big group, of course. People sometimes assume that you must be some sort of genius to reach enlightenment, but that is wrong. You have to be a genius to solve complex math or physics problems, perhaps, but if you can smell coffee as it brews and marvel at its dark color and rich aroma, you have all the tools you need to reach enlightenment.

I, myself, am extraordinarily average. Many who have known me, teachers, bosses, colleagues and friends, might even be happy to tell you that I am below average. "That guy? Not even average, in my book." Of course, every year I get cards from my children on my birthday telling me I am the "world's best" father, or something like that, so in that regard maybe I might even be average, or a little above. Or, maybe that is just what really terrific kids do on their dad's birthday. All in all, on a good day, I am pretty average. I am your average awakened human being.

You say it takes very little time to achieve enlightenment, is that really true?

Yes, it depends on the person and his goals, but there's no reason why it should take more than a few weeks to work through the first four or five steps. Remember that you are a living miracle. Recall that you have already been, at certain times, aware and awake; it is simply a question of systematizing your approach to enlightenment. Of course, the final step of planning and embarking on specific *quests*, described in Chapter Eleven, by definition, will take longer, months, perhaps, or even years, and continue for the rest of your life. And, enlightenment is not like buying a car, where once you drive it home it sits in your driveway and there it is. The first step in awakening is to perceive the world correctly. You can't just do it once, say on a Monday or a Thursday, and be done. Once you start perceiving the world fully and comprehending the "suchness" of everything, you have to continue to perceive in that way each and every day, each and every moment. Perceiving the world fully must become your daily practice, that's why these steps are also called practices. This is the power source that lights your high-powered flashlight, as it were. If you do not continue the practice, then your batteries will fail, your light will go out and you'll go back to the unenlightened world you were in before. In that sense, enlightenment is not a condition or a static state, but a process.

Picture in your mind a master fly fisherman, someone who has achieved absolute mastery of his skill. Do you see someone who, once and only once, a long time ago, read everything available on fishing, and then bought all the best gear and practiced with it at home and then, during one single year, travelled to the six best rivers in the world and fished, using his gear and skill? And then packed it all away? Or do you see an older gentleman who has fished every free moment of his eight decades on earth, and who is now sitting late at night in his study crammed with books about rivers and geography and fish species and fishing technique, constantly studying and thinking about fishing, and working with his specialized tools to create new flies to try out? This is the practice, the drill, of enlightenment.

Once you achieve awareness, or enlightenment, can you expect to be happy all the time?

No, you can't. Enlightenment is enlightenment, it is not happiness. It may lead to more situations where you find yourself "happy" or "content," but also to more situations where you will be unhappy, not content and just plain uncomfortable. Most people spend their lives aiming at, and wishing for, happiness. Surprisingly, happiness, at least in the "sustainable" form most people are looking for, doesn't really exist. Happiness is a temporary glow which a particular situation or set of circumstances or individual moment provides. In my mid-twenties while visiting my parents one summer, I remember sitting with my sweet father late one afternoon having a scotch with him in the backyard. We spoke quietly of various things. He told me he was proud of me. Birds were singing, the barbecue coals were almost ready for the steaks and the light and the temperature were perfect. I was exquisitely happy. But that feeling only lasted perhaps ten minutes. That's the way happiness is. Once that magic moment and concoction fades or vanishes, then so does "happiness." What is happiness? Is it the feeling you get when you bring that warm puppy home for the first time and he trails behind you in the yard? (It certainly isn't the feeling you get when you see your favorite rug later that day.) Is it gazing at the sunset with your girlfriend when you are seventeen, or is it a summer long adventure which takes you on the interstate across the western states at twenty? As the Tom Jobim's Brazilian samba states: *Tristeza não tem fim, felicidade, sim,* "Sadness has no end, but happiness does." But, enlightenment, since it bridges happiness and sadness, joy and grieving, comfort and discomfort, need have no end.

You said, rather than accept this method of attaining enlightenment on faith, we should test this for ourselves. How can we do this?

Testing these propositions and these steps might seem hard at first but it is actually quite simple. Everything in <u>Sustainable Enlightenment</u> is provable. Before we get started, can you accept that you are a miracle, that you are an individualized manifestation of the miraculous in life, that you are a part of the miracle of life on earth, and that you are alive on a miraculous planet? If you accept this, then first, test that your perceptions are not only the key to your survival and your sanity, but also your connection to the universe. Do some of the subtle experiments at "disconnecting" yourself which I wrote about in Chapter One and see how long you can continue to "exist" in any meaningful way. Second, using your perceptions, test your thoughts and intentions. Can you control these? Once controlled, can they lead you to a higher, more enlightened state? Can you, for example, simply *will* yourself to feel grateful for the next breath of air? If not, hold your breath for a longish while, and try again.

Third, can you now control your expressions in light of your perceptions and thoughts? Fourth, can you decide on and carry out actions in line with your thoughts, intentions and expressions? Once carried out, can these actions lead you to a higher state? Fourth, can you sit quietly for ten or twelve minutes a day, quiet your reactive mind and train it in the ways discussed in the text? Fifth, you can quite easily now review your work and career and test it against who you are (which you now know). Finally, you can decide on an appropriate quest to take you beyond where you are, to scale a "high peak," something which now appears to you as a challenge and appeals to your desires to stretch your life's journey.

What was the most important moment of awakening for you?

The most important moment of awareness for me, or anyone, is right now, wherever I am. So, sitting here typing this out, breathing, looking, listening—all of it is the "most important moment" of awakening. Enlightenment is not an "event" which you can actually point to. The goal is to try to maintain as high a level of awareness, constantly; thus it is "sustainable enlightenment," and not a single moment, a blinding epiphany. But there have been bigger, more memorable moments in my life, as there are in everyone's. As I wrote in Chapter Eleven, Outward Bound had the end effect of shaking me "awake," for lack of a better term, when I was just sixteen. Outward Bound, my first "quest," instilled in me something I have described as the "High Peak Effect," a sort of beneficial fever, or virus. I have done my best since then to stay in this state, but I don't believe that I stayed "awake" as long as I might have, at any time in my youth and college years, and particularly at *that* time. After all, I was sixteen, I was in high school and played on sports teams, I had a girl friend and my father's car to drive around. F. Scott Fitzgerald famously said, "There are no second acts in American lives." He was a first-rate novelist (Gatsby is one of the great books of all time) but this quote is not only third-rate, but wrong. All lives not only have second acts, but an infinite series of acts, waiting for you make your entrance beginning this very moment.

In any event, the following year, in summer of 1971 when I was seventeen, the experience of traveling alone two thousand miles away from home to live and work on hay ranches in Wyoming, and then climbing the Grand Teton, was also awakening, to say the least. At twenty, I moved to Spain and lived there for a year; it was another adventure in awareness.

I remember, however, three specific moments during my Peace Corps time in Korea which were very awakening. The first occurred during a heat wave in July, 1977, the second was at a dinner later the same year; the third was at a picnic lunch in May, 1978. I was not aiming for awakening or enlightenment at the time, but I know that after these three moments I never really perceived the world the same again. Except for in relation to my life, they are not important moments at all, but I'll go into them in a little detail because they may trigger a memory of something similar in your life which you may want to revisit.

My particular Volunteer group had spent its first ten weeks jammed together in tight quarters for training in the hot and steamy southern city of Cheongju in the summer of 1976. Understandably, by the end of the training period, we had managed to get on each other's nerves; and then suddenly we were scattered on a Peace Corps "diaspora" to sites dotted up and down the Korean peninsula.

In life, we have all had down moments, bad times, and the blues. Even though I think of myself as a perennially sunny person, for some reason everything seemed to go wrong by late June, 1977. I had just completed my first year of service and I had what I was certain was a great plan. I was going to take a vacation from my village and live for five whole weeks in the provincial capital of Chuncheon. I was going to write short stories and chapters in my planned novel, get my black belt in taekwondo, and continue seeing one of the teachers from my school with whom I had fallen deeply in love, who happened to come from Chuncheon, and who would be there, at her home, during the vacation period.

Almost as soon as I settled in, however, everything went south in a hurry. A swampy heat descended on the Korean peninsula and my tiny room in the *Hwang-geum Yogwan*, the Golden Inn, turned into a 6 feet by 4 feet sweltering chamber, twenty-four hours a day. People said it was the hottest summer in thirty-five years. Each morning I tried to write and found that I could barely pen a lazy, meandering paragraph of gibberish before I surrendered to the heat. The teacher I wanted to see had been forbidden to see me by her parents (a reasonable edict, seen in hindsight—I was a nobody and a foreigner, any virtues I had were pretty much invisible to the Koreans and, as a foreigner, I would be here today and gone tomorrow, as it were). I stayed in my "cell" and read and slept off and on and, before long, except for the taekwondo sessions in the evening followed by a cheap (60 cents) meal of badly fried rice, I was simply lying on the

226

futon all day and all night long, sweating and drifting in and out of sleep. The yogwan I was staying at was an inexpensive one; I was awakened at all hours of the night by drunken squabbles among the visiting salesmen who were loudly entertaining themselves late into the night playing the raucous Korean card game, *hwa-tu*, drinking and consorting hooting and cackling with ladies of shady repute, with the other guests and with the earthy and quite rotund woman who owned the yogwan—it all seemed to be an endless, looping nightmare, something out of Fellini. This heightened each day for almost a week as the heat intensified, and with each day I seemed to grow more and more listless. I was as alone as I have ever been, and I guess I was clinically depressed. I remember that I tried on 7/7/77 to change venues, to move to another yogwan, where I lasted just 30 minutes before dragging my backpack and book bag back and sorry ass back to the Golden Inn. So much for lucky sevens.

The innkeeper eyed me as I returned to her establishment, it seemed a withering look, and said, "Ah, you come back, yeah." At least the Golden Inn was a familiar if literally depressing abode, and I needed to cling to something. I felt like I was twisting, no more than half awake in a conscious coma. Nothing changed for two more days, but I had surrendered to my fate. I could not swim against this tide. Fortunately, the evening of the 10th began to cool off perceptively, and the next morning I was able to rise and begin to function, at least a little. I was, moment by moment, re-entering the world. I was still not permitted to see the teacher I was pining for during the rest of my time in Chuncheon, and never was able to write a thing, but I somehow managed to read and exercise my way through until the five weeks ended and my teaching duties began again, in a new town. I had been down and managed, somehow, to simply wait it out, wait for cooler nights to come and the heaviness outside and inside to pass.

I know that, in the scheme of things, my mini-depression would not even register a blip on the psychiatry radar; it was no dark night of the soul, no voyage to the depths. And, although a few months later I would feel physically much worse and shed twenty pounds in a week (amoebic dysentery), nothing in my life has ever compared to my despair on 7/7/77, nor to the relief I felt as I slowly emerged.

The second event occurred later that year, on one freezing evening in Seoul in November, 1977. All volunteers serving their second year in Korea had been invited to a U. S. Embassy facility for Thanksgiving dinner. Now, on this particular cold evening, I was thinking about how, within six months or so we would "muster out" of the corps. Each person had a different plan—one to return to Boston, another to travel to Africa, another to fly to Europe. During my service so far, I had been mostly isolated from the other Americans during my first year in the village of Won Tong, and during my second year in the fishing town of Sokcho, on the Sea of Japan (what the Koreans call the East Sea), two fairly distant locations from everyone else. To be frank, I liked being far from the other Americans, and the feeling might have been mutual, to a degree. I believe I had a reputation for aloofness and bluntness, and probably worse, but as I sat there after the meal, looking over the dishes with their congealing ponds of turkey gravy, the various bowls of stuffing and plates of leftover cranberry sauce, its gelatin still showing the rings from the cans it came in, I realized how special and beautiful each of my fellow volunteers was, and in fact, how rich and wonderful the world was. Time, while not standing still, was ticking by at such a lovely, slow pace. I do not know why it happened then and there, but it felt wonderful to be alive and to be seeing and sensing everything in each moment. I realized that I would never see these volunteers all together like this again, and perhaps I would never see some of them ever again. For some reason that evening I began to perceive the world and each moment with more clarity. My feeling extended to the workers who were serving us, and even to the cold Seoul night which awaited us in a very short time, with its black sky and sparkling stars. I must have looked unusually content, because one of our group, Ellen, said, "You look like a cat who just swallowed a goldfish. Why are you so happy?" I answered, "This may sound strange, but this is a great evening, and I somehow know that I will have an incredibly wonderful life. For some reason, I just know it. But I am going to remember all of this, especially this night, for a long long time." Over thirty-three years later, I still remember it, all of it.

The third enlightening moment occurred at my site about six months later, late one morning in May of 1978. The total student body of the girls middle school where I was teaching assembled in front of the school and hiked three miles to a large fold in the eastern facing slope of the Tae Baek Mountains, what might be termed a piedmont area. I had less than two months to serve in my two-year hitch in the "Corps," and had decided not to extend for a third year since I was getting married. This particular hollow was an indentation in the mountains I had never seen before, and would most likely never see again; it was as distant—at 8,000 miles or so—from my home outside Philadelphia or my college in Charlottesville as I could imagine. And now more than a thousand middle school girls in identical navy blue sports suits settled on the slope, looking from a distance like nothing so much as a thousand dark blue butterflies, flitting from spot to spot, now alighting for a moment, and going about the serious business of having a school picnic with their principal and teachers. I gazed at the scene, the chaos of cooking *pulgogi* and the organized distribution of the rice and a myriad of side dishes, *kimch'is*, pickled legumes, and tiny anchovies fried in sugar and oil (*myolchi*), fresh lettuce and hot peppers, and I perceived each person differently than I ever had before. I had never been in such a large group that was still, somehow, so personal. Everyone there knew my Korean name and knew who I was (that was easy, I was the only American, not only there, but for at least two hours in any direction). I felt the richness and true sweetness of each life arrayed on the mountainside—I could imagine each heart beating—and I drank in the lush bounty of the setting, the soft meadow grass, the brilliant sun, the sweet breeze. I also knew immediately that I was less than one one-thousandth of this particular swarm, like one worker bee in a hive or one laboring ant in a colony. At first, that thought was a little unsettling to me, that I could be *so insignificant*. But then, remarkably, the whole of it suddenly seemed quite lovely. I was so *absolutely* unimportant. Fantastic, I thought. I was free to find my own way, to live as I chose, to do whatever I wished, without ever having to be important. Everything was more numerous and bigger than I was, and it was wonderful.

(I would be remiss if I did not mention the birth of my two children as further, completely illuminating moments. I felt a complex mix of wonderful emotions when Son, and then a few years later,

Daughter, were born: joy, bliss, rapture, gratitude to my wife and to the world as a whole, and a kind of overwhelming love for these two helpless creatures who had been, miraculously, given to our care. Again, time slowed for me, waiting for me to see, hear, taste, smell and touch those wonderful moments—the suchness—on January 24, 1983 and again on November 12, 1985. I began to understand, at least in part, my own parents and all parents, and began to fill in more details about the tremendous gift that is life.)

You are not an ordained minister, a theologian or a monk. Why should anyone accept anything in this book?

Perhaps *because* I am not a minister, theologian or a monk. Enlightenment, awakening and awareness is not theology. I have certainly sat through scores of deadly dull and shallow sermons and homilies, disquisitions which lacked the candlepower of a single stick match. How about you? Read what's here and reach your own judgment. What I am telling you is a truth you can test for yourself. Nothing here needs to be taken on faith, everything can be subjected to your own rigorous examination. Test everything. This book either works for you or it doesn't. If these chapters don't make any sense to you, stop reading and find that book which does. However, do ministers and priests generally make this kind of learning more accessible or less? How often is their response to one of your questions, *Well, in this matter you must take it on faith*? Maybe in their traditions they have forgotten that, for enlightenment to mean anything, it must be accessible to everyone and anyone. If there are six billion people on the planet today and only one or two have achieved true "enlightenment," (say, the Dalai Lama and a player to be named later), what good is that? What if most or almost all of the six billion could achieve enlightenment and live in greater peace and clarity every day of their lives, and not after paying for t-shirts and chakra beads and spendy webinars and teleseminars and cruises, or after twenty or thirty years of struggle or asceticism or mysticism or jihad, but after only a few weeks of practicing simple, understandable steps? What if people could, by the millions, begin to achieve their own destinies? Would that be worth a try?

Never ask a barber if you need a haircut, and never ask a guru or a monk how difficult it might be to reach awareness or enlightenment. The barber thinks you could always use a trim, and it would undercut the entire purpose of the contemplative life, not to mention the decades of chanting and wall-sitting, to find that enlightenment is, well, relatively easily attainable and sustainable.

What you call "full perception" seems too easy. As I see it, all you are doing is really focusing, for that moment, on any object that may be at hand.

Well, once we realize that the very first step is to use our senses and perceive one, single thing fully and correctly, and we look at the texture, feel, smell (if any), shape, color and shadow of it, or listen to it if it makes a sound; we are beginning to understand its unique "suchness*," without any meaning.* These "things" don't *mean* anything, you know. We have to get away from the meanings we and others have ascribed to them, their labels, and simply perceive them as they are. Initially perceiving in this manner may be a little hard for some. This does not mean that we must react coldly to everything. If we see the sunset on the lake one evening and it makes us miss a loved one or recall a beautiful time, and creates a related emotion within us, that is fine. It is not the lakeside sunset which is sad or grateful, but our emotive response which is sad or grateful, and is part of our unique perception.

Perception is our magic doorway, if you will, into the universe, a portal which we have walked by thousands of times each year without knowing it. It takes practice to turn our perceptors on, especially if we have not *really* used them for years or decades. Once we have fully perceived an object, though, now we may think about where it came from and how it got here. If it is a rock, then we might consider what forces (glacier, flood, volcano, deposited sediment, plate tectonics) brought it here; if it is a tree, then we might think about where its seed came from, how it took hold and managed to survive the years of its existence. If it is a manufactured item, then let's ask who designed it and for what purpose, who first owned it and how it got to us, how long it might be staying with us, and where it might go after it leaves our possession (if indeed we ever actually possess it). Take any item, a steel letter opener, a plastic extruded medicine bottle, an orchid which has not bloomed in a few years, a cracked plastic CD case, yesterday's sports section, and perceive them fully. Once we do this for a while (say, for a week or two), we begin to discover a world of variety and richness we either once knew and forgot, or never knew existed, on our desk or out our back door, and we will begin to finally perceive the universe and our own position within it.

At the same time that we begin to fully perceive whatever we are focusing on, we are letting go of labels and judgments, of memories and expectations. That is, we are freeing ourselves from the prison of the past and the anxiety of the future, and residing in the absolute glory of the present moment.

But what good does it do you to perceive this rich world? Isn't it just a mind-game? Does it make any difference?

Imagine you are alone working after hours late one Friday evening in the third sub-basement of an office tower, a place where they keep old records and files. You have set up a temporary workspace in a room, and are going through some fascinating documents on a research project. Suddenly, the power fails and you are plunged into darkness. Even though your eyes become accustomed to the darkness, because there is absolutely no light at all down there, you can see nothing—literally nothing. There is simply no light which can be focused on the photo-receptor cells in your retinas. You don't have a candle, a match or a lighter, and your telephone is in your car. You can feel the bottom of the chair you are now sitting in, and you can trace the edge of the table you were working at. You are not comfortable getting up and moving about, because you are not familiar with the layout here and you have left some boxes of records on the floor which could send you sprawling. You grow resentful of your decision to take on this project, and begin to list out in your mind whom you might blame for getting you into this. At the same time, you begin to worry about the future, tonight, tomorrow, Sunday . . .You might have to stay here until Monday morning when the new week begins, without food or water, perhaps having to urinate in some corner, if you can even find one. It is unlikely that you will die or suffer grievous injury from this ordeal, but it is not a pretty picture you see, looking forward to the next 50 or so hours. It will be embarrassing, uncomfortable, to say the least. Suddenly you remember that you have a very small L.E.D. light on your key chain. You pull out your keys and press the button. You are exhilarated to have even this little bit of light and, while you carefully navigate your way to the emergency stairway, the exit, the parking lot and your car, you marvel in gratitude for this little trinket you have been carrying with you for years without ever using.

Before you found your little light, you could perceive the world but only in a poor way—by touch, sound, smell, and hearing—and you were facing circumstances which were unpleasant, to say the least, literally benighted. Once you found your little light, you could make your way carefully through the dark, and still in a relatively poor way, but you were so *happy* to have even this little source of light. But, what if in the middle of groping your way out, the power had been suddenly restored and everything properly illuminated, or if you had found a very powerful flashlight, so that now you could fully function with the full perception of where you were? This is clarity, this is enlightenment. What good is that to you? Each of us has to answer that question in accordance with our own experience fumbling in the shadows and darkness of life so far.

Why don't you think it's useful to use koans?

They may be useful to some people; I just doubt that they are of much use to most people. There is a long tradition of using koans, and I think we know a couple of things about long traditions. The first is, practices do not become traditions without some efficacy. Obviously, koans have been useful in getting ardent students to move away from their linear, discursive, intellectual thought processes so that they can grasp the suchness of things, from a small commodity measure ("three pounds of flax") to the nature of enlightenment itself ("the nature of the Buddha"). But another thing we know about long traditions is that they often continue with lives of their own, for no better reason than "we've always done this." We type on awkward and inefficient QWERTY typewriters for no better reason than this array kept the original mechanical machines from jamming, and now it is our "installed base.". In a digital world of word processing, why wouldn't we switch to the DSK (Dvorak Simplified Keyboard)?

So, my question to you is, if you can already understand the suchness of things and can practice perceiving it, and you can meditate and practice bifurcating your mind, do you need to study paradoxical questions which guide you to this exact same knowledge and realization? If so, use them. If not, dispense with them, since you have already learned what they have to teach.

I've tried meditation and it doesn't work, nothing happens.

Of course, nothing "happens," because the essence of meditation is that nothing, at that moment, is happening, and nothing will happen. Our reactor is going to rest, completely, for at least a few minutes. If anything is "happening," it is our job to stop it from happening further. It is the nothing that is happening (or, "not happening") that we seek. We want nothing to happen, or, said another way, we want all the somethings to stop happening. The problem is, we've been so conditioned to a world where *something* is happening, or is about to happen, that we need to stretch our minds even to begin to comprehend the reality of *nothing* happening.

No one has any problem with the idea of turning off a car engine or a generator for a while, or taking a much needed vacation from what we call "work." Why is it so troubling or difficult to try that with our consciousness?

While we can't turn off the world, we want to turn off, at least for a while, all the something that is happening in our heads, our brains racing around and bringing up random and discursive thoughts which serve to entertain us and to distract us. Our reactor is a little like a comedian, it doesn't want its audience to rest too long between yuks, but our commander must take over as the host or emcee of this particular variety show. "A giraffe walks into a bar," the reactor begins. "Not now," the commander says and sweeps that away. If we sit quietly for ten minutes or so and gently push aside each thought which arises, then meditation is working, and we are taming the reactor to serve us. Trust that it is working, and just sit and keep moving those thoughts away.

What's the benefit of pushing aside my thoughts for ten minutes, and then going back to normal? My thoughts, worries and anxieties just come back, and nothing has really changed.

First of all, by "pushing aside your thoughts" you are establishing the two elements of your mind, which we have discussed above: the commander and the reactor. Think of it as a training session, where you are taming or training your reactive mind to obey you. As we continue to hold our mind in two partitioned sections, as it were, and use one part to train the other, we gain control of our reactor, so it can't, so to speak, "go off." After meditating for, say, ten minutes each day, we will be more aware, and awakened and enlightened, for the other 1,430 minutes of each day. We do not wish to be enslaved to the chaotic nature of the world, we do not wish to allow circumstances or other people's words and actions to "wind us up" or "set us off." You may think that your thoughts, worries and anxieties have come back just as before, but think again. When did you notice them coming back? Before meditating, weren't they *always* there? So, if they are coming "back" now, it means that you gained control of them for that period of time, and that you have taken steps to come to terms with those thoughts, worries and anxieties. You are beginning to master them, to command them. Therefore, everything has changed.

If I can meditate for 30 minutes a day, or even an hour, wouldn't that be better than just 10 or 15 minutes?

Maybe, maybe not. Sometimes more is not more, you know. Sometimes more just takes more of our time, with only slightly more efficacy, or the same efficacy, or less efficacy. There is also the vital question of *sustainability*: almost anyone can find ten or fifteen minutes a day to meditate, five days a week or so, but every time you raise that bar and look instead for thirty minutes, or an hour, you make it harder, not simpler, to sustain. Just as an example, a master horse trainer may know that a two-hour workout on the track, done well, is the right amount of practice and preparation for his prize steed. A two-hour session creates the correct circumstances for more efficient workouts in the days which follow and, eventually, an excellent performance on race day. A shorter session and the horse and jockey do not have enough time to work on the physical and cooperative nature of their task. A longer session and the horse and jockey become jaded and worn out, the next day's workout suffers, and the next one as well, and they do not achieve their goal. I personally like the efficiency of ten minutes of training (meditation) and 1,430 minutes of living, each day. That seems a sustainable ratio. But longer meditation may increase some health benefits which science is beginning to attribute to the practice. In the end, you may find a different recipe, or ratio, works better for you, and so long as the extended session remains *sustainable* over the long haul, then it obviously would do no harm.

I'm not sure what correct actions are. You seem to emphasize physical actions such as hiking or running, and eating correctly. But when I think of right or correct actions, I think of doing the correct thing, being nice to everyone, contributing to charities, volunteering at the school and at my church, voting in elections. Aren't those the correct actions?

Those things you describe, they might be right, they might be wrong. It all depends. Our actions, to be correct and to lead us toward our true destiny, need to be guided by our intentions and thoughts, which need to be correct. Before that happens, however, our intentions and thoughts need to be informed by, one, an acceptance of the miraculous nature of our lives, and two, complete perceptions of the world we live in, the real world in all its detailed richness (which we call its suchness) and our own particular suchness. Those perceptions will be personal to you, and will need to be renewed each day. Once we are properly guided by full perception and correct intentions, then we will see the world with clarity (enlightenment) and it will be easier for us to take correct actions. It won't be impossible to take wrong actions, of course, but it should be clear at the time that such actions are doubtful or even wrong.

Maybe you are not meant to smile and cluck at everyone, to make small talk and ask insincerely how they are doing. Maybe that's not "who" you are. And if you proceed to do that smiling and clucking because it's "nice" or "right," then you are cutting across the grain of your own suchness. If you are going to church or being nice to everyone or contributing to charities because someone told you to do that, or because you would be ashamed in front of your neighbors and family if you did not do that, or because it makes you (overly) proud of yourself and you can think about yourself—or talk about yourself to others—in a way which enhances your status, then it is probably not the correct action for you. No action can be the correct action, no matter what the rest of the world thinks, unless it arises from within you, from your own suchness. Correctly.

I'm not sure I understand how a "quest" is really any different than a series of correct actions.

Yes, there is a certain fluidity between correct action and a quest. A quest is when you combine a number of correct actions into a planned effort to accomplish something which you are not certain you are even capable of doing. My biking buddy, Paul, participated in Cycle Oregon's week long bike trips for many years and then, for some reason, decided he would like to bicycle across the USA. He wanted to start from Oregon and end up with his front tire touching the Atlantic Ocean, Maine to be exact. He researched gear and routes (and tried to interest me a little in the voyage, but it was not *my* quest), and started out one day in May, 2010. After a series of steps and missteps, freak winter storms in the Rockies and hot summer blasts across the Midwest he ended up on the Atlantic shore. His quest was finished, and I wonder now what his new quest will be.

Let's say we determine that hiking is what we like to do, that it is in line with our perceptions and intentions, and by hiking every Saturday morning for three hours in the nearby woods we feel more attuned to the world and all that is within it. We hike and figuratively drink in the woods, the rivulets, the meadows and the small promontory that looks over our valley, and each time we do this we make new discoveries of rocks, plants and creatures which exist along the trail throughout the seasons. We see new, richer patterns in the textures, sounds and smells of the woods. We can do this, almost without thinking, in perpetuity.

Now, someone offers us the opportunity to go on a multi-day, long distance "expedition style" hike into the Rockies or high Sierras, which will require map and compass or GPS, better equipment and planned meals, and which will present a certain amount of discomfort and challenges and, frankly, dangers, which we haven't faced in our weekly hikes. It will take place in an area with cougar and bears, we will need to pack bear spray, and take bear precautions both on the trail (bear bells, careful watching for any sign of bears) and at camp (keeping the tents clear of any scent which might attract a bear, the use of a bear canisters for storing food, etc.). We are excited by the prospect, but not quite sure how to cope with three or four rugged 15-mile days in a row, and wondering whether we can even do it. Now, when we first go on this particular expedition, it is a *quest*, in that it is the exertion of correct intention to command the mind and body to persevere for an extended period of time with a larger goal in mind. The larger goal does not need to be any grand "moral" goal that society approves of; it will be enough if it meets the above criteria for us.

And, three years later, after going on several of these multi-day, expedition-style hikes, it is entirely likely that such an expedition will have become simply a correct action, since it will arise out of our enthusiasm and be guided by our perceptions and intentions, but it will *no longer* require any extraordinary exertion of our faculties to accomplish it. Its novelty and risk (two elements which made it into a quest in the first place), in a sense, will have become familiar or even worn off, and its dangers and challenges, although exactly the same as they were three years prior, will no longer require an extended exertion to achieve the goal. Such a hike will simply have become "something we do," an action. Our next "quest" might be a technical climb of a high alpine peak, or an extended sea kayaking expedition. But it need not be something physically harder and / or connected to the previous quest in any obvious way. The next challenge might be something completely different, informed by something we saw or heard or did on the previous expeditions, or it might have grown "organically" from an interaction we had with nature or with our fellow adventurers, or out of some other collection of perceptions and intentions. Or the next quest may not be connected in any way to a previous action or quest, it might simply be the next quest we are meant to attempt. The only thing we can know for sure is that it will flow out of our full perceptions and correct intentions, and be a series of connected actions with a larger goal in mind.

What if the "quest" you decide on is too dangerous? What if you decide you are going to surf the north shore of Oahu or ski off an out of bounds cliff, or go on a multi-day trek in the Himalayas and get caught in an avalanche? How is dying going to be part of awakening or enlightenment?

First of all, a quest is the seventh step in this process. Only after you have perceived the world and yourself correctly (that is, you have connected to the world and to yourself intimately), and worked on your thoughts, expressions, actions, mindfulness and livelihood, do you even get to consider a quest. Quests are not, necessarily, dangerous or semi-dangerous outdoor activities, although they will require struggle and perseverance. As you have read, a quest can be almost any series of connected or linked actions which stretches you beyond your previous comfort zone. It could be embarking on a new course of study, starting a new business, or any number of extended efforts and actions which carry no unusual physical danger whatsoever.

By the time you determine to undertake a quest, you already understand more than others how precious and valuable (miraculous) your life is, as well as how precious and valuable each moment is. No enlightened person would simply decide to undertake some life-threatening activity without first determining that *that* particular activity was in line with his own suchness. To do so would not be undertaking a quest, it would be simple, vacuous thrill-seeking, and perhaps suicide. However, by way of example, if the person in question is a serious, practiced mountaineer who has undergone rigorous training, has acquired and learned how to use the highest quality climbing and safety equipment, has mapped out a reasonable (under the circumstances) expeditionary course with other, highly skilled climbers in his team, has analyzed carefully the terrain, weather and other risk factors (and continues to do so during the course of the expedition), and has accepted the risks involved in tackling Mt. Everest or K2, then climbing such a mountain would appear, for him, to be a valid quest. Certainly there is no way that I could question those decisions and his actions. If he dies in the Khumbu Icefall under a 6-story block of ice, then, that is the end of his life. But that is all it is. His dying, that moment when his breath and his consciousness ceased, was no part of his enlightenment, but his living was.

Except in hindsight, we cannot say that any quest was too dangerous. Life is fraught with dangers. The mere act of being born ensures that death will end it. From time to time, cars jump up on the sidewalk, planes fall out of the sky, buildings catch fire, buses crash, and terrorists bomb railway terminals. Are we to avoid walking on sidewalks, constantly watch the sky for falling planes, never enter buildings or ride a bus, and never take a train or subway again? Whenever you drive down a road (or ride in a car), you are undertaking an act of faith that all of the cars coming in the opposite direction won't, either for a lark, or out of negligence or even malice, suddenly veer across the line and ram into your vehicle, head-on. Risk is always out there, awareness helps you to perceive it and evaluate it, and live more comfortably with it

Is it necessary to become a vegetarian, or give up rich food, caffeine, smoking or alcohol to achieve enlightenment?

No. Of course, if the consumption of those items interferes with our perceptions, thoughts, expressions, actions, meditation, livelihood or efforts then we will want to take action in that regard. An alcoholic should never drink alcohol, a Celiac should never ingest gluten. It would be difficult for me to fully appreciate the "suchness" of Thanksgiving with my family without the familiar fragrances and tastes of turkey and stuffing, yams and seasonal pies, and a glass of wine. I am not looking to deny myself and to practice asceticism, I am only looking to perceive, think, express, act and meditate correctly.

I would add, however, that the use of tobacco, whether in cigarette, cigar, or pipe form, so blunts and diminishes the sense of taste (and smell) that it acts to deaden one or two of the basic powers of perception. In that sense, you should probably forego use of tobacco in all its forms.

The things people do constantly irritate me, whether it's smoking on the street where I can't avoid it, or the way they drive. I don't know that I'll ever get to the "bless them and move on" stage.

Among a laundry list of irritating habits they possess, drivers in my town of Eugene, Oregon have a very selective approach to using the turn signal. I can drive behind someone in a 35 mph zone and find him suddenly slowing to 10 mph, for no apparent reason. No signal is ever given and, after slowing down, he may turn right, or turn left, or continue slowly, or pick up speed and decide to drive more or less normally. I can also drive behind someone, driving with a right or left turn signal on for 20 city blocks, who has no apparent inclination to make any turn at all. I can be waiting to turn left from a side

241

street and see a single oncoming car with his right turn signal on. If he turns right onto my street, then I was free all along to turn left onto the main thoroughfare and continue my journey. Of course, in our town, only a foolish driver believes that a right turn signal means the driver is actually going to turn right—it *can* mean that, of course, but am I willing to risk my life and my property? If I assume that risk, then as I assess the damage to my car and wait for the ambulance I already know what the other driver will say: "No, my turn signal was *not* on," or "I *was* preparing to turn but not on this street, on the *next* one," or "I didn't know my signal was on." Of course, other drivers will continue to irritate my reactor, and that won't stop with enlightenment. But enlightenment will train the reactor, once irritated, to calm down, and train the commander who sits above it all to monitor the situation and order the reactor not to react, to simply let it go.

Is this really just a quick and too easy summary of and guide to awakening, isn't the truth actually contained in older, more established texts?

Einstein's Razor is the subtitle here, which should point you toward efficiency of thought and action. My wife and I went to Italy recently and took two types of guide books. The first type was the Michelin's full guide to Italy, a somewhat encyclopedic tome that listed all the hotels, all the restaurants, all the tourist and scenic spots, and laid it all out in almost excruciating detail. To use it you needed to research very diligently, absorb all the information, locate the various sites on a map, categorize them, take notes and then list them in descending order of importance to the travelers, then cross-check what you wanted to see with where the sites were on the map in relation to your hotel, and finally decide how much time you had to go through your list. It was like an entire research project, each and every evening, just to prepare for the next day, and it quickly became fatiguing and burdensome. The second guide book was a Rick Steves' guide, one of those handy and concise tomes where he has done all the research and presented it in a useful format for the tourist on site. For example, in Rome, he simplified everything: if you just had just one day in Rome, you could do these four things, if you had two days, then you could follow this itinerary of perhaps nine things, and if you had more days then you could follow a more extensive travel plan. It was brilliant and soon we left the Michelin's back in the hotel and took the Steves' guides with us in Rome, Florence and Venice.

Enlightenment is simply too *important* to be left to others, the seminar promoters, the *tchotchke* sellers, the gurus and religious hierarchies, and even the ancient texts and practices. And it *is* fairly straightforward: train yourself to use all of your powers of perception all of the time in order to think, talk, act, concentrate, work and exert yourself correctly. Have the courage of your perceptions. That's it, in a nutshell. Certainly, read all the texts which have stood the test of time, enjoy them, but don't put off awakening or enlightenment for one more day because you haven't had a chance to read the entire King James Version or to study the Ramayana or parse the Lotus Sutra.

Does your approach have anything in common with *The Power of Attraction* or *The Secret*, two popular (and related) approaches to fulfilling a person's dreams by connecting to the universe?

I don't think so. I'm not an expert in those programs by any means, although I am familiar with their basic approach. To a certain extent, it's true that if you think limiting thoughts (for example, *I'm not good enough*, or *I'll never have much money*, or *That just can't be done*), then those thoughts can act as self-fulfilling prophecies or at least self-limiting beliefs. There is a real power to positive thinking, and there is a magical power to belief. So, like many things, there is a kernel of truth to the "power of attraction". People are more than happy to create products to sell based on expanding that kernel to unrealistic promises of wealth, beautiful cars, exciting love interests and the life of a celebrity.

But I don't believe that you can simply imagine or visualize your way to a *truly* rich or fulfilling life, or intone magical incantations to achieve your life as it might be destined. The reports I see usually feature the promoter, sitting in a house by a pool or at some luxurious location under palm trees, telling you that all he did to achieve this wealth was to visualize it, or post a picture of it on a bulletin board at home and focus on it, or mutter some intense affirmations, or create some sort of neural network, and *voilà*, within a year or three years there it was. According to these types of programs, the universe, running perfectly on its own, was simply waiting for the promoter (and those who buy his books or videos, etc.) to get in sync with the Infinite, to create the correct vibrational harmony with the spirit of the Cosmos so that all his dreams (mostly in the form of house and pool and cars) could be answered. And very quickly. Of course, the down payment and the mortgage payments for the house (and the gardener and the pool boy) apparently come from the sale of seminars, workbooks, software, personal appearances and trinkets on the website. Human beings seem to want, more than anything, some sort of expedited path to a big house, an imported (and important) car as proof that somehow they got it right. Ah, money—the proof of election. When I see these ads and infomercials, I am reminded of the Italian proverb about chess and life: "After the game, the king and the pawn go back in the same box."

I remember another promotion that involved something called *The Prayer of Jabez*, which is a very minor bible verse in Chronicles. Apparently God wants you to be rich, but decided to hide the code in one of the most obscure characters in either testament. I doubt even bible scholars could have answered "Jabez" correctly on a multiple choice test before the Jabez ado. According to the Jabez *formula*, in order to break open the Christian piñata and shower its fortune upon your shoulders, you apparently must mutter a secret incantation, which strangely turns out to be something like, "God, bless me, make me rich, stay with me, and protect me." Talk about expedited grace. The original book sold about 9 million copies (well, it appears to have answered the author's particular prayer of Jabez), and spawned a cornucopia of peripheral items including a special Jabez book "for women," Prayer of Jabez journals, Prayer of Jabez children's versions, as well as key chains, mugs, a jewelry line, backpacks, Christmas ornaments, scented candles, and mouse pads.

I don't see that the power of attraction stuff and the Jabez foofaw differ all that much from the normal infomercial brand of get-rich-quick schemes, whether it's no-money down real estate (from a government auction), affiliate or multi-level marketing, or calcium pill promotions.

The truth is I don't know, and you don't know, what your destiny is or how it should unfold. And I will never know because I will never bring to the table your unique background and history, nor can I plug into the universe the way you will be able to. But you might be able to do all this one day, if you are willing. One certainty is that imagining life as the owner of a luxurious estate in the Hamptons or a 100,000 acre ranch in Montana or a private island in the South Pacific has absolutely nothing to do with your awakening and your enlightenment. It may be that, after connecting to the universe and going through the seven practices, your "station" in life might change. Or, it might not. In fulfilling your destiny it may turn out that you do *not* move up to a mansion, but rather downsize from your current 2500 square foot house to a 1200 square foot condominium or a 900 square foot cabin, giving up more than half of your belongings, your car and your garden to pursue what you are meant to do during your time on the earth. Even if you could command wealth, women (or men) and fancy cars through some power or some prayer, that might be worst thing you could do with your life from an enlightenment point of view, and your destiny. Remember Richard Cory, who was:

> *. . . rich – yes, richer than a king –*
> *And admirably schooled in every grace:*
> *In fine, we thought that he was everything*
> *To make us wish that we were in his place.*
>
> *So on we worked, and waited for the light,*
> *And went without the meat, and cursed the bread;*
> *And Richard Cory, one calm summer night,*
> *Went home and put a bullet through his head.*

~ Edwin Arlington Robinson ("Richard Cory")

You mentioned Positive Psychology in Chapter Six. Isn't this awakening or awareness just a repackaging of positive psychology?

In certain ways, this book's view of enlightenment shares a lot with the Positive Psychology movement.

Traditional Psychology, which we can call "Pathological Psychology," looks toward small segments (say 2 to 3 percent) of the population, those with certain pathologies, such as neuroses, psychoses, bi-polar disorders, schizophrenia, etc., and works toward bringing those sufferers more toward the norm. Put another way, it focuses completely on those people having a sub-optimal or subnormal experience of life and tries to remove or at least alleviate the pathology so that they can try to experience a *more* normal experience of life. Its goal is to try to help 2 to 3 percent of humanity.

Positive Psychology, however, focuses on the two or three percent of people having a *super-optimal* experience of life and tries to figure out how they do it, what are the elements of the super-optimal life, and then prescribes *that* for all people. Its goal is to try *to help 100 percent of humanity.* Everyone can take certain steps to optimize their lives, no matter where they are on the psychological spectrum. And the steps (gratitude, generosity, enthusiasm, robustness and authenticity are among them) are much the same for everyone. I think of life's strata as something like a series of escalators at a big department store, say, Macy's in New York City. For those already on the top floor, the *super-optimals*, life just can't get any better, but for those on the next floor down, the mere *optimals*, they can still do certain things differently to get on the escalator going up. And it turns out that those on the next floor down, the *low-optimals*, can do the very same things to get on their escalator going up to the optimal, or even super-optimal, level. It is the same with the *high normals*, the *normals* and the *low normals*. And even those in the sub-basement, the *sub-normals*, if they will engage in the same successful (gratitude, generosity, etc.) practices, they, too, can ride the escalator up into the low normal and perhaps normal floors in the store. In this way, Positive Psych can be helpful to everyone who tries, and not just a tiny percentage of us.

As in Sustainable Enlightenment, although with different emphasis, in Positive Psychology it turns out that correct perception is the key to most of what ails us. Seligman calls it "explanatory style," the way you explain the world to yourself. In other words, the first thing you must do is perceive the world, but perceive it *correctly*. If you perceive (explain) everything bad that happens in the world as "permanent, pervasive, and personal," which is to say that bad stuff *always* happens, it happens *everywhere* and it happens to you *personally*, then you will have a miserable life. But if you do that, you are not perceiving the world, but only mis-perceiving the world. Seligman wants you to "dispute yourself" when you find that you are perceiving the world incorrectly, he wants you to find out that certain things which happen are, in fact, merely temporary, limited in scope and impersonal. But I don't want you to dispute yourself from the beginning, I want you to understand first what an absolute miracle your existence is, and then to perceive correctly everything that is, and the *suchness* of everything. Then there will be no conflict, no reason to take arms against your explanatory sea of troubles. It is not a question of becoming a Pollyanna or a Dr. Pangloss; it is a question of perceiving the true nature of everything.

Richard Wiseman's The Luck Factor shows how people can and do nurture and create their own good luck. It's a fascinating read. His four elements of luck are: remain open to the world (perceive the world), listen to your intuition (again, perceive fully), have positive expectations (think and intend correctly) and have a resilient attitude toward adverse events.

Although Nathaniel Branden's excellent book, Six Pillars of Self-Esteem is not, technically, part of the Positive Psychology movement, in substance it is. Branden's six pillars can be summarized as: 1) living consciously (perceiving and acting correctly), 2) self-acceptance (perception of one's own suchness), 3) self-responsibility (meshing perception with thoughts, expressions and actions in a web of responsibility), 4) self-assertiveness (right expression, correct action), 5) living purposefully (correct actions, right efforts, right livelihood) and 6) personal integrity (right thoughts and intentions, right expression, right actions).

I encourage everyone to read everything they find absorbing in Positive Psychology, spiritual writings (including Zen studies), the Bible and biblical commentaries, and the self-help field. See the appendix for a short list of good places to start. <u>Sustainable Enlightenment</u> is really meant to be the simplest possible (but no simpler) guide to achieving that awareness and awakened state we all not only desire, but deserve.

How long do you think a person can stay enlightened? Until death? After death?

I don't know, but I assume that once you have done everything described here, there's no reason why you should ever "lose" enlightenment. I suppose if old age dementia were to set in, then perceptions and even the ability to think clearly might be eroded to the extent that awareness, just like the rest of life, would begin to deteriorate, to spiral downward. Barring that, there's no reason why octogenarians and older should not be the *most* enlightened people on the planet, after all, they would most likely have been aware for the longest time. After death? I don't concern myself with that, and sometimes find it hard to understand why others do.

That is the point of the section early in the book, the *Parable of the Banquet*. Life is so rich and delightful now, it seems a sin to ignore that and lose ourselves in anxiety about the future. I am reminded of high school girls growing up who can't wait to be older, to wear older clothes, paint themselves with makeup and "pass for" a girl five or ten years older. When they are finally ten years older, they will get upset if they can't pass for five years younger. This life, this moment and all we have now—call it Creation—is not only so rich but so *commanding*, that I don't want to lose any of it. Hidden away in another chapter is the *Parable of the Car*. Let's also not forget that this lucky life does not come to us from our own efforts, it is a great gift bestowed on us by our ancestors who made many sacrifices and difficult choices in order to pass it down to us. It is up to us to maintain it and care for it.

In baseball, what might happen to a batter at the plate in the first inning who begins to muse about this afternoon's game? How many more times might he get up to the plate, if it is going to be five times, why then he might be able to get five hits and one of them could very well be a homerun, and then he might be a sports highlight that same evening, and wouldn't that be great? Meanwhile, the pitcher has thrown three strikes past his sternum, and now the manager has pulled him out of the game. This is our game now, we are up to bat and each moment we need to open our eyes, watch the pitcher begin his windup, and see the baseball the minute it leaves his hand.

*   *   *

Afterword

By now, you have read through this short book and absorbed everything in it. I assume you have already begun to perceive the world as fully as possible, or at least more fully than before, and have begun to examine your thoughts, expressions and actions to see that they are in line with your values. To aid you in your practice, from time to time you may close your eyes and imagine loss and suffering, a world of want and pain, and then magically end that nightmare by simply opening your eyes and restoring your rich world. Or, if you prefer, go to your local pool and swim 25 meter laps on one breath; you'll feel like the Zen monk in Chapter One as you gasp for breath, and see how delicious even an indoor pool's chlorine-laden air can taste. Any time you get disconnected you can simply pause, perceive, and immediately reconnect. You may have begun your jockey and horse training sessions—meditation—and this is all wonderful. You are finding it easier and easier to "unpack" or "unlock" the dense files which the universe lays at your feet every moment of every day wherever you are. All you have left to do, carefully, over time, is to review your livelihood and to begin to focus on which kind of initial quest might be particularly suited to you. That quest will be the first of many, and I wish you good luck and safe passage on all of them.

So, you may have already begun to see results in yourself, and you and perhaps others have begun to notice that you are different, frankly better, than you were before. And now you may begin to ask, *not*, "Does enlightenment work?" but "*Why* does enlightenment work?"

The answer is quite simple, in fact it is as simple as possible (but no simpler). Up until recently, you may not have fully realized how miraculous you really are, and most of your miraculous machinery (your senses and your mind) may have been turned off, or running at such a low level that the machinery might as well have been turned off. No one who truly understands how miraculous the world is, and how miraculous each life is, could ever be anything but enthusiastic, grateful and generous. No one who really understands this miracle could ever want for more than to perceive more and more of it—*to witness life fully*—and then to interact with it on higher and higher levels.

Through these simple steps you have commanded yourself to switch on your own cog, your very own connection machinery (perceptions) and then ordered yourself to use those perceptions to *create* your own highest and best use: good thoughts, good expressions, and good actions. By doing this you have brought yourself out of the dark and out of the shadows, and into the light. Now that you are in the light, everything is illuminated. You now meditate, very efficiently, and achieve a kind of self-control that all people are capable of, but few actually have, and you have this new power at your beck and call every moment of every day. You examine, or re-examine, your life's work and can make intelligent and personally moral decisions about what you are doing to earn a living and provide for your loved ones. You are now set up to decide on larger challenges—quests—which are in line with all that you are about, and which will not only reward you with the process and the achievement of the quest itself, but also reward you with a new, expanded, and more transcendent self to go forward with.

There simply is nothing more to awareness and enlightenment than these steps, and to repeat them each and every day of your miraculous life.

*   *   *

July 4, 2011, Eugene, Oregon

Further Reading

These are books which might serve as starting or jumping-off points for you. Read everything, but test it, always:

Diane Ackerman, A Natural History of the Senses

Tara Bennett, Emotional Alchemy: How the Mind Can Heal the Heart

Claude Bristol, The Magic of Believing

Nathaniel Branden, Six Pillars of Self-Esteem

Dale Carnegie, How to Win Friends & Influence People

Mihaly Csikszentmihalyi, Flow: Psychology of Optimal Experience

Victor Davich, 8 Minute Meditation: Quiet Your Mind. Change Your Life

Ralph Waldo Emerson, Selected Essays, Lectures and Poems

Victor Frankl, Man's Search for Meaning

Daniel Goleman, Emotional Intelligence

Steve Hagen, Buddhism Is Not What You Think

Steve Hagen, Buddhism Plain and Simple

Jonathan Haidt, The Happiness Hypothesis

Napoleon Hill, Think and Grow Rich!

Ellen Langer, The Power of Mindful Learning

Maxwell Maltz, New Psycho-Cybernetics

Abraham Maslow, Toward a Psychology of Being

Christopher McDougall, Born to Run

Norman Vincent Peale, The Power of Positive Thinking

Richard Wiseman, The Luck Factor: The Four Essential Principles

Martin Seligman, Learned Optimism, Authentic Happiness

Tal Ben-Shachar, The Question of Happiness, Happier

Henry David Thoreau, Walden; Or, Life in the Woods

Alan Watts, The Way of Zen

Douglas McCarty

Acknowledgements

This is only a partial list of my creditors, that is, the people to whom I am indebted for instruction and gentleness they showed me along this path called Life. A full list would resemble a telephone directory. Some named here are no longer alive, and others I have lost contact with, but I still would like to acknowledge them and their interactions with me: the McCarty family of Northern Ireland, Kentucky and West Virginia (all 6 generations), William Louis McCarty, Thomas and Janie McCarty, Madelyn and Dwight Steele, Donald Hancock McCarty, Ernesto Canales, Frieda E Reed, Mark Coffey, Pierre Cintas, Yun Anja, the Jon family of Korea (all 55 generations), Edward Purnell, Mark Standley, Edward W. Wagner, Jerome Alan Cohen, Dennis Hersch, Phyllis Korff, Gordon Chapman, Robert Wolfe, Paul Roline, Desiree Robinson, and Joseph Lieberman.

ABOUT THE AUTHOR

Douglas Wilson McCarty was born in Charleston, West Virginia and grew up near Philadelphia. He is a graduate of the University of Virginia, Harvard University and Harvard Law School. He is a former Peace Corps Volunteer, Fulbright Scholar, international lawyer, a linguist and an avid outdoorsman. <u>Sustainable Enlightenment</u> is his first book.

www.ingramcontent.com/pod-product-compliance
Lightning Source LLC
Chambersburg PA
CBHW071954040426
42447CB00009B/1328